Southern Literary Studies
Louis D. Rubin, Jr., Editor

The
SOUTHERN REVIEW
and
MODERN LITERATURE
1935–1985

The
SOUTHERN REVIEW
and
MODERN
LITERATURE
1935–1985

Edited by

LEWIS P. SIMPSON, JAMES OLNEY,

and JO GULLEDGE

LOUISIANA STATE UNIVERSITY PRESS
BATON ROUGE and LONDON

Designer: Sylvia Loftin
Typeface: Perpetua
Typesetter: Composing Room of Michigan
Printer: Thomson-Shore, Inc.
Binder: John H. Dekker & Sons, Inc.

10   9   8   7   6   5   4   3   2   1

Permission to use the following items is gratefully acknowledged: the Introduction, adapted from "The *Southern Review* and a Post-Southern American Letters," which first appeared in *TriQuarterly* (a publication of Northwestern University), XLIII (Fall, 1978), and subsequently in Eliott Anderson and Mary Kinzie (eds.), *The Little Magazine in America: A Modern Documentary History* (New York, 1978); the text of "The Death of Huey Long: A Photographic Essay," "Politics and Education," and "Conference on Literature and Reading in the South and Southwest, 1935," all of which first appeared in the *Southern Review,* n.s., XXI (Spring, 1985); "The Origin of the *Southern Review,*" which first appeared in the *Southern Review,* n.s., XXII (Winter, 1986); and "T. S. Eliot and the American South," which first appeared in the *Southern Review,* n.s., XXI (Autumn, 1985). "The Gift of Tongues" is copyright © 1987 by Robert Morgan and is reprinted from *At the Edge of the Orchard Country* by permission of Wesleyan University Press. Photos are courtesy of LSU Office of Public Relations.

Library of Congress Cataloging-in-Publication Data

The Southern review and modern literature, 1935–1985.

(Southern literary studies)
Contains most of the papers presented at the
Conference on Southern Letters and Modern Literature,
held at Louisiana State University in 1985, along with
a few pieces from the Southern review.
Bibliography: p.
1. American literature—Louisiana—Baton Rouge—
History and criticism—Congresses.   2. American literature—20th century—History and criticism—Congresses.
3. Southern review (Baton Rouge, La.)—Congresses.
4. American literature—Southern States—History and
criticism—Congresses.   5. Literature publishing—
Southern States—History—20th century—Congresses.
6. Southern States—Intellectual life—20th century—
Congresses.   I. Simpson, Lewis P.   II. Olney, James.
III. Gulledge, Jo.   IV. Conference on Southern Letters
and Modern Literature (1985 : Louisiana State University,
Baton Rouge)   V. Southern review (Baton Rouge, La.)
PS267.B3S68   1987   810'.9'975   87–21384
ISBN 0–8071–1424–3

For
the past and present contributors to
the *Southern Review*

CONTENTS

ILLUSTRATIONS

following page 115

PREFACE AND ACKNOWLEDGMENTS

The one hundred and twenty-fifth year since the origination of Louisiana State University, the year 1985 also marked two other occasions of note on the campus. It was the fiftieth year since the university's establishment of the original series of the *Southern Review* (1935–1942) under the editorship of Charles W. Pipkin, Cleanth Brooks, and Robert Penn Warren, and it signified the completion of the twentieth year of the second series of the journal, inaugurated in 1965 under the editorship of Lewis P. Simpson and Donald E. Stanford, coeditors, and Rima Drell Reck, associate editor. Anticipating the anniversary year, the editors in charge of the *Review*—Simpson and James Olney, who replaced Stanford on his retirement in 1983—conceived of signaling it by various undertakings. For one thing, several special issues were planned. The first, under the rubric "The Southern Writer," came out in the spring of 1985; a second special issue, devoted to Afro-American writing, came out in the summer of the anniversary year; and the third, entitled simply "T. S. Eliot," appeared in the fall. The appearance of the Eliot number was virtually coincident with the realization of the second part of our plan to honor the anniversary, the convening on the LSU campus of a national literary conference devoted to the theme of "Southern Letters and Modern Literature." With the publication of the present volume—drawn from the proceedings of this conference (held October 9–11, 1985), together with a collection of relevant materials from the spring, 1985, and winter, 1986, issues of the *Southern Review*—we at length realize the third part of our plan to distinguish the anniversary year.

We here reproduce from the proceedings of the 1985 conference only the papers presented during the various panel sessions and a taped transcription of the session of the Afro-American panel. What we necessarily omit—readings by Ernest Gaines, Walker Percy, Robert Penn Warren, and Eudora Welty, and the prerelease showing of the notable documentary on the life of Huey Long directed by Ken

Burns—will be recalled vividly by readers of this volume who were among the large audiences present at these events. Those who attended the conference no doubt will recall too the intangible atmosphere that we cannot reproduce: the intellectual and emotional ambience of an occasion that brought together teachers, students, writers, and members of the public at large from all regions of the United States and from abroad for two and a half days to share a common interest in the writing of the twentieth-century South as an expression of literary modernism.

Yet while we cannot represent the full proceedings of the conference of October, 1985, still less its intangible aspects, we have attempted to enhance its historical context by a substantial addition to the papers presented during the first session. Perhaps most importantly we have replaced Thomas W. Cutrer's brief summation of the Conference on Literature and Reading in the South and Southwest, held under the auspices of LSU, at a downtown hotel in Baton Rouge on April 10 and 11, 1935, with Cutrer's edited version of the transcript of this conference. One event during a week-long celebration of the university's seventy-fifth anniversary, the 1935 Baton Rouge literary conference, as Cutrer explains in his introduction, served not only to announce the inauguration of the *Southern Review* but to project its relation both to the contemporary southern literary flowering and the twentieth-century literary renaissance. A reprinting from the spring, 1985, special issue of the *Southern Review,* the transcript of the 1935 conference is accompanied by two other items from the same issue: an essay by Charles East on the significance of the death of Huey Long, which occurred scarcely two months after the publication of the first issue of the *Southern Review* in July, 1935; and a short address Long gave at a luncheon held on the LSU campus during the week of the 1935 conference. One other supplement to conference materials is a clarification by Cleanth Brooks and Robert Penn Warren (from the winter issue of the *Southern Review,* 1986) of the circumstances surrounding the inception of the *Review.*

Introduced by a consideration of the relationship between the original and the new series of the *Southern Review* by Lewis P. Simpson, our compilation of materials from the conference and the magazine suggests the involvement of both its earlier and later series in a variety of literary and cultural issues. A number of these issues were raised at the 1935 conference by the editors of the original series and by such participants as Allen Tate, John Gould Fletcher, Lambert Davis, Ford Madox Ford, and Caroline Gordon: What effect has the lack of a public had on the nature of literary production in the South? Is the problem of the lack of a proper public special to the South? What are the problems of editing a magazine in the South? What are the problems of directing a university press in the South? What is provincial literature? A number of questions that were to become vital were not raised in 1935, notably those presented by the members of the Afro-American panel. In fact, no difference between the conference in 1935 and the one in 1985 is more striking than the presence of several distinguished black writers at the latter. No black writers were invited to the first conference.

In eliciting contributions for the program of the conference, we suggested general subjects to participants but made no effort to specify how a given subject might be approached. Thus no section is tightly focused. The final section, "T. S. Eliot, the South, and the Definition of Modernism," even though it may seem to be the least focused of all, serves to suggest, quite correctly we think, that the continuity between the *Southern Review* of 1935 to 1942 and the *Southern Review* of the later day bears a distinct relation to the decisive influence of Eliot on twentieth-century Western letters.

We wish to express our deep appreciation to several institutions without whose generous financial assistance the conference on "Southern Letters and Modern Literature" would not have been possible: the National Endowment for the Humanities, the Louisiana Endowment for the Humanities, and the Louisiana State University Alumni Federation, College of Arts and Sciences, and Department of English. A number of individuals who rendered great assistance to the conference include the following LSU officials: James H. Wharton, chancellor; Sean McGlynn, vice-chancellor for research; Carolyn Hargrave, provost and vice-chancellor of academic affairs; and William C. Cooper, dean of the Graduate School. The editors of The *"Southern Review" and Modern Literature, 1935–1985* further gratefully acknowledge the indispensable help of Beth LeBlanc, editorial assistant to the *Southern Review,* and Ann Humphries, student assistant. We acknowledge with utmost gratitude the truly invaluable assistance of Evelyn Heck, business manager of the *Southern Review,* throughout the process of planning, holding, and closing out the conference. Many other persons kindly assisted in helping us out, including Elizabeth Cahoon, coordinator of grants and contracts, College of Arts and Sciences; and Joanna Hill, designer of the conference poster and the program. Let us finally not fail to thank the distinguished writers, scholars, and editors who chaired the various conference sessions: Ellis Sandoz, Martha Lacy Hall, David Culbert, Donald E. Stanford, Dan Littlefield, Charles East, John R. May, and Thomas A. Kirby.

The Editors

The
SOUTHERN REVIEW
and
MODERN LITERATURE
1935–1985

INTRODUCTION
A CERTAIN CONTINUITY

The historical character of the literary periodical is immutable. It cannot for a moment be separated from its context in the accumulative literary record. Unlike a play by Shakespeare, an ode by Keats, a lyric by Wordsworth, a novel by Joyce, a periodical never achieves—in a single issue, in a single volume, in its whole serial run—even a quasi transcendence. Its implication in history is germane to its origins in the seventeenth and eighteenth centuries, when the extension of printing technology brought literature and printing into a primary and ever expanding relationship, and literature became almost wholly identified with what is made public in printed form. The periodical responded to a constantly increasing need for literary news. Its aura of historicity became more distinct when it took the form of the critical journals of the nineteenth century, like the *Edinburgh Review* and the *Quarterly Review.* Conveying a critical debate or dialectic about the nature, function, and influence of literature as an institution, the literary periodical became a record of the struggle of literature for self-interpretation and historical definition in a civilization that, in embracing science, technology, and industrialism, had entered into a state of continuous revolution. When we pick up, say, a fifty-year-old number of a "literary quarterly" (as distinguished from a "scholarly quarterly" or a strictly "critical quarterly"—a hybrid form, a mingling of the scholarly journal, the critical quarterly, and the general literary magazine), we may find in it a poem, a story, or an essay that we have long regarded as speaking with its own luminous autonomy. We are slightly shocked to see it in this context, where it assumes the appearance of an artifact of literary history. Nothing is so old as yesterday's news, and this includes the literary news. The literary periodical bears the stamp of its origin. Many of us have probably not heard of the journal or the editor, but the archetypal literary periodical is Pierre Bayle's *Nouvelles de la République des Lettres,* published from 1684 to 1718.

I set down these observations not for what they may be worth as summary wisdom, which is no doubt very little, but because they have grown out of my effort to inquire into a seemingly small and specific question: the circumstances under which the publication of the *Southern Review* at Louisiana State University was renewed in 1965 after a lapse of twenty-three years. The circumstances—I realize to a greater extent than I did two decades ago—were something more than adventitious. Indeed, the historical connection between the new series of the *Southern Review* and the *Southern Review* of the 1930s and 1940s is fundamental to the *Review*'s place in the present-day spectrum of American literary quarterlies.

The preface to the first number of the new series of the *Southern Review,* in January, 1965, recognizes the outward circumstances of the resumption of publication. These were unexceptional. Certain persons who were strongly interested in renewal were located in the right niches of power at LSU, including the late Nathaniel M. Caffee, professor of English and dean of the Baton Rouge campus of the university; the president of the university system, the late John A. Hunter; the dean of the Graduate School, Max M. Goodrich; and the chairman of the English department, Thomas A. Kirby. In 1963 an administrative decision to renew publication was implemented by the appointment of a faculty committee to assist in planning the resumption. This prepared the way for appointment of Stanford and Simpson, of the Baton Rouge campus, as coeditors; and Reck, of the New Orleans campus (now the University of New Orleans), as associate editor. Patt Foster Roberson was appointed as the first business manager.[1] By mid-1963 we were in business, and before long had arranged to engage the services of Franklin Press in Baton Rouge, printers of the 1935–1942 series. Save for an alteration of the cover design, the editors decided that the second series of the *Southern Review* would appear in a format close to that of the original series.

There was an element of the fortuitous in our engagement of the

---

1. Professor Reck served as associate editor of the *Southern Review* from 1965 to 1984. Ms. Robertson served as business manager from 1965 to 1969. Subsequently this post was held by Karen Paterson in 1970; Sarah East, 1970–1978, 1979–1980; Susan Polack, 1978–1979; and Joan Seward, 1980–1981. Since 1981 Evelyn Heck has been business manager. The post of editorial assistant was created in 1969. It has been held successively by Joy D. Dykhuizen, 1969–1971; Cheri M. Pancake, 1971–1973; Jackie Weatherford, 1973–1976; Maureen Carleton, 1976–1979; Jacqueline Riester, 1979–1980; Carol M. Dole, 1980–1981; and Jo Gulledge, 1981–1983. In 1983 Ms. Gulledge was named assistant editor. Since that time fellowship students in the graduate program in English have filled the post of editorial assistant: Martine Brent (1984); Beth LeBlanc (1985–1986); Paul R. Connell (1986–   ).

printers of the original series for the second series and in our adaptation of the format of the old series to the new. Even though we did not seek it as a matter of deliberate editorial policy, we found the expression of a symbolic continuity pleasing. When Cleanth Brooks—who, with Charles W. Pipkin and Robert Penn Warren, served as an editor of the original series—was questioned about the direction the reinstituted *Southern Review* should take, he remarked that it should be a direction as different from that of the earlier publication as the literary situation demanded; and this, he thought, might mean that the second series would take a quite divergent road from the first.

The road we took, however, was only a relatively different one. To be sure, we might have taken another road, if we, the editors of the new series of the *Southern Review,* had been younger. But having been college students in the age of the first series, we possessed a literary education acquired in the days of the "second flowering of American literature" (Malcolm Cowley's term) and its attendant phenomenon, the first "Southern Renaissance," both of which had their context in the general renaissance in Western letters in the two decades between the first and second world wars. Our response to literature could not fail to be governed in considerable part by the sensibility of an age that was marked by avant-garde techniques but, as understood today, found its leading motive in a struggle by men of letters to recover the use of letters as a functional arena of civilization, a public space of discourse, a literary *res publica*. The struggle was against an increasing sense of the loss of all forms of transcendent order and the consequent diminishment of all concepts of permanence in human relationships—against, that is, the concept of the historicity of man, society, world, and God that had announced itself in, to use T. S. Eliot's famous phrase, the seventeenth-century "dissociation of sensibility," and had by the twentieth century become decisive. In the vacuum left by the separation of sensation and intellect, the poets and philosophers of the post–World War I world perceived with crystal clarity the historicity not only of expression but of perception itself. And yet to some poets and philosophers it seemed not too late to defy the closure of the capacity for transcendent vision by an appeal to the classical-Hebraic-Christian amalgam of thought and emotion that constituted the tradition of the West. Asserting that the function of literature transcends the historical process—that it is a continuous assimilation of literature to the mystery of existence, which is, properly speaking, the reference of history—

they sought to vivify the reality of tradition by asserting the living force of the past in the present.

The effective representation of the arena of discourse—of the realm of literary order—has been through the portrayal in poetry, fiction, drama, and essay of a struggle between history and tradition as modes of existence. But as this myriad conflict has become more and more weighted on the side of historicism—on the side of scientific determinism in the interpretation of the consciousness of man, society, the world, and God—the historicist interpretation has tended to erode the power of the Republic of Letters, the public space of letters that by the fifteenth century had emerged as in effect a third realm in the institutional structure of Western civilization. Distinct from the realms of Church and State—a secularization of the ecumenic world of letters and learning established by the medieval university—this peculiarly modern realm of moral and spiritual literacy, with the rapid rise of printing technology in the sixteenth and seventeenth centuries, underwent an unprecedented expansion.

The American republic has a major source of origin in the widening of the public space of literacy. In revolutionary America, it was assumed by the men of letters who led the rebellion against the Crown that the nation they were making would be synonymous with a lettered citizenship. It would, one might even say, incarnate the image of the Republic of Letters. But after the Revolution the extension of literacy was soon seen by cultural conservatives to imperil rather than to promote the autonomy of the literary polity. During the first two decades of the new nation indeed the Federalist literati prophesied the distinct possibility of an American destruction of the literary realm. One of the early nineteenth-century New England periodicals, the *Monthly Anthology and Boston Review,* clearly expresses the fear that the Americans may convert the literary polity into an amorphous "democracy of letters." From this time on, we can trace a quarrel in American magazines between an endorsement of the prescriptive custody of literacy and the advocacy of its democratization. In mid-nineteenth-century America the issue was neatly dramatized in the opposition between the *Whig Review* and the *United States Magazine and Democratic Review.* But it is too simple to say that the one magazine supported a traditionalist view of culture and the other the historically determined rise of democracy. Writers were often pulled different ways. It was not always easily possible to belong to either the establishment or the movement—in Emersonian terms, to the "Party of the Past" or the "Party of the Future." In truth Emerson, although denying the past at his back, never entirely divested himself of classicist attitudes. Internalizing the dialectic of tradition and history, he was, in his very vision of an antitraditionalist, autonomous self triumphing over history, the participant in the literary dialectic that maintained the realm of discourse against the threat of assimilation either to the democratic state or to a compelling historical determinism.

The literary situation in the nineteenth-century South was not the same as that in New England and the East. In the South the realm of public literacy was virtually closed by the defense of slavery. The dialectic of history and tradition ceased.

Chattel slavery, as it existed in the American South, was not a traditional but a novel institution, which, originating as a historical expediency, became a historical necessity in the planting states. When the "peculiar institution" came under attack, its defense demanded its identification with the state. This meant that ultimately both the realm of religious expression and that of literary expression would be assimilated to the state. Before this finally happened, the Southern literary mind tended to evade the relationship of literature to slavery by isolating literature in a classical piety. Such a motive is evident, for example, in Hugh Swinton Legaré's depiction of the holy commonwealth of secular letters in the leading essay of the first number of the first quarterly to bear the title the *Southern Review* (published in Charleston, South Carolina, from 1828 to 1832). A classical literary education, Legaré says, will let a young man "into that great communion of scholars throughout all ages and nations—like that more awful communion of saints in the Holy Church Universal," and he will "feel a sympathy with departed genius, and with the enlightened and the great minds of other countries, as they appear before him, in the transports of a Vision Beatific, bowing down at the same shrines and glowing with the same holy love of whatever is most pure and fair and exalted and divine in human nature."

As the assimilation of letters to the state proceeded in the Old South, the purity of the literary realm began to be defined in prescriptive terms—that is to say, in terms of whether or not literature in any way questioned the institution of slavery. When the editor of the *Southern Literary Messenger* was accused of "injudicious leniency towards Northern books and authors," Paul Hamilton Hayne of *Russell's Magazine* offered a curious defense of his fellow editor: "Now, it seems that when a work is purely *literary*, interfering in no way with the peculiar institution, or our rights under it, common honesty requires that it should be reviewed without reference to the birth-place of its author, or the locale of its publication. A true literary spirit is essentially liberal, and the Editor who should arraign Irving's Washington or Hawthorne's Tales, upon the charge that their authors were Northern men, would be guilty evidently of the grossest absurdity." That a young Southern man of letters could thus depict the relationship between letters and slavery in the late 1850s indicates the extent to which the literary order and the world of the slaveholders had been joined.

The reopening of the public space of literacy in the South after the Civil War was signified by the inauguration of the second quarterly to be named the *Southern Review*. Published in Baltimore from 1867 through 1879, the second *Southern Review* was edited by the aging Albert Taylor Bledsoe. Known in the antebellum South as a proslavery advocate and in the Reconstruction as an unreconstructible fire-eater, Bledsoe was withal a man of letters and mathematician of very considerable learning. In the first essay in the initial number of the Baltimore *Southern Review*, taking as his point of departure the works of Vico, Lessing, Hegel, and Schlegel, Bledsoe in spite of his commitment to the Old South anticipates the disposition of the twentieth-century Southern literary mind to enter into the deeper levels of the relationship of tradition and history. "The history of civilization," he says, "is nearly, if not absolutely, the same as the Philosophy of History, or the Education of Mankind." (This statement is prefaced by the remark, "The Philosophy of History is one of the creations of modern genius.") The sense of history as the symbol of civilizational existence, expressing itself in one way in the formation of an Old South–New South opposition, was embodied in William Porterfield Trent's founding of the *Sewanee Review*, a magazine which, in view of its continuous publication since its inception, is justly entitled to its claim to be the nation's oldest literary quarterly. A few years later, a similar sense of history was embodied in another continuing periodical venture, the *South Atlantic Quarterly*, launched in 1902 by John Spencer Bassett at Trinity College (now Duke University) in Durham, North Carolina.

Other significant periodical ventures responded to the impulse of the Southern literary mind to reconstruct the literary polity. Among these were the *Texas Review*, established at the University of Texas in

1915 (transferred to Southern Methodist University in 1924 and re-named the *Southwest Review*), and the *Virginia Quarterly Review*, established at the University of Virginia in 1925. Meanwhile the reopening of the literary realm in the South evidenced itself in the appearance of several independent little magazines, among them the *Double-Dealer* in New Orleans and the *Fugitive*, published in Nashville from 1922 through 1925. Like the *Dial* of Emerson and Margaret Fuller in New England eighty years earlier, the *Fugitive* of John Crowe Ransom, Donald David-son, Allen Tate, and Robert Penn Warren exerted a lasting literary power. It not only expanded the realm of literary discourse in the South but pushed its boundaries outward to embrace the modernist discus-sion of history and tradition.

> Poetry, the oracle, is gone. Our time cleaves to no racial myth, its myth is the apotheosis of machinery. Perhaps Oswald Spengler is right: a man is a fool to be an artist or a poet in this age. But at least our poet is aware of his own age, barren of any art though it may be, for he can't write like Homer or Milton now; from the data of his experience he infers only a distracting complexity.

This is Allen Tate in the *Fugitive* in 1924 continuing a "discussion of the future of modern poetry" begun by Ransom in the preceding number. Within a few years several of the more prominent Fugitives would inaugurate the Agrarian movement, which, although it has been widely misinterpreted as a political movement—a misunderstanding promoted by the Agrarians' own misinterpretation of their basic mo-tives—was a literary movement. As the Transcendental movement opened the New England mind to nineteenth-century literary dis-course, the Agrarian movement opened the Southern mind to the discourse of the twentieth century. In so doing, it substantiated the modern realm of letters in the South and provided the context for the establishment of the third Southern quarterly to be called the *Southern Review*. The most effective periodical expression of the South-ern literary flowering, the Baton Rouge journal appeared at a point when the dialectic of history and tradition, focused and developed by the *Fugitive* group and the Agrarians, was ripe for consolidation on a broader, more reflective, and more sophisticated level.

The story of the publication of the *Southern Review* at Louisiana State University in the years of the Louisiana hayride has acquired an aura of legend. Looking back on that time, Robert Penn Warren commented,

"After Louisiana nothing has been real." He was no doubt thinking about the strange improbability of certifiable circumstances in the Louisiana of the Huey Long epoch. Among these was Warren's reunion at LSU with the slightly younger Cleanth Brooks. Both graduates of Vanderbilt, both fresh from the experience of being Rhodes scholars at Oxford (Warren, B.Litt., 1930; Brooks, B.Litt., 1932), both close to the Agrarian movement (although Brooks had not been a contributor to *I'll Take My Stand*), they were joined in academic destiny as though by happenstance. But it was, in good measure, owing to a greater im- probability of the time: the appointment of Charles Wooten Pipkin to the deanship of a fledgling LSU Graduate School. Pipkin, a native of Arkansas, was thirty-two years old when he became the graduate dean at LSU. He too had been at Vanderbilt; he too, after a short period at Harvard, had been at Oxford. A political scientist whose fame in his field made him a full professor at twenty-eight, Pipkin exemplified the recrudescence of Jeffersonian cosmopolitanism in the post–World War I age. A twentieth-century *philosophe*, a forceful advocate of the League of Nations and of the "redemption of the South through educa- tion," Pipkin, according to one of his LSU colleagues, Alex Daspit, was a critic of university programs which "had grown from catechisms of denominational colleges to the vast catholicity of curricula which mean nothing." Deploring the "animated academic circus of mediocrity and miscellany," he condemned the "righteous contentment of many col- lege professors who are embalmed within the shroud of a Ph.D." Surveying the result of much of what has passed for academic research, Pipkin even observed that if Dr. Johnson were alive, "he would not overlook the vast possibilities of the word 'research' as the last refuge of the scoundrel."

For Pipkin the minimum objective of the LSU Graduate School must be "a greater immediate realization of the inherent capacities of the southern regions and a more vital reintegration of the regional culture in the national scene." While neither his emphasis on employing graduate education in the pursuit of, as he said, "the optimum conditions of the good society," nor his contention that "the American is a world citizen inheriting his internationalism from the great power of the industrial potential of the United States," was compatible with the Agrarian perspective, Pipkin's stress on the Southern intellectual as a cultural redeemer who must marshall all "the skills necessary to utilize the existing resources of the [Southern] land and the people" provided an ample rationale for his association with Robert Penn Warren and Cleanth

Brooks. Opponents of the industrialization of the South though they might be, they were among its promising cultural resources, as was Albert R. Erskine, Jr., a student at Vanderbilt during Warren's brief teaching stint there following his Oxford days. (Erskine, the first business manager of the *Southern Review,* also assumed editorial responsibilities. When John Palmer, like Brooks and Warren a Rhodes scholar, replaced Erskine in 1940, he was given the title of managing editor.)

Another important figure in the mix of persons at LSU was the president of the university, James Monroe Smith. While his flamboyant misuse of university bonds eventually resulted in his incarceration in the state penitentiary at Angola—a photograph in *Life* shows Smith in striped prison garb at work in a prison sugarcane field—Smith had a regard for the university as well as for himself. It was Smith who, in accordance with the administrative style of the Long era, one Sunday afternoon in late February, 1935, drove up to Robert Penn Warren's residence in Baton Rouge and invited Warren and his guest, Albert Erskine, to go for a ride, during which he announced his willingness to support a literary quarterly at LSU. The story is told by Brooks and Warren in their introduction to *Stories from the Southern Review.*

> While the official black Cadillac crunched the gravel of the back roads, President James Monroe Smith revealed the motive of his invitation. Was it possible, he wanted to know, to have a good literary and critical quarterly at the university. Yes, was the answer he got—yes, if you paid a fair rate for contributions, gave writers decent company between the covers, and concentrated editorial authority sufficiently for the magazine to have its own distinctive character and quality. There was one more stipulation: that quality must not be diluted or contravened by the interference of academic committees or officials. How much would it cost? Toward $10,000 a year.

Smith suggested that Warren and Erskine confer with Pipkin and Brooks, and promised to authorize funds for the magazine upon receiving a statement of the plans for it. He received this statement the next day. In the amazingly short period of three months, the fledgling editors produced Volume I, Number 1, of the new quarterly, dated June, 1935. The masthead carried Pipkin as the editor and Brooks and Warren as the managing editors. So in an improbable time and place—in a time of bizarre political corruption mingled with intellectual and literary excitement, in a provincial state university in the Deep South—a distinguished literary magazine came into its being. A few years later, when the scandals broke at LSU and Smith went to prison, the unlikely circumstances which had created the *Southern Review* disappeared. The entrance of the United States into World War II seemed to be sufficient reason to the institution, still affectionately known in tribute to its origin and its continuing military mission as the "Ole War Skule," to remove the *Review* from its budget, this in spite of nationwide protests against the action.[2]

The first number of the Pipkin, Brooks, and Warren *Southern Review* was preceded by a prospectus avowing that the chief aim of the quarterly would be "to define large issues" and "to attempt interpretation of the contemporary scene." To this end it would publish essays on "social, economic, political and literary topics, fiction, poetry, and reviews of current books"—these to be written by a cosmopolitan authorship which would include not only established writers but new ones, their works to be judged uniformly on the basis of "significance and artistic excellence." It was within the amplitude of such intentions that the *Southern Review* would "aim at presenting and interpreting Southern problems to a national audience and at relating national issues to the Southern scene."[3] To the extent that the original series of the *Southern Review* carried out its ambitiously broad editorial policy—and this was to a considerable degree—the new series is obviously not continuous with it. Our policy, set down early in the planning stage of the resumption, is more narrowly literary. But, it may be observed, the continuity of the original series and the new series is not to be judged merely on the basis of subject-matter emphasis; it lies in similarity of tone and temper.

Some of our readers have remarked, as a matter of fact, that our critical program has been chiefly retrospective. Their attitude is not without justification. The first issue of the new series begins with an essay on Ransom and includes essays on the Agrarians, Yeats, Céline, Faulkner, and D. H. Lawrence. Throughout the first twenty-one volumes of the new series, similar attention is given to writers who had their beginnings in the twenties and thirties. No special numbers have

2. *Cf.* Cleanth Brooks and Robert Penn Warren, "The Origin of the *Southern Review,*" *Southern Review,* n.s., XXII (Winter, 1986), 214–17, reprinted in the first section of this volume.

3. I am indebted to Rhonda Cabot Tentarelli for the quotations from the prospectus, which she discovered in the files of the LSU student newspaper, the *Reveille* (April 16, 1935). See Tentarelli, "The Life and Times of the *Southern Review,*" *Southern Studies,* XVI (Summer, 1977). This essay places the first series of the *Southern Review* in the context of the thirties.

been devoted to appraisals of writing during the sixties, the seventies, or the eighties. But special numbers or special sections of the magazine have been devoted to Frost, Wallace Stevens, Yeats, Caroline Gordon, Faulkner, Mark Twain, and Yvor Winters. Other special issues deal with such general subjects as the French literature of the past 150 years and the literature of the twenties. Ten numbers given over to the subject of writing in the South have tended to look backward.

If I am giving the impression that the continuity between the original and the new series of the *Southern Review* has the character of a pietistic response to a brilliant past, I must qualify my remarks. Whatever piety there has been in our regard for the company of Yeats, Eliot, Faulkner *et al.,* has been dominated by a more complex impulse toward continuity: the perpetuation of the dialectic of history and tradition. Although this motive has never been formally recognized by the editors, it was implicit in the historical act of resuming the publication of the *Review.* Once, I discover, we made it virtually explicit in a policy statement prepared for an advertising brochure during the fourth year of the new series. Addressed to potential contributors and subscribers, it states in part:

> The new *Southern Review* is maintaining the original high standards [of the 1935–1942 publication] by drawing on the resources of writers from the South and other regions of the USA and abroad. It continues to bring the readers a variety of poetry, fiction, critical essays and book reviews of lasting merit. The editors believe that a serious interest in literature starts from the present and that contemporary literature matters because it is the consciousness of our own age. Emphasis is on the twentieth century, although criticism that furnishes fresh insights into the literature of the past and essays that deal with the culture and history of the South are also published. There are frequent bilingual poems and essays dealing with contemporary European literature. Emphasizing technical discipline in fiction and poetry and clear thinking in critical essays, *The Southern Review* invites you to recognize new talents and rediscover established writers.

Looking back at it now, I may say, I find this statement both puzzling and illuminating. (Of course I do not speak for the other editors.) What is meant by the declaration that "a serious interest in literature starts from the present"? What present? What is meant by the term *contemporary?* By the phrase "the consciousness of our own age"? What, in fact, is meant by "our own age"? And why are readers and other writers invited to "rediscover established writers"? In 1968, when the above statement was published, had established writers become so disestablished that they needed "rediscovering"? Who are "established" writers anyway? Our advertisement of our virtues in 1968, it seems to me by hindsight, is ambivalent. If the editors attempted to devise a similar statement today, would it be less so? I doubt it. In its uncertainties the 1968 statement reflects a long-term situation in America, one in which an unprecedented degree of literary activity is accompanied by an unprecedented literary eclecticism. It is a time when not only a great literary movement—modernism—is ending but the very power of literature as a civilizational order seems to be suffering depletion.

Yet, while it can be seen in the light of its lengthening history that the *Southern Review,* new series, has assumed a certain retrospective quality, we have nonetheless, I think, sought to influence the literary future. When in the thirties the modernist recovery of tradition often bore the paradoxical guise of an avant-garde mission (T. S. Eliot being the exemplary instance), the original series of the *Southern Review,* in its association with the New Criticism, seemed prospective instead of retrospective. Its editorial staff proclaimed that a "serious interest in literature starts from the present," for the present comprehends the past and in this comprehension implies the future. The *Southern Review* of the sixties, seventies, and eighties has remained within the aura of modernism. We have seen contemporary writing not as postmodern but as the continuing expression of modernity in its sense of history and tradition as conflicting modes of existence.

The original series of the *Southern Review* commented on this conflict in the first number in 1935, in which the leading essay is "Culture Versus Colonialism in America" by Herbert Agar, who a year before had won the Pulitzer Prize in history for his book *The People's Choice.* Accepting the Spenglerian cyclical view of history, Agar questions whether the struggle between "the deep instinctive faith which is the essence of the Culture and an abstractly rationalizing self-destructive element which is a feature of man's mind" must necessarily be resolved in favor of doubt, disillusionment, and death. America's large cities, he contends, are colonial outposts of Europe; in them America imitates an "alien . . . old age." Declaring that the saving native American tradition lies in the provinces, Agar expresses the general hope of the *I'll Take My Stand* group: the redemption of America by a provincial assertiveness, particularly on the part of the South. The fundamental significance of Agar's essay to the history of the Pipkin, Brooks, and Warren *Southern Review* is that, appearing as the initial essay in the first issue, it projects the dialectical drama of history and tradition as the contextual image of the magazine.

We have sought to perpetuate this image. We have said, if mostly by inference, that the later decades of this century are not a time of literary origination but the time of a falling off from the literary intelligence. We have said, if only by implication, that the falling off from the literary establishment—which has included the disavowal of Eliot and Hemingway, though not so much of Joyce and Faulkner—has left a vacuum. In contrast to the disassociated personalism of post–World War II poets and novelists, the writers of the second flowering in the twenties and thirties represented the tradition that literature is integral to the corporate structure of civilization. Aspiring to contribute to the literature of civilization, their thrust was toward the restoration of this structure. The *Southern Review* of the new series, aspiring to recover the impulse of the second flowering, has represented a critical effort that might be dubbed the recovery of a recovery. Like our most direct competitor, the *Sewanee Review,* we have tried to affirm the validity of the great literature of restoration created by the "traditionalist moderns." Underlying this critical redundancy is the concept that the literary quarterly functions, as Allen Tate said in the *Southern Review* in 1935, through the "conviction of being a part of literature."

Recalling Tate's vision reminds me forcefully that I have been stressing the resemblance between the critical programs of the original series and the new series of the *Southern Review* to the neglect of what is an equally, if not more, important aspect of continuity, the community of authorship.

The *Southern Review* of 1935–1942 was a young writers' enterprise. Writers in their fifties, like John Crowe Ransom and Wallace Stevens, constituted a minority of its authorship, which included several poets (among them W. H. Auden, John Berryman, and Randall Jarrell) and a number of fiction writers (among them Andrew Lytle, Peter Taylor, and Eudora Welty) who were barely beyond apprenticeship. Robert Penn Warren was only a slightly older presence among the poets and storytellers of the original series. The original series also included several youthful poet-critics, notably R. P. Blackmur and Allen Tate, who by the time the *Southern Review* appeared in 1935 was, at the age of thirty-six, a fully mature man of letters. The *Southern Review* series beginning in 1965 displays a more numerous and diversified authorship than its predecessor. But among its important contributors are more than thirty writers who appeared in the original series. These include Ransom, author of three essays, one being his significant revisionary estimate of Eliot; Warren, the author of numerous essays and poems; and Brooks, the author of several essays, one of these being a significant evaluation of T. S. Eliot and the South. Other contributors to the present series who had been associated with the Southern movement of the twenties and thirties are Welty, Katherine Anne Porter, Caroline Gordon, Donald Davidson, Jarrell, Lytle, and Tate. The numerous writers of non-Southern origins who appeared in the 1935–1942 *Review* include several who have reappeared in the new series, among them, Kay Boyle, Mary McCarthy, Josephine Miles, Kenneth Burke, Howard Baker, and Arthur Mizener. I must not fail to mention Joseph Frank (author of distinguished essays on Chernyshevsky and Dostoevsky), Yvor Winters ("Forms of Discovery" and "The Poetry of T. Sturge Moore"), and James T. Farrell (an evocative prize story, "An American Student in Paris"). Malcolm Cowley has already been mentioned. Although he appeared in the original series of the *Southern Review* only as a correspondent, he was—with his unparalleled acquaintance with the American literary scene of the twenties and thirties—an outstanding contributor to the new series for several years before ill health put an end to his work as a writer. His essays—on Conrad Aiken, on the concept of literary generations, on a visit with the Agrarians in the depression years—are rich in literary history and in critical suggestion. Cowley's contemporary, the late Matthew Josephson, was another contributor of valuable reminiscent views of the thirties.

Writers of first importance in the new series whose careers originated in the twenties and thirties but who cannot be conveniently categorized are the emigrés René Wellek and Eric Voegelin. Although not a contributor to the original series of the *Southern Review,* Voegelin may especially be noted. When he left his homeland in the thirties he came to LSU, where he wrote much of his monumental *Order and History.* The impact of Voegelin's mind on historical, political, and philosophical studies is at present just beginning to be grasped; the relation of his thought to literary studies has as yet been no more than suggested, although something of its significance may be derived from a reading of his essay on Henry James's *The Turn of the Screw* (new series, VII, winter, 1971).

But the older generation of writers by no means dominates the new series; a mingling of generations is evident in most numbers. Brooks, Warren, and others of the generation of the twenties and thirties appear along with writers whose careers originated in the late forties and in the fifties. Writers of the Brooks and Warren generation also share our pages with writers whose careers originated in the sixties (or slightly earlier) and in the first half of the seventies. As the roster of *Southern Review* authors who have written only for the new series has grown, the number of contributors from the older time has inevitably decreased; but even writers whose literary origins belong to the later seventies and the eighties have appeared in the company of writers whose first publications belong to the twenties and thirties. The authorial continuity between the original and the new series of the journal is evident, it should be added, with respect to native authors only. While the original series published Eliot and Auden, it did not by policy seek foreign writers. The new series has sought and published, in addition to emigrants like Wellek and Voegelin, a number of Continental, British, and Irish authors. Our bilingual publication of such poets as Osip Mandelstam, George Seferis, Pablo Neruda, and Eugenio Montale has been notable. The publication of George Macbeth, W. W. Robson, Mary Lavin, and Denis Donoghue (now an American resident) has afforded us a singular measure of distinction.

The mention of various storytellers and poets associated with the present and first series of the *Review* suggests another element of continuity between them, a mutual devotion to fiction and poetry. Although the space given to poems and stories in individual issues has varied somewhat more in the new series than in the original series, we have—allowing for issues designated as poetry or fiction numbers—*in toto* assigned something like half our space to them. At times we have published fiction of seminovella length, and on a few occasions have brought out poems of some length. Our attention to fiction and poetry has recognized that the sources of publication for these forms, particularly for serious fiction, are more limited than in the 1930s, when several monthly magazines of good literary quality provided not only a market and an audience for writers but to some degree a sense that the literary polity still existed.

In the late twentieth century the best news the literary journal can report from the failing Republic of Letters is the feasibility of its restoration and perpetuation. Approaches to this subject in the new series of the *Southern Review* include, for instance, (as a result of the editorial energy and acumen of Donald E. Stanford) the essays in a special issue (winter, 1971) both by and about Voegelin. Other new series essays pertinent to this movement are those both by and about Brooks and Warren; and several essays by Cowley, including one in the winter, 1976, number on the concept of literary generations. Then, too, there are the writings of authors of the generation of the sixties, who may be referred to as neorestorationists; for example, essays and poems by the Kentuckian Wendell Berry, whose search for a relation to the land is at once a repudiation of Agrarianism and a quest in its own right.

But it must be admitted that our sense of the restorationist motive is haunted by the suspicion of its mere redundancy, especially in the South. The twentieth-century Southern literary flowering was not a second flowering but a first one, which, moreover, holds no promise of a second. In the last quarter of the twentieth century, we may well have reached the point from which we can look back on Southern writers from 1920 to the 1960s as belonging to a distinct phase of modern literature. In spite of their diversity, they constituted in sum a literary movement, one distinguishable from the cosmopolitan modern movement by its own historical coherence, yet deeply identified with it. By 1960 the Southern movement, like the nineteenth-century New England movement in 1860, was reaching a stage of exhaustion. Unlike the New England movement, the Southern movement was not, it would seem, to have a long aftermath continuous with a still unfolding literary modernity. The Southern E. A. Robinsons, Robert Frosts, Robert Lowells will not appear; for the Southern movement (continuous with Proust, Yeats, Joyce, Mann, Kafka, Pound, Eliot, Ford, Auden) has symbolized literary modernity in its finality, and itself has been one of the final phases of modernity.

When it is hinted that the "postmodern" world—announced by Hiroshima but struggling to be born long before Hiroshima—may take the shape of a nonliterary world, we are extremely resentful of such a notion and are helpless before it. We cannot discuss a nonliterary world, for a world in which the public space of literacy has disappeared is undiscussable. Seeming to stand in the evanescent margins of the dialectic of history and tradition, we seek the shape of postmodernity by trying to imagine a world without the antithesis of history and tradition. Realizing that the shape of such a world has been formed and made familiar in existentialist interpretation, we are inclined nonetheless to see existentialist concepts as versions of historical interpretation and to oppose these to traditionalism. Wanting desperately to hold on to the tension between history and tradition as modes of existence—for in this tension we have defined the modern mode of existence we call literature—we ask if the tension is any longer a vitalizing experience, a ratification of being, even in the literary mind of the South, which recently knew it strongly and intimately? The evidence of the lapse of the literary dialectic, as variously recorded in the *Southern Review,* is powerful at times, as in Walker Percy's essay "The Delta Factor," or in Walter Sullivan's essays "Death by Melancholy" and "The Decline of Myth in Southern Fiction." The dialectic of the secular realm of letters provided a context for the discussion of the opposing theories of man as organism (physical and social) and man as soul; for the drama of the divinization of secular letters (Hegel called this the "secularization of spirituality") and the rise of the writer as pseudopriest. Are we left in a void created by the depletion of the literary dialogue? Do we have left only our anguish about the meaning—the meaninglessness—of language and the literary vocation?

The three special issues of the *Southern Review* published during the anniversary year of 1985 question the negative implications of such speculative questions. As logically plausible, as inevitable even, as these implications are, we would seem to find in the issues appearing under the rubrics of "The Southern Writer," "Afro-American Writing," and "T. S. Eliot" a juxtaposition of ideas, attitudes, and emotions that suggest the possibility of not only a continuation but a fruitful expansion of the dialectic of history and tradition in the *Southern Review.* Among other ways, a widening of the *Southern Review*'s critical program is suggested by the special Afro-American issue. Edited by James Olney, who was appointed to the coeditorship upon the retirement of Stanford, this issue is based on Olney's highly knowledgeable acquaintance with twentieth-century African and Afro-American writing. At the same time Olney has brought to the journal a strong interest in its concern for Yeats, Eliot, and the school of "traditional modernists." Sharing the interests of Olney, Fred Hobson, who has filled the vacancy on the editorial staff of the *Southern Review* created by the recent retirement of Simpson, will specifically continue our commitment to Southern letters.

Yet even as the new editors of the *Southern Review* seek to enhance the meaning of a critical program growing out of the complex tensions between history and tradition, they will be aware of the question insinuated by their effort: Is such a program truly valid? Or have we entered a completely historical age—an age so possessed by history as process that it has no feeling for what Allen Tate at times, with awesome simplicity, referred to as "The Tradition"? If so, what news from the Republic of Letters, save that of its decline? At moments it seems to me that the news we have been reporting for the past twenty years—a century after the lapse of a New England American letters—concerns the coming of a post-Southern, and a "postmodern," American letters. At the same time, with no overt intention of doing so, we have been suggesting the possibilities of Western literature in the condition of detachment from the dialectic of history and tradition. Or, to put this another way, we have been repeating the news about the possibilities of literature under the circumstances of a fully realized historical existence.

Lewis P. Simpson

LSU
in the
THIRTIES
and the
SOUTHERN REVIEW

SOME ASPECTS of LSU THEN

Robert B. Heilman

Looking back fifty years comes easier than looking ahead fifty years. In 1935 looking ahead fifty years, even if one had thought of doing it, would have smacked of hubris. The main task was not going under in a not very comfortable present; aside from the usual vague hopes one did not imagine much of an existence beyond that present. For we were still in *the* Depression. Few will remember that one today. But then it seemed, if not terminal, at least interminable. Universities were generally cutting back, and some of my graduate-school contemporaries in the humanities were anticipating the 1970s by doing what we have come to call "exploring alternative career options." One was lucky to have an academic job, any job. I got my Ph.D. in 1935, but what in advance seemed to be an open door to the profession opened only one door for me—the door to LSU. At the time I did not know what a fortunate door it was.

My having only one door, and then finding that door opening on a richer world than one could expect, sets the tone for a glance at LSU "then," that is, fifty years ago. The door did not look promising to one using it for the first time, just as LSU would doubtless have seemed, to a detached observer, a hardly promising spot for the remarkable developments that were to occur. As a general rule, populist dictatorships do not lead to the establishment of elite quarterlies or posh local military schools toward national university status (and in general one does not expect elite quarterlies to be disestablished, as the *Southern Review* was, under political reform administrations). My theme is, for the most part, such contrasts or even contradictions—not only the contrast between the probable and the actual but also, and more basically, a continuing doubleness, as I shall call it, within LSU. The initial impressions of a newcomer should serve as a convenient and suitable entry into a tale of two cities within the university.

My own life has some small parallels to the public occasion of 1985—the fiftieth anniversary of the founding of the *Southern Review.* I got my degree fifty years ago, as I have noted, and came to LSU fifty years ago. I also got married fifty years ago, and my wife's and my trip from the Northeast to Louisiana was in effect our honeymoon. We were finding ourselves in a strange, often difficult, and at times even intimidating world. State and national highways were paved, but they had an uneven blacktop surface with a high crown in the middle. There were no four-lane highways. State and even national highways were often gravel roads. Detours could wind for many miles over wagon-track back roads; one even involved fording a stream. Dust-swathed and windshield-pitted cars were commonplace. Motels were not yet; we stayed in old hotels, usually with the bath down the hall, or in private residences that displayed signs saying "Rooms for Tourists." Nothing in the experience of the traveler intimated a brave new world that would offer new excitement and light. If one's reading had suggested a description, it might have been "Yoknapatawpha without Faulkner."

We drove along the coast from Mobile. Nighttime introduced us to the most varied, long-lasting, and vehement outpouring of sounds from nature that we had ever heard, from mosquitoes at one frequency to frogs at the opposite one. The lushness of growth everywhere seemed a little frightening. We drove through our first swarms of what we learned were called lovebugs, were virtually blacked in, and wondered whether all life would mean a stop every fifty miles for a windshield cleanup. Daytime temperatures were a stern probation. We watched heavy rain showers around the gulf, welcomed brief downpours, and found that they only steamed things up. The *State-Times* assured us that LSU football practices were going well on "these snappy fall afternoons." Since thermometers were reaching into the nineties everyday, we shuddered at the thought of what unsnappy afternoons would be.

The Baton Rouge in which we arrived—on Labor Day, 1935—was nothing like today's urban center, often striking, often handsome, generally well-to-do in appearance. The population was thirty-five thousand, but the place looked and felt rural rather than urban. No freeways or Mississippi bridges provided easy access to other worlds; on the old Airline Highway to New Orleans one had repeatedly to dodge, or brake violently for, roving cattle. Baton Rouge streets were often badly paved or unpaved. The rich foliage of the present campus did not exist; what are now great old trees hadn't been put in or had just been put in. The university area looked bare and a little hard. It was more brash new than brave new. Nothing suggested a rich imaginative life.

We found an apartment on the second story of a house overlooking the grounds just south of the Capitol. Our refrigerator was an icebox for which a cake of ice was delivered each day. The melt dripped out through a pipe that ended in open air, and roaches used it as an entryway into the icebox and the food. Ants and mosquitoes were likewise in good supply. I do not believe that we had a portable electric fan then. In 1935 the only air cooling available was by means of a fan permanently installed in a window; it would suck in night air and bring down the inside temperature a little. We finally acquired one of these about 1941 or 1942, when we had our own house. Our experiences were representative, I believe; people who were going to write, edit, and think beyond the ordinary demands of life were not much coddled by creature comforts.

So much for the general scene, which hardly suggested large intellectual and literary happenings. Then there were forbidding events. On our seventh day in Baton Rouge we hiked over to the Capitol, sat in the gallery at the rear of the lower house to watch the legislature of our new state in action, and saw visiting United States senator Long genially and light-fingeredly direct the proceedings. After a while he and others left, and then we heard beneath us the firecracker rat-a-tat-tat of the shots that killed Dr. Carl Weiss and fatally wounded Long. We wondered, is this the way they always settle political differences in Louisiana? How would it be in higher education? The shock was followed by the surprise of seeing hundreds of mourners come in from all over the state and camp on the Capitol grounds for the several days before the funeral—a singular response to a man whom, through the Northern press, we knew only as a dangerous threat to American political well-being. Several days later, another shock: Dr. William A. Read, then head of the English department, dropped in at our flat to tell us that he wasn't sure that the university would open on schedule the next week. Longer mourning period was my first thought. But no; Dr. Read evidently feared that Senator Long's death would totally disrupt all the institutional processes of the state. This was a frightening possibility for a new instructor fresh out of graduate school, heavily in debt, skilled only in ordinary classroom procedures, and at the bottom of the totem pole in what would continue to seem, for some time, a quite alien world. Happily Dr. Read's fears were not borne out by fact. We began teaching on schedule, though still shaken.

One of my wife's freshman-English classes included Russell Long, the son of the senator who had just died; the next year he appeared in a sophomore class of mine. If we had any trepidations about having the son of a political dictator in class, they were groundless, for Russell was a well-behaved, hard-working, solid B+ student. After all the shocks, this fact provided some reassurance on the instructional front. A year or two later Russell was to become the first, I believe, of spectacular undergraduate politicians, a campaigner of new flamboyance. He once used a plane for campaigning, dropping leaflets and perhaps some kind of small presents for those who could grab; I vaguely recall, also, a handout of ice-cream cones to the electorate.

Term opening revealed an aspect of heavy-duty faculty life that perhaps went out when the Depression gave way to the War. All faculty members were supposed to work at registration, sitting in long rows behind tables in front of which students lined up for instructions and advice. This was in a gymnasium or some such large space. We new-comers to the game were given hasty instructions about requirements, sectioning, and so on, and then turned loose to impart information and wisdom to the students who were stuck with us. I never could learn about catalogs, I was a flop at registration, and in time I began to cheat by being mysteriously missing on opening day. Did Brooks and Warren also serve, if only by sitting and waiting? My sense of it is that LSU was not then making, for people of special attainment, any of the conces-sions which are now familiar the country over.

Like the city and the university, the English department was small: it did not have the magnitude that we ordinarily presuppose as a basis for large enterprise. Unless my memory is even worse than I take it to be, there were just nine people in the professorial ranks—Dr. Read, the head (*head* was not yet a four-letter word), and Professors Bradsher, Uhler, Bryan, Joan Miller, Brooks, Warren, Olive, and Downey; there was also a considerable subprofessorial staff concerned largely with freshman English. It was a boost to our sorry financial situation when my wife was given a spot in this cadre; as I remember it, she was called an associate. Her schedule was fifteen hours—five 3-hour courses—and I do not believe that it changed during her ten years of teaching. Her 1935 salary was $1,100, and it went up little, if at all, in ten years.

As an instructor I had the same fifteen-hour teaching schedule. In my first year I taught two sophomore classes and three freshman classes. The former averaged 75 students, the latter 30; so my student total was about 240 per term. The 90 weekly themes I read myself. For the sophomore classes I had a student assistant, whose task was to grade the true-false, multiple-choice, and fill-in examinations on which we largely relied (as we likewise did in the freshman-English finals).

After a year I was promoted to assistant professor, and my teaching schedule went down from fifteen hours to twelve. This seemed a relatively easy load, at least in the sense that it was what I had mostly had since I began full-time teaching in 1928. Toward the end of my time at LSU I believe I got down to nine hours for a term or two; perhaps Tom Kirby was able to say that for the other three hours I had been assigned to do research. My impression is that Brooks and Warren never got below nine hours, even during the seven heavy work-load years of the *Southern Review.*

My incoming salary, when I had my degree and six years of teaching experience, was $1,800. With my promotion to assistant professor I got a tremendous raise—to $2,400. It was my first salary over $2,000, which I had received in the pre–Depression year of 1928–1929, when I was still only A.B., but which I had been below ever since. That $600 raise was my largest at LSU. After that my salary rose slowly. Between 1936 and 1948, when I left, it had gone up from $2,400 to $4,700—an average of not quite $200 a year. Obviously summer-school teaching was desirable, indeed close to indispensable, and I stuck to it for about ten years. A standard teaching schedule was fifteen hours, that is, three 5-hour courses. In the summer of 1936 the salary for that load, at my rank, was $350. It must have gone up after that, but the figures escape me.

To cite these figures is in no way to complain or to introduce the well-worn how-tough-it-was-in-my-day motif. The figures may have some general antiquarian interest that is not out of place in the historical context of this volume. But the principal function of the figures is to help give a concrete impression of LSU *then.* They clearly show that LSU was in most ways a parochial Depression place—penny-pinching, narrow-gauge, getting by, in no aspect of its style suggesting the capability of imaginative outlays for venturesome projects. It was, so to speak, not a place in which the *Southern Review* was a probable event; it might not be overstating the case to speak of it as an impossible event.

On the personnel front, too, there was little to suggest plan, program, or vision. Procedures seemed casual and hit-or-miss. Today, Brooks and Warren would be brought in, after the usual "national search," and expected to do big things. Then, they just happened to be here and, as far as LSU was concerned, were, I suspect, no more than a couple of guys that Charles Pipkin happened to know, or know of, as fellow southern boys who had got Rhodes scholarships. I got my job at LSU simply on the personal say-so of A. J. Bryan, who had been in the department for some years, and whom I knew as a fellow graduate student at Harvard. An old boy vouched for some friend who then showed up as a new boy. I have no sense of there having been much, if any, institutional search and screening. Perhaps because of the Depression, perhaps because it was a different world, we who came did little screening of the university—certainly nothing of the tireless scrutiny that became rather too familiar when later on I was conducting an appointments process elsewhere. What research grants do you have? How good is your research library? How is your university press? Does it look to the English department for manuscripts? No, on both sides things were quite informal. I received no blueprints of what was expected of me; I heard nothing about standards for tenure and promotion. At this stage of the game the usual emotional cycle is Ph.D. exhilaration, post-Ph.D. depression, and then pretenure anxiety. Though I had enough anxieties to be quite conventional, I can't remember tenure tension. I do not remember whether I ever formally received tenure. One more or less assumed that a job was a lifetime affair, even if students did not entirely love one. There were, as far as I know, no teaching evaluations. The term "publish or perish" was not yet invented, and I don't think anything was ever officially said or implied about publication as a professional activity. Still, the subject was somewhat and somehow in the air. A friend of mine in another department, adopting a *faux naif* stance, jested ironically: "What's this about writing? What do they want me to write? If they tell me what they want me to write, I'll do it."

When I say that writing in no way seemed to be officially expected of faculty, but that the idea of writing was much in the air, I of course describe an aspect of that doubleness which, at the outset, I set forth as an identifying characteristic of the LSU of fifty years ago. The 1935 picture was remarkable and even now seems fascinatingly unexpected: on the one hand, the Depression, messy politics (they would get even messier in the late 1930s), a dictatorship, violent death, mass mourning, the fear of general collapse; on the other, the presence of gifted persons, a fusion of minds and personalities in an influential intellectual and literary flowering, all this evident in such phenomena as the founding of the Louisiana State University Press, the big literary conference in the spring, and the founding of the *Southern Review.* So far I have been mainly describing the aspects of that world which would lead one to expect institutional ordinariness rather than the extraordinary developments which justify a 1985 backward look. I want now to sum up or expand somewhat the contrasts or contradictions which create the "doubleness," and then to go on to a fuller look at the excellences which have become memorable.

The immediate outside world would hardly have seemed conducive to a major literary enterprise or a think-tank world. Yet it is clear that a small Southern city, not very centrally located, and not yet endowed with many comforts that we take for granted, did not impede a new creative outburst in the university. A certain spirit, however generated, triumphed over terrain, location, and discomfort.

LSU was an undistinguished institution which, as we have seen, had many of the stigmata of the Depression university. On the other hand the Huey Long way of doing things, which included both securing new tax revenues and indulging a singular passion for LSU, supplied the university with funds that enabled it to expand, at least in parts, when numerous comparable universities were retrenching. Brooks and Warren joined the English staff just before 1935; three new appointees came in 1935, and two more in 1936. Within five years seven newcomers were added to the professorial ranks, which rose to a total of eighteen by 1947 (with at least the same number in other ranks). And given the general salary range in the 1930s, the outlays for the *Southern Review,* as well as for the School of Music, which was taking on a comparable distinction, were relatively enormous.

Much of the expansion and improvement seemed casual and unplanned—indeed almost accidental. Appointments did not represent the rigorous calculation of betterment that we now know. Yet the *Southern Review* was formally programmed, and the programmatic action began at the presidential level.

Scholarship and writing were neither prescribed nor recommended, and the dominant local tone hardly prodded one toward it. Yet writing was somehow in the atmosphere. Indeed, it got done here and there. Dr. Read had been writing prolifically about place names (I still remember his delight when he hit upon an etymology for the well-known Louisiana surname *Cazedessus*). Warren had already published a biography and was publishing poems and essays; Brooks was writing essays. Likewise people in other departments were writing. In some way the university had acquired members who wrote spontaneously, autonomously. Individual talent modified local tradition; we had personal examples rather than institutional imperatives and codified stepladders.

It is this aspect of doubleness which brings into the open the question that lies behind all the contrasts and inconsistencies that characterized the LSU of the 1930s: how explain the doubleness? More specifically, how did that LSU manage to bring in, in effect welcome, and perhaps even stimulate a number of fertile, creative minds that permanently changed the air? That problem leads more to speculation than to explanation. We may have to settle for that concept of chance which we usually phrase as the presence of the right people at the right place at the right time. But that tells us little. I want to make a guess which, while it still leaves the matter rather abstract, unanchored to precise historical facts, at least improves on the idea that all was chance. My guess is that what happened at LSU—specifically the remarkable influx of talent—had its ultimate roots in the imaginativeness evident in the very complex makeup of the man who ruled Louisiana for a time. It was an imaginativeness which could grasp ends beyond profit and power. Huey had it, and I suspect it influenced his appointment of some underlings who had the same quality, notably President James Monroe Smith. Smith was a very imaginative man (unlike Huey's statehouse followers, singularly unable to imagine the probable consequences of conspicuous looting). And aside from that more or less direct channel, the impulse to imaginative leaps could conceivably have been carried more or less unconsciously by lesser university people than Smith who had some influence on the way things went.

Questions of source aside, the influx of some quite gifted people led to a certain internal doubleness in the thirties: the one between the productive or creative individuals who moved toward a more ecumenical intellectual or professional life, and the comfortable academic citizens who were pretty much content with life in the parish. Initially this was not much more than a contrast in style, with perhaps some reciprocal feelings of annoyance or irritation between what we might call new boys and old boys. (In no way, having been a new boy then, do I want this to be a diatribe against the old boys of the day. Throughout academe, new boys tend to bring with them a sense of the excellence of the ways of doing things at the places they come from, and a desire to transplant these ways to the place they have come to. Hence they tend not to have a very high opinion of the resident old boys. Having now lived long enough to have grown from several new-boy-hoods into old-boy-hood, and to have seen different versions of both classes, I am no longer sure that our own criticalness was as entirely objective as it seemed then.) Then the doubleness of attitude took more solid form in overt action. Some of the more restless faculty tried to have some influence on institutional direction—procedures, standards, appointments, and so on. Nineteen of us got out a rather modest manifesto suggesting some alterations, by no means revolutionary, in LSU; the basic idea, I suppose, was the one put into words by Tom Cowan of the Law School, that LSU should be "more like a university." We probably achieved some stylistic abrasiveness, but I doubt that we stated more than academic truisms. Still, what a furore! In reply, 176 faculty members issued a countermanifesto asserting that LSU was absolutely first-rate just as it was. This was unusual school spirit by faculty members. The doubleness had an amusing side: one faculty member signed both manifestos. Comic doubleness within the individual soul.

The make-it-new versus keep-it-the-same division did not involve two other kinds of doubleness, one of which we might historically expect, and the other of which was alleged at the time. If it was in some sense new boy versus old boy, it was not scholar-critic versus non-scholar. The 176 included some good established scholars, mostly, if my memory is correct, on the science and engineering sides. Again, certain defenders of the status quo complained about some alleged no-goods for whom the going term was "Yankee troublemakers." But the division was, happily, in no way northerners versus southerners. The nineteen were about as evenly divided as a prime number could be between Northerners and Southerners, and the 176 had a healthy infusion of good old Yankee boys. The system of doubleness was not quite the simple affair that a doubleness can sometimes be.

Finally, there was one other doubleness, though rather more elusive than those I've noted. This one faintly reflected breezes blowing from the State Capitol. Some campus characters always seemed to have vague statehouse ties; some could quietly but audibly hint at a Long connection. Thus one could feel, in spots, a faint derivative air of quid-pro-quo-ism. (Minor example: one department secretary managed to let some staff members feel that professional goodies could be arranged if, and so on.) On the other hand, there were campus characters who hated Long and all his works and methods and successors. But these contrasting styles never shaped up into a clear-cut good guys versus bad guys split. Things were more complicated than that. After all, the statehouse characters, whatever they were up to on their own political and economic front, were committed to the Long tradition of magnifying the university. So they might gain tolerance, if not total forgiveness. At any rate, one expectable alignment seems not to have occurred: namely, that the "make it more like a university" group would also become a political-purity faction demanding total divorce between campus and capitol. We tended rather to utilize any slender political resources that might be tapped, or tactics that might be invoked. Rigid partisanship was doubtless made difficult by an ironic doubleness in the state as well as in the university. One aspect of this situation was nicely put by Bob Harris, then head of the Department of Government, after the 1939 scandals had made an official reform movement politically feasible. Harris said, "We have to vote for stupid reformers or bright crooks."

To sum up: at its seventy-fifth birthday LSU was in a transitional period marked by many contrasts in aims, attitudes, and indeed sensibility. But the conflicting elements on different axes never came together enough to create an all-out polarization of objectives and styles. In retrospect one sees energizing differences rather than a possibly disastrous irreconcilability.

Let me now focus on the central doubleness—that of a local tradition under the impact of individual talent. Not only was LSU partly expanding during a depression, but it was making some outstanding appointments. You might call it luck, or surmise the unusual availability of gifted people in a depression. On the other hand, when these people came here, the place did not discourage them or reject them. That's the big point. There was some sort of institutional vitality that could live with difference, even superiority. I have suggested a subterranean imaginativeness under the surface of ordinary humdrum existence, an undefined readiness for institutional adventuring, an intangible susceptibility to "conversion." But on the whole we can describe better than we can interpret.

Of gifted newcomers, Brooks and Warren are of course outstanding examples. But there were others who would achieve different kinds of distinction. Of the new people in English in 1935, Tom Kirby was to become a medieval scholar and a department head with an incredibly long reign, and Nate Caffee was to become provost of the university. Two new people came in 1936: Bosley Woolf would later become a principal editor at Merriam-Webster dictionaries, and Arlin Turner a nationally prominent Americanist. There were strong and striking appointments in various areas in arts and sciences. Various new appointees discovered considerable congeniality. LSU was at that time small enough to encourage a good deal of interdepartmental association, for no one was enclosed in departments of the massive dimensions I have known since then.

There were, of course, some more spectacular eminences whom one knew about rather than knew. I think of those brilliant arrivals from the Metropolitan Opera, Louis Hasselmans and Pasquale Amato, both short and paunchy and equipped with canes and stiff straw hats like a vaudeville duo, to which, of course, they had no other resemblance. There were quite a few younger newcomers that one kept running into in social and campus affairs and feeling generally at one with, whatever the areas of disagreement. I remember Christian Jordan, the pianist; Mac Hebert, Jefferson Fordham, Mel Dakin, and the witty Wex Malone of the Law School; Bob Clark and Karl Arndt in German; Pete Taylor in romance languages; the excellent Rudolf Heberle, who arrived from Germany in 1938, in sociology; the incredibly energetic T. Harry Williams in history; Allen Stanley and Bob Melampey in biology; the sculptors Armin Scheler and Duncan Ferguson, one of whose wonderful bronze cats we yearned to own but never could afford; the painters Conrad Albrizio and Caroline Durieux, the latter with the marvelous comic sense and the experimental spirit and the inventiveness that continued into late years; Ralph Wickhiser, the art historian; in physics Max Goodrich; and in geology both Russells, Chalmer Roy, and Fred Kniffen. This is, I know, a quite skimpy sampling (I am probably forgetting names that I certainly ought to remember) of an academic generation in which there was great personal and professional vitality, and many beginnings of distinction. But I have still to mention what was then called the Department of Government (Bob Harris insisted that the field was not a "science"; he quoted a Vanderbilt professor, a historian and poet, who said, "I speak with authority not because I am called a scientist but because I am a poet"). I had some good friends in that department—Alex Daspit, the LSU alumnus and Rhodes scholar who went on to a long career in the United States State Department; Alden Powell, the genial midwesterner who arrived when my wife and I did, who gained the confidence of established figures on the campus, and who hence was often very valuable as a mediator; Bob Harris, one of the distinguished Vanderbilt representatives in the faculty, later a dean at Virginia, and a notable wit (it was he who said of a member of another department, "Yes, he is bilingual; he is illiterate in two languages").

Three people who came a little later were all to remain, I am proud to say, my lifelong friends. The last of the three was Harold Stoke, a political science person who came as president in my last year at LSU: he was the first non-Southern president in modern times, and the university's appointing him surely evidenced the adventurousness that is one of our themes here. If he did not gratify all the constituencies that besiege presidents, nevertheless his style won many longtime admirers. My other two friends in political science have in common only a similarity in life-span: born within a few months of each other at the turn of the century, they died on the same day in January of 1985. The *American Spectator* mentioned their deaths in the same sentence and asserted that their departure "lowered the I.Q." of the nation. I refer to Charles Hyneman, who came in 1937, who was long a distinguished professor at Indiana University, and who was at one time president of the American Political Science Association; and to Eric Voegelin, who came in 1942 and who has been generally recognized as one of the leading philosophical minds of our day. With their vast differences, they illustrate the extraordinary range and flexibility that LSU had nearly half a century ago. Charles Hyneman was the pragmatic political science man for whom theory was not a formal issue but was implicit or taken for granted, for whom the public machinery of American democracy was an absorbing subject, and who loved, at least in his LSU days, to maintain active relationships between professors and state political figures. He told me once of a happy interview with governor-elect Sam Jones: they sat with their feet on the table and talked the same language. Charles was an easy, articulate, and forceful speaker; in faculty debates on university policy, he was the one good floor leader for all of us who felt that we wanted to "make it more like a university."

In Eric Voegelin LSU showed its extraordinary capacity for cherishing a totally different breed of professional scholar—the pure theorist for whom the truths of political life were inextricably interwoven with the history of ideas, with philosophy, with theology, and indeed with the practices of the traditional aesthetic modes. What we call practical politics did not interest him except insofar as it illustrated problems of theory; from the start he understood what Nazism meant, and he was a heroic intellectual antagonist of the Nazis. He had to flee Vienna when they came in. With his enormous gifts, his formidable intellectual equipment, and his inclination to tell the truth as he saw it, he scared off more than one major political science department in American universities. He did not scare off LSU, he was made to feel at home, and in his fifteen years at LSU he not only won many student admirers but was an enormously productive scholar.

Eric Voegelin and Charles Hyneman, polar opposites as they were in professional life, were remarkable in having in common one interest that, as far as I know, neither spoke about. Eric was a gifted pianist with a mastery of many classical scores (he knew them by heart, I believe), and Charles had amassed, and used, a great collection of recordings of classical compositions.

To sum up: the traditional political philosopher, European in intellectual and personal style, combining graciousness with formality and punctiliousness; and the American pragmatist, a folksy, slangy, midwestern small-town boy, were both welcomed and made at home by a provincial state university, still strongly attached to its military tradition, and just emerging from obscurity at its seventy-fifth birthday. Its basic doubleness was to be its hereditary self and yet to be hospitable to these outsiders who would change that self; and its corresponding doubleness was to entertain such strikingly different immigrants. All this tells us something about its range, potential and actual. That range is otherwise reflected in the birth, fifty years ago, of the *Southern Review*—on the one hand, LSU as a medley of old boys, parochialism, and a more recent existence as institutional pet of a populist dictator; and on the other hand open to, and having a singular gift for, the kind of appointments that brought in a Brooks and a Warren. These times were not merely old times; they were extraordinary times.

The ORIGIN of
the *SOUTHERN REVIEW*

Cleanth Brooks
and Robert Penn Warren

Man is the King of the Beasts because he is the master maker. Birds make nests, bees make honeycombs, but man makes paintings, constitutions, and nuclear bombs. He also makes fictions, some pieces of which are called history—history being concerned not only with established facts but with attitudes and interpretations. The truth is not in man, except sometimes on oath and only if objectively established facts are at stake. In general, man cannot report a fact without reworking it a bit, if only unconsciously, as something of a creative artist.

The "history" of the *Southern Review* is a case in point, though *history* is not quite the right word here. We would do better to speak of histories, because in the folk imagination, as embalmed even in accounts in print, there are various contradictory tales. But the account to follow, though possibly containing some minor slips, would be given on oath if such were required.

Soon after R. P. Warren came to the Louisiana State University in the fall of 1934, Charles W. Pipkin (who held a D.Phil. from Oxford University, was professor of government and dean of the Graduate School), Cleanth Brooks, and Warren (Brooks and Warren being assistant professors in the English department) went to Shreveport, Louisiana, to meet John McGinnis and Henry Nash Smith, editors of the *Southwest Review,* published by the Southern Methodist University of Dallas, Texas. The meeting had been arranged to discuss the possibility of LSU's joining with SMU in editing the *Southwest Review* and in financing it. Undoubtedly, Pipkin had earlier been discussing the matter with the president of LSU, James Monroe Smith, but neither Brooks nor Warren had had any conversation with the president or any other official, and had had no word from Pipkin except the bare outline of the mission. In any case, after the meeting in Shreveport, Brooks and Warren had no special inclination in favor of such an arrangement, even though their names were later to appear on the masthead as "contributing editors." Their attitude toward large editorial boards may be summed up in the old saying that a camel is a "horse designed by a committee." Not many months later, with LSU's funding of its own publication, the *Southwest Review* reverted to its former status.

The first official conversation, or any conversation with either Brooks or Warren about the founding of a review at LSU, occurred in the late winter or early spring of 1935, when one Sunday afternoon the limousine of President Smith—*mirabile dictu*—drew up in front of the house rented by Warren on the outskirts of Baton Rouge. The mission of President and Mrs. Smith was ostensibly to show the newcomers something of the countryside. At this time Albert Erskine, an old friend of Warren and then a graduate student at LSU, was living in the Warren house, and so was asked to join the party.

After some idle conversation, perhaps about the Louisiana landscape, the real mission of the president was disclosed. He asked if a quarterly review published by LSU could get "good" contributors. Warren's answer was "yes." After more landscape, the president said that Warren might get in touch with Brooks and Pipkin to draw up a prospectus of such a quarterly review. He added that he would be ready to sign the authorization the next day.

Brooks and Warren called on Pipkin the next morning. The prospectus was drawn up and offered to President Smith, who signed it. Pipkin was to be editor, Brooks and Warren, associate editors, and Erskine, business manager. There was not much business for him to manage as far as subscriptions went. Local enthusiasm was not great; typically there were fewer subscribers in New Orleans than in Tokyo. Erskine was in fact one of the editors along with Brooks and Warren, reading manuscripts and participating in decisions.

This is definitely the whole matter of the *Review*'s origin as far as Brooks and Warren can reconstruct the past. It has been reported that President Smith had earlier discussed the creation of the *Review* with Pipkin. Such discussion may well have taken place, but if so, Pipkin never reported the matter to Brooks and Warren, not even by any glancing reference to it. Whatever dealings Pipkin may have had, or probably did have, with the administration or any official person concerning the *Southern Review* were never disclosed, or even hinted at, to the associate editors.[1]

1. Only the *Southern Review* is referred to here. Before the trip to Shreveport to meet John McGinnis and Henry Nash Smith, Pipkin had given merely a bare outline of the situation, but concerning the *Southwest Review* there is another detail. Late in 1929 or fairly early in the next year, Warren had had, at Oxford, a

The funding of the *Southern Review* by LSU was set at ten thousand dollars a year. This funding was clearly one aspect of the general expansion of the university, and money available for this expansion was the result of the state legislature's voting additional funds for LSU as well as for various other state activities. (LSU's funding is still the responsibility of the state legislature.)

It is clear that this new and unprecedented generosity of the legislature was due to pressure exerted by Huey Long and a function of his political power in the state. He meant to provide the citizenry with paved roads, hospitals, better schools and universities; and LSU, in all sorts of its activities, including football, profited from the flow of funds. But there is no evidence that Brooks and Warren know of to suggest that Long ever planned the creation of, or even knew of the existence of, the *Southern Review.* Long was preoccupied with his own national career and his hope to win the 1936 Democratic nomination for president of the United States.

In any case, for the associate editors there was no direct *financial* reward. The new assignment provided neither promotion in rank nor rise in pay. It did cut the teaching load of each from four courses to three, but the reading matter brought in by each day's post far outweighed the student papers one freshman class could provide.

---

pleasant acquaintance with Pipkin, then on leave from LSU. Some years later, when Warren was teaching at Vanderbilt University, Pipkin wrote (he must have written because there was no telephone in Warren's house, some miles out in the country) that he was to be in Nashville and would like to come by. After dinner at Warren's house, Pipkin mentioned the possibility, with no details, of the merger between LSU and SMU in the editing and financing of the *Southwest Review.* At this early date Warren had had not even a wild surmise that he would ever be on the faculty of LSU. But along the way in the conversation Pipkin asked if Warren had any new poems handy. This seemed a trifle odd, or polite, for Pipkin had not shown any previous interest in Warren's poetry or other contemporary poetry, though Brooks remembers that Pipkin occasionally quoted traditional poems and professed a real interest in poetry. After a little time with the new poem, Pipkin said that he would like to print it in the *Southwest Review.* He had just remarked on a possible merger of LSU and SMU in regard to the *Southwest Review*—or was about to remark on the matter. In any case, he now said that he would like to pay for the poem now, and would collect from the *Southwest Review* later. He produced fifteen dollars. Did he ever collect? Did the poem ever appear there? Warren cannot say.

It may be proper to say a word about Pipkin's earlier acquaintance with Brooks. Brooks first met Pipkin when he was interviewed for the Rhodes Scholarship in 1928. (Pipkin had been a Rhodes Scholar and was on the examining committee.) Later, during his first year at Oxford, he saw something of Pipkin, as did Warren.

Though Pipkin would not presume to offer Brooks a teaching post in a department other than his own, he did later introduce him to the head of the English department and suggested that he might be invited to give a lecture. In the summer of 1932 Brooks was offered a lectureship in the department.

Brooks remembers that Pipkin hoped that Warren could be invited to come to LSU and undoubtedly used all proper influence. But Warren's previous acquaintance bears more specifically on the origins of the *Southern Review.*

There is one expression of the creative imagination that has appeared in several slightly variant forms. It attributes to Huey Long's direct hand the creation of the *Southern Review.* Maybe so, but not a crumb of such evidence has ever come to Brooks's and Warren's attention. William Faulkner, in his long story "Knight's Gambit," provides another account, this one avowedly the product of Faulkner's imagination. Faulkner has his character Chick Mallison quote his uncle, Gavin Stevens, on the subject of Long and the *Southern Review* as follows: "Huey Long in Louisiana had made himself founder owner and supporter of what . . . was one of the best literary magazines anywhere, without ever once looking inside it probably nor even caring what the people who wrote and edited it thought of him."

Brooks and Warren are grateful to Faulkner for putting this generous comment in the mouth of the resident intellectual of Yoknapatawpha County. But what is more important is that Stevens' surmise seems to them to have the ring of truth.

The one opportunity to test whether Long really didn't care "what the people who edited [the *Review*] thought of him" was cut short by Long's death. About the time of Long's death there appeared in the second issue of the *Review* an article written by Norman Thomas, who at the time was sharply critical of Long. Had this article been called to Long's attention, Pipkin, Brooks, and Warren might have learned how brave (or foolhardy?) they were in their editorial policy. They shall, of course, never know.

CONFERENCE on LITERATURE and READING
in the SOUTH and SOUTHWEST, 1935

With an Introduction by
Thomas W. Cutrer

Nineteen thirty-five, said Malcolm Cowley, was "the Year of Congresses." Meeting in April in New York, the first American Writers' Congress resolved to "strike a blow at the growing fascist enemy, the rapidly developing white guard and fascist criticism, and the Roosevelt-fostered national-chauvinist art." Its leaders, all of whom were "enemies of reaction in the cultural field," included Granville Hicks, Waldo Frank, Malcolm Cowley, James T. Farrell, and Kenneth Burke. Complete party domination was assured by restricting invitations to "reliable writers"—writers, that is, who had "clearly indicated their sympathy for the revolutionary cause."

In June, close to three thousand European, American, and Asian communist and socialist intellectuals convened at the Palais de la Mutualité in the Latin Quarter of Paris to discuss "the conditions of literary creation and relations between the writer and his public." As in the case of the American gathering, the Paris meeting neither invited nor welcomed centrist and right-wing thinkers. Presided over by André Malraux and graced by such distinguished men of letters as André Gide, E. M. Forster, Léon Blum, Aldous Huxley, Bertolt Brecht, Boris Pasternak, and Tristan Tzara, the First International Congress of Writers in Defense of Culture was efficiently organized, well attended, and sympathetically reported. It heard speeches, created committees, adopted resolutions, and adjourned with the distinction of being the largest gathering of writers and artists since the Middle Ages to attempt the mobilization of art and letters around a single political ideal. Its insistence upon party loyalty, however, doomed it to literary futility. Good poets, it has been said, make bad strike leaders. In retrospect, Malraux called the congress an "impassioned confusion."

Also in the spring of 1935, bracketed between these two massive and closely scrutinized writers' congresses, was a third important but largely forgotten meeting of internationally prominent men and women of letters. In an isolated corner of the republic of letters, far from the cultural capitals of New York and Paris, a crossing of the careers of Huey P. Long, often characterized by the left as a proto-fascist American dictator, and Cleanth Brooks and Robert Penn Warren, two of the brightest stars on the American literary horizon, resulted in a writers' conference which would signal a significant burgeoning of literary effort on the campus of Louisiana State University.

In 1935 the university was celebrating its seventy-fifth anniversary, while enjoying an unparalleled period of growth under the capricious but generally benevolent hands of Louisiana's "Kingfish," Senator Huey P. Long. The origin of LSU went back to the establishment of the Louisiana State Seminary of Learning and Military Academy at Pineville, Louisiana, in 1860, with Colonel William Tecumseh Sherman as superintendent. This tiny school had closed, reopened, and closed again during the Civil War, reopened after the war, burned in 1869, and reopened at last in Baton Rouge. Named Louisiana State University in 1870, the institution was joined in 1877 to the Louisiana Agricultural and Mechanical College—a union that still exists. In 1925 the university began to move from its location on the grounds now occupied by the state capitol to its present location. The spacious new site afforded the opportunity for the institution to transcend its origin and move beyond a small-school mentality.

Nowhere on the campus was the hand of change felt more decisively than in the Department of English, which in the 1930s suddenly acquired a crop of talented young assistant professors with graduate degrees from Harvard, Berkeley, Oxford, and other prestigious universities. Foremost among this band were Cleanth Brooks and Robert Penn Warren. They had a good deal in common. Both were natives of Kentucky, both had been undergraduates at Vanderbilt, where they had been more or less closely associated with the *Fugitive,* the short-lived but extremely influential poetry magazine, and both had been Rhodes Scholars at Oxford. Additionally, Warren had been one of the Twelve Southerners who defended traditional Southern values in *I'll Take My Stand,* and Brooks, though not a charter member of the conservative movement, was in strong sympathy with its principles and goals. Both Brooks and Warren, moreover, were tremendously excited by the change in the practice and teaching of poetry wrought by T. S. Eliot, I. A. Richards, and others of the nascent schools of modern poetry and the New Criticism, and sought to take the university into the vanguard of these literary movements. After funding for the establishment of a quarterly journal at LSU was provided in February, 1935—and Charles W. Pipkin, dean of the Graduate School, had been named editor with Brooks and Warren associate editors—an announcement occasion of the university's new publication was planned as a part of the "Ole War Skule's" Diamond Jubilee celebration. As conceived by Pipkin, Brooks, and Warren, this took the form of the Southern writers' conference to be held on the roof of the Heidelberg Hotel in Baton Rouge on April 10 and 11, 1935.

A number of literary notables were invited to attend the conference. Some—among them John Crowe Ransom, Donald Davidson, Stark Young, and William Faulkner—sent regrets or simply failed to come. But forty men and women of letters participated in the event, while a mix of spectators looked on. Robert Penn Warren served as chairman. Although several Agrarian allies—Allen Tate, Caroline Gordon, John Gould Fletcher, John Peale Bishop, John Donald Wade, and Frank Lawrence Owsley—took part, the participants also included Southern writers and editors more attuned to the New South movement than the Agrarian persuasion: Lambert Davis, managing editor of the *Virginia Quarterly Review;* William T. Couch, director of the University of North Carolina Press and editor of the influential anthology *Culture in the South;* Savoie Lottinville of the University of Oklahoma Press; B. A. Botkin, Oklahoma folklorist and editor of two short-lived journals in Norma; John McGinnis of the *Southwest Review;* and Hodding Carter, Brooks's Tulane roommate and editor of the fiercely anti-Long Hammond *Daily Courier.* Adding their prestige to the occasion were the two reigning lions of the Louisiana literary scene, Roark Bradford and Lyle Saxon, as well as Manson Radford and Kenneth Thomas Knoblock, lesser-known New Orleans writers. Representing local English departments were Richard Ray Kirk of Tulane and LSU's John Earle Uhler, whose name had become something of a scandal in Louisiana in 1931 with the publication of a controversial novel, *Cane Juice.* Also attending were James Rorty, a Northern journalist of leftist political persuasion who covered the event for *Forum* magazine; Edward Donahoe and George Milburn, Oklahoma writers, both of whom were working on first novels and were to publish short stories in the first volume of the *Southern Review;* and Frederick S. Wight, a New York–born artist and writer with deep affinities for the Southern land and people. Perhaps most notable among the participants was Ford Madox Ford. Founding editor of the *English Review,* the famous novelist was a lifelong admirer not only of Stonewall Jackson but of a culture he associated with his love of "green growing objects" and those who nurture them.

Ford remembered that it was "insupportably hot" on the morning of Wednesday, April 10, when Warren called to order the first session of the Conference on Literature and Reading in the South and Southwest on the roof of the Heidelberg Hotel, the very location from which Senator Long managed the affairs of Louisiana when away from his Washington office. In his opening remarks Pipkin called for the repudiation of provincialism by the group and invoked a spirit of "genial tolerance and congeniality" among its members. Although the planners of the conference were quick to point out that they were "not intended to limit, or even necessarily to direct the discussion, but rather to provoke and suggest possible developments," Pipkin, Brooks, and Warren proposed seven rather broad areas of discussion for the two-day event. Each question was to be formally addressed by the session's chairman and then opened to general discussion. Not by chance, the seven questions coincided precisely with the problems that the *Southern Review* would face. Contrary to Pipkin's expressed hope, the ensuing two days of prepared statements, debate, and "literary chit-chat" were characterized by disagreement between the conference participants who called for a powerful center of publication in the South and a literary secession from Northern presses, especially those of New York, and the more moderate participants, who agreed with Saxon's assessment that "New York has treated us perhaps better than we deserve."

Overshadowed as the conference was by the larger literary events taking place in New York and Paris, it is hardly surprising that its results received but little assessment at the time and has had not much since. The New Orleans *Item,* which cited Roark Bradford and Lyle Saxon as the only clear heads in the group, called the conference "amusing" but "completely ineffectual." After reading the transcript of the proceedings, the arch-Agrarian Donald Davidson wrote to Warren that the liberals and progressives (like Bradford and Saxon) were "the villains, and the Agrarians among the heroes quite clearly." For the conference hosts, however, the outcome was not one of right or wrong or left or right. "The sporadic 'Conferences' and 'Congresses' of writers in different sections of the country have . . . tended to define differences of opinion rather than concord," Warren observed in an early *Southern Review* editorial. "Certainly no program or dogma has emerged." For him and his colleagues, the true purpose of the Baton Rouge writers' conference was not to forge a unified world view or an artistic stance to support a political philosophy such as the New York and Paris meetings had hoped to achieve. The conference was rather a symbolic statement to the effect that the *Southern Review* would serve two states, the state of the South and the state of letters. The presence and participation of so many outstanding spokesmen for so many divergent points of view clearly indicated the *Review*'s commitment to responsible literary pluralism within a regional framework. During the seven-year period of the publication of the original series, it seemed to some that the realization of this commitment was sufficient to indicate a shift in advanced literary thought and creativity from the left bank of the Seine to the left bank of the Mississippi at Baton Rouge.

B. A. Botkin served as recorder for the Baton Rouge conference, transcribing the comments of each of the speakers and distributing copies of the transcript to each of the participants. These copies have become quite rare, and I am indebted to the late Professor Walton Patrick of Auburn University, a first-semester graduate student at the time of the conference, later to become the LSU English department's first Ph.D., for making his copy available to me.[1]

FIRST SESSION
WEDNESDAY, APRIL 10, 1935, 9:30 A.M.
(Mr. Robert Penn Warren, presiding, introduces
Dean Charles W. Pipkin.)

DR. CHARLES PIPKIN: I want to say with what genuine feeling I speak for Louisiana State University. Of all the Jubilee events this is nearest to my heart and interests. For you and I believe in ideas. There are so many things that happen whose passing seems momentous. But the ideas and ideals are important. You who manage to put this into words are thinking of the past and looking ahead to the future.

The chief purpose of this group is fellowship—a community of ideas. Genial tolerance and congeniality must characterize it. I am glad we are southern writers. We do not meet as provincials this morning— how dare we, how could we, meet as provincials, surrounded by the

---

1. The story of the Baton Rouge conference is told in greater detail in Max Webb's "Ford Madox Ford and the Baton Rouge Writers' Conference," *Southern Review,* n.s., X (Autumn, 1974), 892–903, and in Thomas W. Cutrer's *Parnassus on the Mississippi: The "Southern Review" and the Baton Rouge Literary Community, 1935–1942* (Baton Rouge, 1984).

crash of the world, many of whose phases are ended. What is important is that we think of the South today as a way of life toward the future. And it is to that future we have given ourselves.

MR. ROBERT PENN WARREN: To Dr. Pipkin's welcome I want to add my own. And I want to thank those who have come for their cooperation. I have regrets from Donald Davidson, John Crowe Ransom, Elizabeth Madox Roberts, T. M. Pearce, Arthur Campo, Caroline Miller, Ellen Glasgow, and Irita Van Doren. William Faulkner may or may not appear—he was undecided Saturday. . . .

The aims of this conference particularly are to discuss reading and literature in the South. The questions as originally proposed are something like this:

First, why don't people in the South buy and read books?

Second, the question of magazine circulation.

Third, why do the colleges and universities fail to provide a responsive and responsible public?

We shall probably arrive at no prescriptions. The program is informal. The questions on the mimeographed sheets represent the subjects for short talks. John McGinnis was to talk on the first topic, but he is not here yet. John Peale Bishop will talk on the second, Allen Tate on the third, Irita Van Doren was to have talked on the fourth, Lambert Davis will talk on the fifth, W. T. Couch on the sixth, and Ford Madox Ford on the seventh. Today the first three topics will be given. We shall open with Mr. Bishop and Mr. Tate.

Question two: *What effect has this lack of a public had on the nature of literary production in the South?*

MR. JOHN PEALE BISHOP: I want to begin that very generally—the question of the artist in general to his public. When you get a public and its artist having the same reactions and those are significant reactions, you have great art. The last time you had that was in the seventeenth century. It was not a matter of patronage, but you had the same taste and sensibility. That began to go to pieces in the eighteenth century. Then the artist and the person who paid for the art had the same taste and sensibility but it was not artistic; it was social—furniture, conversation, journals, etc. In the eighteenth century the middle class rose, and you began to have the evil of the purely instinctive way of life. This was not favorable to literature, painting, and sculpture. You began to get

sentimentality and pornography—two of the things that vitiate literature. You get Madame de Pompadour—the first example of a middle-
class person patronizing the arts. She became the king's mistress, but
she was of the middle class. She patronized the pornographic note (in
Boucher, whom she made court painter), the sentimental and blue-
stocking note.

Now I dwell on that because civilization in the South was the same.
You had a society very much like eighteenth-century England. The life
of Virginia was very much like the life depicted by Fielding. The
planters were very much like Squire Western. There was that very
definitely limited interest. They were provincial people, country people. You get no capital city. You had important cities like New Orleans
and Charleston but no capital.

This continuity means there was no definite break as in New England
and all parts of the country settled from New England. I feel it in New
Orleans. New York has a long history, but it is impossible to feel back
before 1870. You get it in Paris. But the South was primarily pioneer.
The frontier is everywhere around us—a stabilized frontier—though
we speak of the passing of the frontier. Both these audiences—the
eighteenth-century gentleman and the pioneer—did not read.

I don't think that the position of the writer in the South is vastly
different from the position of writers elsewhere. Since the middle class
came into power, the position of the writer has been a very lonely one.

When you get into the nineteenth century, you get a very great
divergence of taste. The middle class left all those things to the upper
classes, though even the latter became bourgeois. (This is not a matter
of birth but a way of thinking.) The parallel can be drawn between the
South and France between 1830 and 1880. In 1830 you had the
complete triumph of the middle class—a complete hopelessness. The
author tries to please his audience, but knew there was no immediate
audience or a very small one.

What are the qualities that developed out of the loneliness of the
artist? The artist should not have to set his own problem. That should be
set by the man who pays for it. The artist should give the solution only.
The man who pays is no longer capable of setting problems. You ought
not both to build the hurdle and jump it. The result is certain eccen-
tricities—self-indulgence—doing things he wants for himself. That
obscurity, eccentricity, perversity, and self-indulgence are found in a
man like Faulkner—a very distinguished writer. You find it especially in
his early books, before he found his public.

Yet those same qualities are found in the French. The same thing is found in poetry. The Fugitive group is an obscure group. You get it developing after the middle of the century as in Rimbaud—writing for oneself. You get it in Proust—who is very self-indulgent.

Also you get an antisocial quality. When you get complete disregard by society, the artist tends to take it out on society. *Tobacco Road* is one of the best things that has been done in this country, but it is antisocial. You get a great deal of horror and obscenity, parallel with French naturalism, as in *Madame Bovary* and Zola. The same protest was raised against them. These are the effects of loneliness—of having no corrective or feeling no corrective from the public.

I do not consider the practical qualities resulting from this loneliness. If you have no audience, you have to find one. The potential audience for a serious book in the United States is 400,000—ridiculously low. What you have is a criticism of Southern life from standards not Southern but New York, as in Mr. Stribling and Isa Glenn—what the non-Southern audience expects. That has been condemned a great deal by Southern writers, but there is another side to it. It is unfair to judge a way of life by standards outside it. You find this in nineteenth-century biography. Lytton Strachey criticized everything from its own standards.

At the same time there is a possibility of Southern writers becoming provincial. Writing should be provincial in space but not in time. Writing should be exported or exportable. Many works lose their value in other countries. I refer to Mr. Ford as an example of the writer who is localized but exported. He is not a Southern writer, of course, except as Provence is South.

The South doesn't like to be written about or talked about even in a complimentary way. I was very much struck by that when I came down to Natchez to find *So Red the Rose* unpopular because, for instance, Stark Young moved a house from the west to the east side. They resent the nice things as well as the bad things you say about them.

The Southern writer cannot depend on the Southern audience for correctives. At the same time the writer should be criticized by his own standards. What you will get, on the other hand, in any book about the South is the "decadence" and "degeneration" of the South. Whenever you write, you are told you have represented very powerfully the decadence of the South. As our chairman said, the world is upside-down and decay is going on everywhere else. A decadent society is one that has lost its sense of form in which to live. In Stendhal you get decadence—the breaking down of the forms in which they live. Mr. Tate is going to speak further on that question. The ultimate point of decadence in society is reached when it has lost its sense of life and substitutes for it abstractions or nothing. The society of *Appointment in Sammara* is decadent—a more complete degeneration than even in Caldwell. There is absolutely nothing left for these people except to get drunk. The people in *Tobacco Road* are pretty far gone but they can still function in some ways. In New York you have the substitution of abstractions. But I leave that to Mr. Tate.

Question three: *What is the position of the individual writer in such a situation?*

MR. ALLEN TATE: I think Mr. Bishop has done entirely too good a job. Mr. Lambert Davis and I were conducting a whispered commentary and agreed that he left nothing for us to say. In a meeting of this kind each talk must be improvised on the basis of the previous one. The problem of the writer is not very different from the one Mr. Bishop stated. You can take one writer and follow his work in terms of that outline.

The arts will disappear because the forms are being broken down and something is being substituted for the hurdle. . . . The split of the public into two parts came in the eighteenth century. In Defoe you have a good example of the journalist. The two publics were parallel until the eighteenth century. There is only one public left—the general public—which must buy the book as a commodity. That is the situation we are in—unfortunately. There is nothing we can do about it. The position of the Southern writer is seen in Mr. Faulkner—in his appeal to sensation, etc. He has no public of his peers. He issues his books in the hope that they will catch on. They do catch on. But that is not the best kind of public.

In the South we have the writer whose society is in one place and whose public is in another. He writes about one to be read by another. The South has no distinctive middle class, so the writer has no public at home. How can the author write about it and sell it elsewhere?

Not one-fourth, probably one-eighth, of the 400,000 readers in the United States are found in the South. Now I do not propose to talk any longer or draw any conclusions. I should like to ask the chairman to turn that over to the audience.

DISCUSSION

MR. WARREN: Mr. Bishop and Mr. Tate have put the basic difficulty in sharp terms that will provoke discussion without its being demanded.

(Mr. Lambert Davis asks what part the author has in setting the problems.)

MR. BISHOP: I was thinking in terms of painting and sculpture. But in poetry practically all the forms were settled by the court and then taken up by the poets. It is only later that you get those forms diffused. The Tudor poets are court poets—the Elizabethans took over and developed those forms.

(Mr. Davis speaks of the function of the editor.)

MR. BISHOP: The editor's function is to set the problem.
MR. LAMBERT DAVIS: The editor is a bridge between the writer and the public. We can only build the bridge, I am afraid.
MR. W. T. COUCH: As one interested in publishing and selling books, I'd like to know why books are not selling. The chief reason is lack of money. The second reason is a large population which is not able to read. When I mention the second, I raise serious questions to the analysis of the previous speakers. From 1460 to 1900 (the time of the development of the rotary press) the reading public was very small. At that time the patrons set the problem. The artist was dependent on patrons, and in setting the problems the patron usually did a very fine job. But this was not always the case. Shakespeare appealed to the mob. I feel strongly that we need in the South a large reading public. The success of the writer depends on that. I hope to come to that when I start the discussion of question six. In summary I should say there are two problems: 1) How are we going to get money for books? 2) How are we going to get a public able to read and understand books—take part in the intellectual life?
MR. WARREN: Mr. Couch has raised another question—the creation of a reading public. That is asked in the first question on the list: *Is the problem of a lack of a proper public special to the South? That is, are there any unique features that differentiate the situation here from that in other sections where there is little buying and reading of books?*

(Mr. Warren refers this question to Mr. Bishop.)

MR. BISHOP: That was entirely outside of my question. But it takes too much to publish books. We get 15 percent—the rest goes into distribution even more than into printing. It goes to the people who are trying to sell books and into the bookshops.

QUERY FROM THE AUDIENCE: You say the writers are writing for non-Southern readers and that is not fair?

MR. BISHOP: *So Red the Rose* was published for the Southern audience. Stark Young has preserved the Southern point of view remarkably. Stribling writes from the outside point of view.

MR. DAVIS: Southerners are naturally sensitive about their private lives. So many Southerners, for instance, ordered their letters to be burned. It was a matter of personal integrity.

MR. REYNOLDS: Both speakers assume that the writers are aristocratic and write for the bourgeois tradition of the South. I think the situation is the reverse. There are some Southern writers who are bourgeois and have nothing to say to the aristocratic tradition. This sort of writer learned it in school and is merely trying to ape his betters. Must he be proud of the fact that he can walk across a ballroom floor without stumbling? The trouble, as I see it, is that the writer himself is not aristocratic. (Reynolds has not been identified.—Ed.)

MR. B. A. BOTKIN: In his article "The Profession of Letters in the South" in the current *Virginia Quarterly Review,* Mr. Tate points out that in the South politics and the political tradition have always dominated literature and the literary tradition. I should like to ask Mr. Tate to develop that point here.

MR. TATE: The contemporary political situation makes demands on all writers in all sections. We are in a dilemma—capitalism versus radicalism. That is the present phase of political tyranny. May I develop it dogmatically? The communist solution doesn't lend itself to the South. Communism does not grow out of rural life. Caldwell is very dull when he becomes a social prophet.

MR. FRANK L. OWSLEY: The Southern writer has to recognize certain prejudices both as to history and as to writing. Anyone studying the historical writing for forty years after the Civil War will recognize this preconception. It has been aggravated by recent developments of radicalism in the East. There is mutual vilification. The attitude of the South toward the North was that Northerners were cowards—they would do anything for money. The North thought all Southerners were bullies. They did stick to the code of the duel longer than other sections. Into this picture came the slavery controversy, which gave rise to the most intense emotional campaign in the world. Here we encounter the preconception of brutality, lynching, lack of culture and taste. That preconception was intensified by the war itself and Reconstruction. Then another preconception came in—that the South was degenerate and decadent. By external observation of "jeeter" shacks as well as by prejudice you arrive at the conclusion that the South is decadent. Writers have to pander to this prejudice. Many writers have a personal grievance—it is a question *ad hominem*. With reference to the development of an audience, why not take a leaf out of the writing of history? The historian writes for a small audience. The Northern scholar wants the truth as much as anyone. One way to develop a reading public is to tell the truth rather than merely to defend one's section or to pander to prejudice. The South is becoming sensitive because of being defamed by both its illegitimate sons and outsiders.

MR. JOHN GOULD FLETCHER: I think the last remark was very apt and thank Mr. Owsley for it. I came late and didn't hear Mr. Tate and Mr. Bishop. The question should be related geographically as well as historically. Most of the publishing is being done in New York and Boston. Except for the University of Oklahoma Press and the University of North Carolina Press I know of no Southern presses. The problem of creating a public is to publish regional books. Publishing is a commercial enterprise. It has the critics organized on its side. Someone mentioned *So Red the Rose* as an excellent book. It is. It deals with a way of life in a milieu. There is another book dealing with the same life—*Aleck Maury, Sportsman* by Caroline Gordon—but it hasn't sold. The reason is that the American public has heard about Natchez—it has been publicized. On the other hand, the dates of Aleck Maury's life are not given, and the names are fictitious. It is a fictional character and setting, but represents a very important side of Southern life—the backwoods hunter type is just as important as the cotton planter. Mr. Young deals with the latter and is very careful to detail his background.

This shows there is no particular critical standard—there is only a metropolitan one. The publisher goes around to the reviewers and says: This book has to be puffed. All the critics are there in New York. The sensitivity of the South may be due to the realization that we are at the mercy of the paid critics. There are three ways of breaking down the system: 1) the public library; 2) the bookseller; 3) the magazine and newspaper column. 1) The public-library situation is very important. Some time ago an educator went to a backwoods school and asked how many had read a book. Outside of schoolbooks none had read one. Only one girl had read a magazine—*True Confessions*. That is what gave Mr. Mencken his platform of the South as the Bible Belt. The American Legion has been organizing libraries in Arkansas under the PWA. I have the figures here from June to December, 1934. Thirty-two places are listed, with 42,640 as the total population; 5,302 borrowers; 39,000 books in circulation; and 19,904 books in the libraries. This means that every one of these books circulated twice. The books were given by donation, from private libraries; the entire thing was done by amateurs. In one place, Fordyce, every book circulated five times. We have a reading public in the South—even a poor public is anxious to read. 2) The bookstores do not exist because of poverty and because we have been kept away from books so long.

3) The third question—the magazine question—is very important. If you are going to get a reading public in the backwoods (they will read what you offer them), can the metropolitan papers or can the *Virginia Quarterly Review* (which has a suspicion of Southernness on top and is metropolitan underneath)—can it function for the South? I think not. A Southern review should be distinctly Southern. We are economically nationalistic but we can't be culturally nationalistic. Cultural nationalism is the only kind to have. And you can't get any section of this country to think of its culture except as a joke. Take the West. The West is getting into a political turmoil very much like ours in the South. Are we in the South going to sit back and give up to the metropolitan critics? We were almost the intellectual leaders of the country. If we had started five years earlier, we should have been. Three-fourths of the *Virginia Quarterly Review* is metropolitan. Southerners will read a Southern magazine, but it will not get distribution. The chief distributing agency is the American News Company—it has barred backwoods magazines from the newsstands. You are going to have to build up a subscription list. You are going to have to sell door to door. I wish Mr. Botkin would tell us more about his experience with the news agencies on *Space*.

MR. JOHN UHLER: I want to discuss the contradiction raised by Mr. Fletcher. There is a large reading public in the South. Louisiana has only two million population, with 800,000 Negroes. The Negro population is not a reading population. Then, too, reading is a matter of civilization. Civilization is a matter of cities, not of rural districts. We are not urban. When those two facts are considered, we see we have a tremendous reading public just the same.

MR. DAVIS: As to the American News and the *Virginia Quarterly Review,* the American News was glad to handle it. It takes one dollar to produce a copy, however, and if you send out five and the American News returns five covers, you lose five dollars. The news dealer will not display a magazine without a public. We need the public. Any news company would be glad to handle a magazine if it could make money.

MR. JOHN DONALD WADE: I don't see that any particular advantage would be gained by the circulation of more books and magazines. If the world is going to be a clutter of books and magazines I'd dread it. The books have to be worth something. The South sets store by style. The pioneers have an exaggerated conception of cities, and have tended to accept the values established in the cities. The type of writing that has grown up in the world at large and the taste for writing have come out in response to a natural state of affairs. That state of affairs hasn't existed with us. We have a different sort of society—not urbanized. But we want to be in style. We ask, What are people doing in New York? The sort of writing whose circulation would make us proud has to grow out of the state of affairs in the region. That would make it impossible for us to write for the person who is paying the piper. If there is a certain taste and you can't qualify for it, it is a trick of slick artistry to do the other thing. It is something to have to bear up under.

MR. FLETCHER (sotto voce): There is no reason at all.

MR. TATE: Mr. Wade reminded me of a point I should have made at the beginning. What is the reading public we want? Eliot once said that the modern public is simply a collector of points of view. The South appeals to the interest in travel literature—for its picturesque detail. You can't get that in the South. I believe there is something to be said in favor of the South not developing that kind of taste. If it can't get the kind of literature it wants, it won't take any.

MR. JAMES RORTY: I am surprised that the discussion has developed about the setting of problems. The hurdles discussed are mechanical hurdles—problems of distribution and circulation. The connection to be made between Mr. Tate's affirmation that the writer has a social obligation and the other is that the writer has to participate in the setting of the problems. I deny the position of Mr. Bishop. This has never been true except in a partial sense. In a time of transition the writer is drawn into questions outside of his peculiar functions. He much concerns himself with economic and social hurdles.

MR. LYLE SAXON: I have been interested in the tone of bitterness that has come into the discussion. We are all disgruntled about something. Stark Young must have known that everyone wouldn't like the book. That is a general problem. Do you suppose that New England liked *Ethan Frome,* or Russia liked Chekhov, or Norway liked Ibsen? I've written books about the South and some of them have been liked by some and not by others. We haven't done so badly—and New York has treated us perhaps better than we deserve. As to logrolling, the New York critics try to do the best they can. Miss Van Doren asked me to review *The Sound and the Fury,* for instance, and I did. I don't know how much good writing has come from the South—some of it is good and some of it drivel. If we give the country what it wants to read, it will read it. Mr. Wade hit the problem when he said we must write the kind of thing we want to write. Our problem is to write just what we want and let the chips fall where they may.

MR. FLETCHER: I am sorry I can't agree with Mr. Saxon. He speaks for an older generation. I speak for a younger generation. The artist is being driven to write about things he doesn't want to. The Communists are right. We must form a united front. Mr. Saxon could go on writing what he wants for twenty years and then he'd have to throw it into the wastebasket. Mr. Herbert Read recently wrote an article on sweated authors for the London *Mercury.* The author gets 10 percent and the publisher all except 33⅓ percent, which goes to the bookseller. The writers should publish their own books. There is a group in New Mexico doing it, and I am one of them. The artist is in the position of being dictated to by the market demand of mass production industry—like cigarettes, Ford cars, and soap—except that the writer only gets 10 percent. You can break it by creating a strong regional taste and creating regional publishing.

MR. RORTY: I am delighted to hear Mr. Fletcher admitting things I've been admitting for years. I think there is a good deal of logrolling in New York, but critics are more justly to be accused of stupidity rather than dishonesty. I published a book last spring, and my publisher was careful not to suggest to the magazines what person was to review the book. That angered them very much. My book fared well just the same.

What happens is that when writers have a chance to register a blow at the type of system in force, they do—a form of sabotage.

MR. RANDALL JARRELL: Chekhov was almost exceptionally popular and so was Ibsen, though Mr. Saxon said they weren't. Shakespeare made a good income.

MR. SAXON: I meant there were two groups—no matter what work of art is produced it is regarded critically by one group.

SECOND SESSION
Thursday, April 11, 1935, 10:00 A.M.

Question five: *What are the problems of editing a magazine in the South? Are they special?*

MR. DAVIS (editor of the *Virginia Quarterly Review*): I am afraid that after what was said yesterday, what I shall have to say today will seem rather prosaic. In fact, in contrast to the work of the writer, the work of the editor is always prosaic. Editing is a secondary and derivative profession, and very modern. Editors have come into being only with the rise of the modern art which Mr. Bishop and Mr. Tate discussed yesterday—with the dissociation of the artist from his public. As the editor sees it, there seems to be a tension between the function of art as expression and the function of art as communication. There was a time when this tension did not exist, as in the seventeenth and eighteenth centuries, when the community had such a spiritual unity that expression and communication were one. The editor didn't exist then. He arose in the eighteenth century when the tension arose.

The writer and reader today are both specialists, and there is a threat of a breakdown between the two. This calls into being the editor. He tries to create a community. There are any number of communities he could create—on common economic or religious motives or social outlook. But that is the publisher's function rather than the editor's function. As an editor his job is simply to create the (literary) community, using every appropriate device he can devise. Mr. Condé Nast has described the editor as a name broker. He was using this term to suggest the relation between the editor and the advertiser, but it applies to the whole problem. The editor is a practicing sociologist—he is interested in groups and collects data. Unlike many sociologists he tries to use those data. The editor has to look two ways—toward his readers and his writers. That may be why he is called two-faced, perhaps. The good editor is one who can look both ways without getting cross-eyed. He has to find the proper writers for his readers and the proper readers for his writers.

It doesn't matter what his economic views are—he can be a Communist, Agrarian, etc. As a Communist he may sabotage the system that is supporting him. But as long as he is editing he is caught in the nexus of cash receipts.

As to the particular problems that face the Southern editor, I can give my own experience, but can't tell whether these problems are strictly Southern or not. Yesterday we discussed economic poverty—that is a general question now. As to his relationship to his authors, the editor suffers from physical isolation. Except New Orleans, there is no community in the South that supports an active writing group. That limits the flow of ideas. Walter Hines Page said the *World's Work* was a good magazine as long as a dozen people dropped into his office each day. Isolation does serve to relieve the editor of wear and tear on the mind and liver. Because of isolation, it is impossible for the South to support a weekly or monthly devoted to journalistic repartee. Isolation, on the other hand, is an advantage to a quarterly in the way of perspective. With regard to the Southern reader there are two groups which condition the Southern editor. First, there are those who want the New York approval. They believe that a Southern magazine is good if and as mentioned in the New York reviews. This reader wants the Southern review to publish things that New York will like. I am not one that objects to New York. Most writers in the South who are any good have gone through the New York mill and come out grateful for it. The other type is the Southern patriot. (I am not a public speaker, as you observe.) The Southern patriotic speaker acts in the same way as the Southern patriot in magazine editing—he wants to tone down criticism. This type is not limited to the South. We get four-page letters from Iowa or Illinois, one page praising the *Review* and three pages telling that the writer's grandfather came from Virginia in such and such a year.

The editor's function is to play between these two groups and to reconcile them. He should try to make the Southerner with an inferiority complex lose it, and the patriot examine his presuppositions. Under these conditions, if he can create this community, any magazine, regional or otherwise, is possible.

MR. JOHN MCGINNIS (editor of the *Southwest Review*): I was charmed by the preceding presentation of some of the problems that confront the provincial editor. For a number of years my chief activities have been editing, first a book page for the Dallas *News* (the largest Texas paper) and then for eleven years, the *Southwest Review* (the smallest of the Southern magazines). I am glad to meet my contributors. I have introduced Mr. Ford's *No More Parades* to Texas. Of the fifteen or more writers I have met here, I have done a friendly service to most.

It seems, however, that the literary critic in the South is failing in his function. One reason is the apathy of the publishers. Of course, everyone knows that the South is good copy. The publishers break in their representatives by sending them on the Southern circuit and are cold when they come back. When I was asked to found a book page, I wrote letters to all the editors. The first book I received was a Sabatini romance. The stencil of the Dallas *News* may have gotten lost in the office of Little Brown or the Viking Press, and yet one dollar-book company advertised in the Dallas *News* and sold six thousand books. One hundred eighty-one copies of one title were sold in one Dallas store. The publishers are slow to wake up to the markets.

I should like to dissociate myself from any effort to propagandize the arts. I am profoundly cynical about the efforts of editors, publishers, and critics to give direction to the production and distribution of literary masterpieces. But if they can do anything, they can do it by selling more books, Southern and Northern.

If there is any interest in books in the South it is shown by the women's clubs and their book reviews. I know one woman who was arrested for speeding on her way to hear her third review of *Mourning Becomes Electra*—because she didn't know what to think of it and wanted someone to tell her. Southerners are eager to hear about books but don't know what to think of them.

As to magazines, the *Southwest Review* has four hundred paying subscribers—a good deal more of these in New York than in New Mexico, Louisiana, and Oklahoma. I am sure that it is not read as it should be where it goes. A few years after the *Southwest Review* came to Dallas, a literary editor asked the question: Is this magazine edited in the interest of the reader or the contributor? And I could hardly answer. Of course, we had always hoped to get readers interested and to discover writers. But which end we held more dear and which we should hold more dear I can't say. In the South at present, one magazine cannot serve both ends at the same time. The provincial magazine that will get itself read by literary editors who influence public opinion does not yet exist. The critical articles appeal to other critics, but have not a great deal of even remote influence on writing and reading in the South.

In conclusion, although I have said quite frankly that I am not hopeful about Southern magazines, I do want to say that the multiplication of these magazines in the South is a good sign, and in the future we shall have more intelligent readers not only for Southern magazines but for magazines and books in general. The activity of two or three of the regional presses is evidence that books written, printed, and distributed at home may find a circle of the right readers more promptly than if we should depend on Northern publishers. The books of the Chapel Hill press had a wider distribution published in North Carolina than if sent to Nothern publishers. They certainly have been printed as well. And it seems to me that a publishing venture in a Southern city—not an amateur but a businesslike organization—would become a successful enterprise.

MR. BOTKIN (editor of *Space*): I was asked to discuss the ideas of Mr. Bishop and Mr. Tate as related to another type of society, Oklahoma. At least that is the way the question was put to me yesterday, and what I more or less promised to do, with special reference to the problems of editing a magazine in Oklahoma. But that was yesterday. And yesterday doesn't count in Oklahoma. Before I go into that, however, I might say that I am and feel like an outsider, not only in the South but also in Oklahoma—and it is only as an outsider that I can discuss the problems of this conference. And to discuss the problems of this conference rather than the ideas of any of the speakers who have preceded me is what I prefer to do, although I can't help referring to the others, as I hope they will refer to me.

You will notice that as stated in the mimeographed list of questions, "the aim of the conference is to discuss literature and reading in the South and Southwest," though in the special topics the word *Southwest* is omitted. I am reading it back in, however; I am glad the word *Southwest* was included. That lets me and Oklahoma *in* instead of *out*. To be sure, there are a good many Southerners in Oklahoma—some of them first settlers. And to be a first settler in Oklahoma means that you "made the run"—that you ran into Oklahoma out of somewhere else and were even run out perhaps. For Oklahoma was, and may still be, No Man's Land, and for the most part no man went to Oklahoma unless he had to or unless it was on a chance. At the perfectly speechless and enjoyable banquet last night (it reminded me of nothing so much as a boardinghouse where everyone sits by himself and sulks—I enjoyed it, only I wish we had pushed up a little closer), during an impromptu after-dinner speech, Mr. Bishop was giving me the lowdown on the Southern aristocracy, of which he denied being a member. (I hate to take advantage of Mr. Bishop and use his remarks for copy, but they were good.) In fact, I understand there were no aristocrats among the colonists and settlers of America except a few second sons and perhaps "an illegitimate daughter (or two) or an illegitimate son of an illegitimate nephew of Napoleon." Mr. Milburn, who was listening in, immediately claimed descent from Moll Flanders. On the strength of the same claim he wanted to start an aristocracy in the South. We assured him he could get financial backing, and even a few titles, which are cheaper. But the point of Mr. Bishop's remarks was, Why should anyone, any aristocrat, want to come to America? On a smaller scale the same is true of Oklahoma.

Oklahoma, as I have said, was settled on the run, as its literature is being written on the run and read on the run, and even, as I am doing now, criticized on the run. Oklahomans have been, are, and, as far as I can see, always will be on the make. And Oklahoma writers and writing are on the make along with the rest. For a time I thought Oklahoma and Oklahoma writers and writing were *in the making*. And soon after I came to Oklahoma in 1921 I began to lend my efforts to assist and promote the making of what I conceived to be an Oklahoma tradition. Those were the days, you remember, when Mr. Mencken was discovering America. Then we discovered Mr. Mencken. And right next to the "Sahara of the Bozart," in which I am now standing, he discovered the "Oklahoma manner in literature," as he called it. And one of the first things I did for Oklahoma and Mr. Mencken—mind you, I am not bragging—was to discover Oklahoma poets for him. You may remember that the group appeared in the May, 1926, issue of the first *American Mercury* (there have been several *Mercuries* since then, as you are aware). I remember this because I got fifty dollars out of it—half of it for a poem of my own (which I *discovered*) and half of it as an honorarium. Anyway, Mr. Mencken continued to publish groups of state poets—Oregon and Alabama poets, etc., and that was as generous a gesture as Mr. Mencken ever performed. There were no Fugitive poets among them, but recently the *New Republic* continued his efforts in this direction and published California and Southern poets. I defy you to tell the difference, by the way, between some of these California and Southern poets—at least so that you or I or anyone can understand it. In fact, one of the things that strikes the outsider about Southern writing is that as soon as one stops writing prose and becomes a poet one ceases to be a Southerner and even poetic. Someone wanted to know yesterday what the Fugitives were fugitives from. I should say they were fugitives from the South, since one of the first rules of Fugitive poetry as I understand it (and I hope the Fugitives who are here will bear me out in this if I am right or correct me if I am not) is *not to write about the South*—at least not so that you can recognize it. However, like all literary theorists, the Fugitives are best when they violate their theories, and Mr. Tate's "Ode to the Confederate Dead" is, I take it, both "Southern" and a good poem.

Of course, I know that the Fugitives will say that they conceive of the South not as a specific subject matter but as a way of living, an attitude, a tradition. Mr. Tate has defined *tradition* (in the *New Republic,* of all places) as the "writer's decorum in the widest sense . . . the knowledge of life that we have not had to learn for ourselves, but have absorbed out of the life around us—those ways of feeling, those convictions of propriety, those ways of speaking, of which the writer himself is *hardly aware* and from which he cannot escape." You notice the emphasis is put on the *manner* and *manners,* on the ways of feeling and speaking (not of *thinking,* you will note), and also on taking things for granted. To that extent, I warrant, the Fugitives have succeeded—and have succeeded in being Southern. But if I were asked to talk on "What is a provincial literature?" I should say that taking things for granted, especially one's region, and setting attitude and manner, especially of one's region, above subject matter, above facts and reason, is provincial in the unfavorable sense. Mind you, I am not implying that subject matter, facts and reason, should be set above manner and form, though that may be less dangerous and less reprehensible.

In this sense, of course, Oklahoma has no tradition—"no fixed procedures [to quote Mr. Tate again] that we can rely on in the larger pursuit of the good life." Oklahomans, as far as I have been able to judge, are not in pursuit of the good life—at least in Oklahoma. Like my friend Mr. Donahoe, they go out of Oklahoma to pursue it, or whatever they happen to be pursuing. Oklahomans (those who can afford it—and there are many who can't) are frankly interested in good living and in securing the necessary wherewithal for that purpose. In the sense in which you use the word in the South—and I think it is the right sense—Oklahomans are only plutocrats.

If I say there is no tradition in Oklahoma, then, I can say even more emphatically that there is no aristocratic tradition in Oklahoma. The only aristocrat I have been able to discover in Oklahoma and the Southwest is the poor lonesome cowboy—whom, I believe, the Oklahoma Agrarians call the "knight of the saddle," or the "aristocrat of the horse," or something like that.

Oklahoma, in short, has no fixed procedures. Oklahoma has no standard. We say that anything can happen in Oklahoma, as indeed anything can happen in America. To cite one instance, a certain Oklahoma writer of short stories who will go unnamed, because that immediately names him, once wrote in *College Humor* an amusing article on his alma mater, which he dubbed a "college comic college in a comic opera state," or words to that effect. If he had been in the state at the time, he probably would have been tarred and feathered. As it was, he was denounced in the student paper as a traitor, a liar, and a defamer. And that was only one of the times he has been denounced by his state. That was about five years ago. Only the other day he was invited to be the principal speaker at the most important journalistic function in the university's social calendar—the annual gridiron banquet—at which he was reminded by the toastmaster, as I am reminding him now, of his past delinquencies and of his university's and state's inconsistencies.

I mean to show by all this that Oklahoma has no standards except success. And since New York is synonymous with success, most Oklahoman writers, as Mr. Fletcher knows and has said repeatedly, look to New York for their standards and their markets. Only one Oklahoma writer of my acquaintance—Lynn Riggs, the playwright—has abjured New York—Broadway, in this instance—for the simple reason, I imagine, that Broadway will have none of him. His plays have since been making—and making successfully—the circuit of the provincial and university little theaters. The case of Mr. Riggs interests me for another reason. When he, in common with other Oklahoma and southwestern writers, looks about for standards and an environment to write in, outside of Oklahoma and New York, he finds them in New Mexico, where he has now made his permanent home, except for commuting to Hollywood. So, many Oklahomans, when they refuse to go Broadway, go native, by way of the Indian and the Spanish-American. But since these traditions, however much alive in the Southwest, are not Anglo-Saxon, it is seriously doubted whether they can ever become natural as well as native to the Anglo-Saxon—and more than a picturesque cult—part of the heroic legend of the West and the cult of the pioneer that still live in Oklahoma, especially in the western half of the state. For Oklahoma is really not one state anymore than it is one population. It is really two states—Oklahoma territory on the west, and the old Indian territory on the east, the latter really more Southern in culture as well as in landscape. Riggs and Milburn both hail from Indian territory and as a result are concerned more with the adjustments and maladjustments of the individual to society, the conquest of the individual by civilization, than they are with the conquest of the wilderness.

In fact, Mr. Milburn could tell you much more about Oklahoma than I can. He has told it in his books. He has told us among other things that Oklahoma is more or less sold out to the Babbitts and the Rotarians, the go-getters and the boosters. In Tulsa, which is a modern city of wealth and society, the spirit of land bragging, the boomtown fever and mining-camp restlessness, still persist. If your husband is an oil-lease broker or an oil promoter, he will dash off at a moment's notice from one end of the state to the other, and bring you home an oil lease under his belt for breakfast. I mean that Oklahoma is still pioneering, and a pioneering society is not a place for tradition or for literature. Oklahomans are also pioneering in culture. While their husbands are off hunting oil leases, the wives are pursuing culture. Culture in Oklahoma is in the hands of the women's clubs and the men's dinner clubs—thank heavens it hasn't yet fallen into the hands of the service clubs. I maintain that the greatest problem of the writer, editor, and publisher in the Southwest, as indeed everywhere else in this country, is the women's club including the writers' clubs and the book-review clubs. They are a great force and doubtless could be made a force of good, but as yet they are still a force of evil. How can anyone possibly read books, or understand them, when she spends all her time going to meetings, hearing for the third time or giving for the third time a book review that is little more than a summary, or trying to learn to write? I am glad Mr. McGinnis brought up the subject, though I had already intended to bring it up. I don't want to seem unjust or ungrateful. The clubs have done some good—they have brought in writers to read and lecture, from Louis Untermeyer to Gertrude Stein, or rather from Gertrude Stein to Louis

Untermeyer. But on the whole their influence is bad because they still regard writers as freaks and curiosities instead of human beings with serious work to do.

As to the efforts to learn to write, I spend half of my time reading and the other time fighting off the attempts of elderly ladies and young maidens to express themselves. That is why I can't do any writing myself. Yet this is only a just punishment, for I who stand before you, ladies and gentlemen, was once president of the Oklahoma Authors' League.

Let me take a few remaining minutes to give you the benefit of my experience in trying to make Oklahomans read as well as write. My first serious effort in this direction was an annual, *Folk-Say: A Regional Miscellany,* published for four years by the University of Oklahoma Press. Since Oklahoma and Oklahoma writing are still largely close to the folk level, I thought the best way to make Oklahomans aware of their heritage (out there we speak of "heritage" instead of "tradition") was to make them take stock of their folk resources and use them for literary material—which, I have said, from the Fugitive point of view, is a bad thing to do. The Oklahomans must have found that out themselves, for after four years the series was suspended and the last volume was temporarily suppressed because they discovered that folklore is not always fit reading for children. Puritanism, censorship, is still a force to be reckoned with by the artist in Oklahoma as elsewhere.

My other experience has been during the past year, in editing a monthly of sophisticated writing, *Space,* in which I tried to make Oklahoma conscious of modern literature, getting away from the provincial into the cosmopolitan. Although *Space* found many loyal supporters in Oklahoma—half of my three hundred (*three hundred,* not four hundred) subscribers were Oklahomans—as a whole, Oklahoma would have nothing to do with it. And so I have come to the end of *Space* and to the decision that Oklahoma is not a place for a liberal creative medium.

The problem of Oklahoma publishing and editing simmers down to the one of creating a taste and a public. I have tried to do it more or less alone, and I have come to the conclusion that you cannot go it alone. There must be closely knit, cooperative self-conscious groups like the Fugitives, each with its organ and preferably a publishing house. Better still, there should be a cooperation of states and regions to fight or meet metropolitan domination of publishing and editing. I have always been suspicious of cliques and coteries because they tend to fight one another instead of the common foe and tend toward dilettantism and pedantry.

Now in all this, what is the place of the writer, the creative writer, to use a much abused and useless term? I am afraid he has no place except to cooperate morally with the regional editor, publisher, and critic. You asked yesterday whether the writer can both set the problem and solve it. I ask whether the writer can both create the taste and supply it. The answer is obvious. But this does not minimize the need of organized critical propaganda to fight commercial or rather commercialized propaganda. For all propaganda must be commercial; it is expensive and it must have money behind it. Here the regionalist is confronted with the ethical problem of asking the plutocrats to support a propaganda that is definitely aimed against the society that has produced them. The first problem of the writer, then, would seem to be to purify the social atmosphere of moral contagion. But that, you will say, is politics and economics, and here we must be careful that politics and economics serve art and culture, and not art and culture serve politics and economics. Which brings us to the fundamental issue confronting the artist everywhere today, an issue which I raised yesterday but which was dismissed: Can the artist afford to ignore politics and economics any more than politics and economics can afford to ignore the artist?

MR. K. T. KNOBLOCK: Mr. Botkin's speech was completely conclusive.

MR. FLETCHER: Mr. Botkin made a very interesting reply to Mr. Davis. Mr. Davis said that the two groups in the South were the patriots and the New Yorkers. Mr. Botkin happens to have edited an annual for three or four years, which was a deliberate attempt to create a third group—a regionally conscious group. Due to local conditions this attempt failed. I wonder whether those conditions are going to prevail. In the South we must continue to do what Mr. Botkin was trying to do—uphold that group. Is there a third group? Mr. Botkin has given this audience a challenge which this audience must face and does not seem prepared to face—a situation which he faced so bravely to keep the Oklahoma folk tradition from disappearing. I think that Mr. Botkin has given us Southern writers an interesting point of view because he looks at it from the outside. Are we going to preserve our tradition or are we going to accept Mr. Davis' compromise—to give a little of this and a little of that? That is a real, live issue. Mr. Davis said that the function of the editor is to hold the balance between the two types of readers. The best editors (and Mr. Ford was in his time a great editor) think in terms not of the reader but of taste—the high canons of taste—how the thing measures up to the great tradition of literature. Mr. Davis also said something about the editor's being allowed to live (about the cash nexus)—he doesn't see Mr. Botkin's attitude that politics and economics must serve art and culture. They should. But in metropolitan areas, under pressure, art and culture are made to serve economics and politics. I have no objection to Communist propaganda—I have even indulged in it at times myself. But I do object to disguising it as literature.

MR. TATE: Mr. Davis has said that the Southern editor is a mediator between two groups—the Southern patriot and those who want the cosmopolitan or New York standards. It seems that we should try to define them historically and see the mediating function. We must have something positive and not try to juggle them into accepting each other. We have heard in the last forty years that we must avoid provincialism and become cosmopolitan. What are these standards?

From 1850 on we see the rise of the national point of view in politics. We in the South know that this is not national but eastern sectionalism disguised as nationalism. We have been asked to accept nationalism which is eastern. In the arts this is cosmopolitanism—not true cosmopolitanism but the New York standards. New York is a place where things are sold and fashions brought over from Europe have their short day. It seems to me that the Southern mediator must make his mediation a little more positive. It is remarkable that no one here has discussed the moribund humane tradition. It is this tradition that enables a writer to write things that are exportable, in Mr. Bishop's phrase. It is through this tradition that the editor and writer can mediate between the provincial and the cosmopolitan. Otherwise it is a mechanical mediation. Mr. Fletcher said that the editor must judge things on merit, and I don't see how we can do anything else. But what is the culture we want?

MR. DAVIS: The editor should attempt a dialectical position rather than an opposition. He should try to manifest the conflict between North and South, between eastern seaboard and inland, between local groups. An editor, without more than faith in the interplay of ideas, can run a magazine to exhibit these contrasts. I'd like Mr. Tate's comment.

MR. TATE: Two ideas of themselves can't play. Between ideas A and B we must make a choice. We cannot hold both. We are not here to tell Mr. Davis what to do but we expect an editor to direct rather than mediate.

MR. ROARK BRADFORD: Is it the direction of the writer or the reader?
MR. DAVIS: Both.
MR. FLETCHER: Would you recognize the *American Spectator* as a mediator? I think it is a good example. And the ideas in the *Spectator* are an excellent example of what mediation does when you entertain two sets of ideas.
MR. DAVIS: I don't know the *American Spectator* very well. I've seen only a few issues, and I can't answer that question. I think the magazine can enlighten people of open mind by taking a dialectal position. It is not the only community of interests possible but it is the only way we can perform in an age of specialization.
MR. BOTKIN: I wonder what Mr. Davis means by specialization, without taking sides or making a choice.
MR. BISHOP: There is a very great difference in taste between the editor and the writer. The editor has to resolve the contrasts in his mind. He can legitimately sit on the fence. But the writer can't. Like an art collector the editor can present both sides. He can be eclectic.
MR. BOTKIN: Can such a magazine be culturally significant?
MR. BISHOP: It can because the issue is not so clear as all that. One must represent all sides.
MR. FLETCHER: The issue *is* clear. This is the reason I brought in the *American Spectator*. Since Mr. Davis doesn't seem to know anything about it I'll enlighten him. . . . It disappeared at the height of its success. It was a tabloid version of the *American Mercury*—the wisecracking wit and repartee without the bitterness of Mencken—the superficial metropolitan thing. I recall in the last number of the *Spectator* an article that said that American poetry had no tradition except the "frost is on the punkin' " sort of thing. . . . That was a mediator between two ideas—the only thing appropriate under those circumstances is a hard-boiled, cynical attitude toward ideas. I don't think that position can be tenable. We must entertain ideas seriously, at all costs and against all comers. That confronts the American intelligentsia—whatever position they are in. Now as to Mr. Davis, I feel he is uncomfortable in that position. He wants to eat his cake and have it, too. Now let us give the metropolitan point of view a pat on the back, and now the hillbillies. That can't be done. We are despising the man with ideas because he is associated with this playing in and out. I prefer Mr. Botkin's idea of taking the folklore of Oklahoma and glorifying it, though he failed.
MR. BOTKIN: I sympathize with Mr. Davis because I have gone through it

myself. That is why I thought my experience with *Folk-Say* and *Space,* two kinds of specialization, was enlightening. In each I tried to make my choice. In my talk I didn't define the function of the editor because I was trying to do too many things. But I think of that function as forming taste, creating and guiding it through the personality of the editor. Where is Mr. Knickerbocker? Is he abroad? He should be here. I don't want to take advantage of his absence, but I think of the *Sewanee Review* as an example of editing not on the fence or off but on both sides.

MR. TATE: I rise to the position of mediator. Mr. Bishop is right, but he presupposed a condition where taste is settled. In the situation as we have it now our position is not defined. We must define and have a Southern culture. We can't have an Abyssinian culture. But we must see Mr. Bishop's position. Otherwise art will serve economics and politics. If a man becomes so passionate as to defend Miss Glasgow against Mr. Stribling or Mr. Stribling against Miss Glasgow, it is bad.

MR. BRADFORD: Mr. Tate has just taken a view of, and used the term, Southern culture. I think that is the thing we have overemphasized here. (I don't think I know what Southern culture or culture is.) That is perfectly all right if you are going to stay in the South all the time. But when you get out you find that there are middlewestern and north-western writing. But actually there are only two ways of living and writing—good and bad. If you think of Southern writing, immediately you are on the defensive and are suspected of an inferiority complex. I think Mr. Botkin was right in what he said of his experience with *Folk-Say* and *Space* and what Oklahoma thought of George Milburn. Milburn has struck the New York market and become metropolitan. He has gone through the clearinghouse of New York. That doesn't mean that New York readers appreciate him any more than Oklahoma readers. He is appreciated just as much there as *Folk-Say* is, and just as much in Louisiana, Iowa, and Russia. In fact, he has been translated into Russian, French, and German. His audience is small in Oklahoma in one way or another, and that is Oklahoma's misfortune and not that of his work.

Nothing is more individual than the writer, and direction from an editor confuses me. If I write a thing and know it isn't good, I throw it away. An editor may direct a reading public. I don't know. I don't read as much as I used to. I can't come under the head of the reading public. If writers live in a certain community and organization unlike other regions, these problems that seem so complex—the problems of reader and writer and what supports a magazine—become simple. It depends on good taste, and it grows; it cannot be created. If a story is well told, it is good taste, and if it comes out of the South so much the better, but let's not call it a Southern story. The writer should be given a very free rein and let the editor print it or not. Let's not try to guide the writer in a special direction.

MR. OWSLEY: The discussion this morning has centered in a special kind of writing, critical writing. Mr. Bradford speaks of stories, and there you have no point of view in the critical sense. The critical essay, on literature or economics, should have a point of view. Poetry was mentioned, but we haven't discussed the story. I say every good story is definitely placed.

MR. TATE: In reference to Mr. Bradford's remark: "If you think of Southern writing immediately you are on the defensive and are suspected of having an inferiority complex." I want to know if Anatole France had an inferiority complex when he wrote about France and French literature?

MR. BRADFORD: I think all French people have an inferiority complex. And, with regard to Mr. Owsley's remark, I meant not a story but anything readable. I have seen in the *Southwest Review* and the *Virginia Quarterly Review* things which anyone, even in England, may enjoy reading, and yet I have disagreed violently with them. Other things are purely local yet so well written and reasoned out that anyone can enjoy reading them.

MR. FORD MADOX FORD: I'd like to make a few remarks about the magazine before it gets into other matters. Mr. Warren has brought me here to give you whatever benefit my considerable experience with magazines may provide. A magazine has to be either commercial or noncommercial. The periodicals which I have been associated with have been noncommercial. Some capitalist gives the money, and it runs out. It doesn't matter where the noncommercial magazine is published. *Blackwood's* and the *Edinburgh Review*—two commercial magazines— were published in Edinburgh. The *Little Review, Transition,* magazines which changed the face of literature, were published anywhere— Geneva, Virginia. The job of the editor has to be to get out good work. The commercial editor has to take the business manager's opinion. If you want to have a Southern magazine, let it not be necessarily Southern but simply good (and noncommercial) as *a result of the editor's instinct or knowledge of the community in which he works.* The problem is very clear. I talk of imaginative literature—when you talk of factual literature, it is different. The only permanent matter is imagination.

This is a matter of chance. Get the best sort of material you can, and some people will like it. Hemingway, Faulkner, and Stein made their first appearances in noncommercial magazines, such as the *Transatlantic Review*. That is the only real guide for the editor who decides to put forth imaginative literature. The imaginative magazine creates a certain public by a certain snobbishness—the intelligentsia—by getting things talked about. . . . If you keep these distinctions in mind, it will be simple. The imaginative magazine is precluded from commercial success.

THIRD SESSION
Thursday, April 11, 1935, 3:00 P.M.

Question six: *What are the problems of directing a university press in the South? Are they special?*

MR. COUCH (editor, University of North Carolina Press): I think the distance of this table from the audience is symbolic. It is much too far away, and as a publisher I suppose I ought to get it closer, but since the rest of you have suffered under that handicap, I shall bear up. What is a university press? The best answer is found in the Oxford University Press, founded in 1478. Since then it has existed not continuously but fairly so. It was established partly as a matter of accident, not by design—it was not a part of a planned economy or of the national life. Before the invention of printing there were scriveners in every town who wrote out manuscripts for the schools. These were licensed, and the Oxford University Press granted the licenses—to prevent the publication of unorthodox religious and political matter. By a paradox, this censorship grew into the positive and productive function of the university press, devoted to the cultivation of intellectual life.

What are the general policies of the university press as represented by the Oxford University Press?

1) The Oxford University Press does not have to make money. It does, however, have to pay its bills. It is not controlled by the profit motive. Though they make profits, they reinvest their profits in publishing. We in North Carolina do that.

2) The Oxford University Press is controlled by scholars. Its chief purpose is to publish scholarly books. Some scholars think a scholarly book is one that has three lines of text to the page and the rest footnotes. I am often asked to arrange books in this manner to impress critics.

3) The Oxford University Press is generally conservative. Its function is to conserve and maintain tradition. In conserving Southern tradition, the University of North Carolina Press puts an *s* on the tradition. There is no such thing in my mind as *the* Southern tradition. There are many Southern traditions. (I expect to be bombarded.) We try to conserve the best Southern traditions and out of those try to develop others. I think the best of those traditions are not peculiar to the South.

4) Some university presses try to pioneer. In my opinion the interlinear text is a useful way to study a language. I see no reason why university presses should not publish interlinear texts and remove the stigma of illegitimacy from them. There are plenty of books still to be written and plenty of forests still to be cut down and turned into paper. Seriously, however, the reasons for making and reading a book have not yet disappeared.

What, now, are the special problems of a university press in the South?

1) The largest problem is the general lack of interest in books and the feeling that the intellectual life itself is of no importance. I feel that the making and reading of books is important. I can give you my prescription if you want it. At any rate, exchange and conflict of ideas is the intellectual life, and that is the thing in itself and needs no justification. I hope I am wrong when I say there is no general interest in reading books in the South. How can the present interest be increased? I have sympathy with the view that it is needless to cut down beautiful forests, but I prefer the intellectual life to the trees. If we could have a planned economy, we should have both.

2) The financial problem. During the past ten years $150,000 has been raised and spent and lost in subsidizing books by North Carolina. Some of our books are done on a purely commercial basis. Some university presses, like Harvard and Princeton, do very little commercial publishing. Chicago, Oxford, and the North Carolina presses do a good deal—because we have to try to make money to pay the bill for scholarly publishing.

3) The editorial problem. What are you going to publish and why? Scholars differ on this. As one who has to send out manuscripts to readers for opinions, I often find opposite opinions. I have no answer to this editorial problem except for certain elementary things. You should write for the English public in the English language. I don't know what

name to give to the mode of expression scholars use, but they don't always know how to express themselves. We have to do a lot of editing, not always successful. The choice of fields is difficult. We have done things that others do not. We have tried to help the movements of culture in the South. We need books about the Southern United States. It is a large geographical area, with plants and animals. We haven't been enough interested in plants and animals to write about them so that everyone can understand them. Culture depends on the intimate knowledge people have of their environment. There are two definitions of culture: 1) a way of living characteristic of a people; 2) refinements, manners, arts, and sciences. We tend to use both words in the same way, as this morning. We have selected as our problem the preparation of books that would enable the people in the region to know the region. If we know what culture means, the South could not any more avoid having a culture than New England or the Midwest. Culture is not a peculiar possession of any one people. In presenting this material to a Southern audience we have to prepare it so that it is available in different levels—from the first grade through the high school. That is going to become of great importance.

4) The manufacturing of books. We have thousands of printers in the South, but not one printer who knows printing as a craft. That is a disgraceful thing. I have said it for ten years and I have managed to develop two or three fairly good printers. Some printers don't even know the names of the types they use or the history of printing—they don't even know that printing has a history. This loss of taste in the arts is due to the failure of our schools, etc., to acquaint people intimately with the materials they work with. We have lost the apprenticeship system. There are two plants in the South that we use for quantity printing. For other things you have to go to New York or Boston or even abroad.

5) The problem of prices. Taking a book priced at two dollars as our standard, we generally think the author gets 10 percent and the publisher gets the balance. I wish that were the happy scheme of affairs. The actual condition is this: The author gets no royalty frequently—he has to pay for the manufacture of the book. He may get 10 or 15 percent. If a book can sell through the bookstores, a discount of 33⅓ percent or even 40 percent of the retail price has to be given to the bookstore. That may be exorbitant, but look around you and see how many prosperous booksellers we have. No publisher has made an immense fortune on

books. That happens in the newspapers and pulps, where advertising pays for the printing. A two-dollar book will normally cost fifty to seventy-five cents on the first printing—25 percent, more or less, of the retail price. Multiply the manufacturing cost by three, four, five, and you get the retail price. You do this after considering the market. If a book has a large market and the publisher thinks the book will sell more copies at a lower price, he may cut the price. A number of years ago publishers issued paperbound novels for one dollar. If there were a public for that kind of book, they could afford it. It must have at least ten thousand sales. I am as much against the capitalist system as it is as anyone else here. We need something else to reach the maximum of culture. The machinery of production and distribution is very poor. But if you take it for granted, the publishing profession is as liberal with the people it employs as any. I can't feel excited about the New York publishers. We have spent one dollar in advertising for every dollar we take in. This is when you think a book ought to sell, and it doesn't, and you find you've spent as much on advertising as you have made on the book.

6) Reviewers. We prefer good reviews but we use no persuasion. Most publishers would prefer evidence that the reviewer has read the book and taken an intellectual position toward the book, argued with it.

I felt this morning after the discussion somewhat confused. It brought to mind the story of the soapbox orator in Union Square. He was speaking in flaming words denouncing the capitalist system and Park Avenue, painting a picture of the banquet table, including strawberries. Someone said, "But I don't like strawberries." Said the speaker, "Comes the revolution, you'll eat strawberries and like them too." I felt that way when Mr. Tate defined his Southern tradition. We may prefer not to eat it even if we like it. Those who find it must have a metaphysical apparatus. I call it the metaphysical horse. It works something like this. You feed ideas to the horse, and after mastication and digestion the horse has a tradition. But each of us has his own ideas. Thomas Jefferson believed in revolution. John C. Calhoun had interesting things to say on the class struggle. The South has some fine traditions, but the chief difficulty with us is that we don't know those traditions. We must inform ourselves on the past and present of the region in which we live.

MR. SAVOIE LOTTINVILLE (assistant editor, University of Oklahoma Press): It is almost an imposition for me to say anything more. I am most concerned with the business side of publishing. There is an old German saying to the effect that "Nothing good has ever come out of Bavaria." This is not true of the South, but it is true of the Midwest. We are making a mighty effort to establish ourselves with the people about us. We are a pioneering group and need time because of our short history. The University of Oklahoma Press also publishes a magazine little known in this part of the country because of its international appeal— *Books Abroad*—a review of books in languages other than English. It is representative of the most difficult type of magazine to push because the editor and publisher are so far from their market. The point I want to make in reference to the regional magazine is this: a magazine that is not read widely in its region is in danger of becoming sterile. It must be read to be a vital force. The magazine which carries its ideas out has to get circulation, otherwise its authors are like widely spaced angels shouting "hallelujahs" without being heard by each other or by themselves. The difficulty is one of establishing communication between the magazine and its audience. There are one thousand fans for any one book—maybe three or four hundred in the immediate neighborhood. You have to search them out, encourage, and maintain contact. This is one of the really great obstacles in the South or Midwest to a magazine which expects to get somewhere with its ideas.

As a result of this failure to establish communication between the publisher and the audience, there arises the tremendous difficulty of establishing communication between the writer and the audience. There may be a lack of a receptive audience. Consider the newspapers—many literary pages were recently cut out of them because there is not enough demand for them. The newspapers have always written down instead of up. The decline of the old-line magazines is one of the worst things that have happened. For the last five years they have gone down rapidly. The audience doesn't exist or doesn't have the money, and the magazine goes by the board or changes character. *Harper's, Scribners,* and the *Atlantic* have all changed character. In the South there is a third factor—the inability of small journals to get widespread publicity. The national journals are dependent upon it. There must be constant plugging—favorable opinion is not enough. Much has been done to sell books and magazines by imitating the methods of selling a package of rice. Are we going to maintain *Books Abroad,* make it popular, or give it up? A popular magazine could be maintained in the South, but from the cultural point of view is it worthwhile? Why not leave that to the others? Communication between the publisher and the public has to be maintained or you have the failure of communication between the author and his public.

In book publishing there is the idea that some publishing depends on "all or nothing." We recently had such a book. We estimated its sale at one thousand and sold fifty thousand. Publishers are idealists and willing to take a long chance. Richard Simon recently said that all publishers are idealists: they publish books they are enthusiastic about and those do not sell at all. Other books they don't think will sell do.

The curse of William Morris is upon us. The American public, as compared with the English or French public, thinks in terms of the well-printed, well-bound book. My own hope is that the paperbound book may be established. It is not so attractive and the American public refuses it. We have been talking about spreading ideas of cultural value: why not attack it from the marketing end? The absence of bookstores is the greatest difficulty in the South and the Midwest. This is a reflection of reading habits. Of the two bookstores on my list in a Southern city one sold copies of the Bible and the other dollar books—-no royalty on the one and very little on the other. The question of the bookstore is bound up with the communication between the author and the public. A New Orleans bookseller complained that it costs thirty-five cents to distribute a book—there is not sufficient patronage and a small margin to carry the store along.

We have a small list. We have nevertheless disregarded the metropolitan whim. We were told that the country was not interested in Oklahoma or Indians, but we issued an Oklahoma Indian book, and the country was interested. We have a feeling of responsibility to the region and to untried writers. We haven't yet entered into poetry and fiction. We serve as critics for young writers—thereby we serve a real function and to that extent are justified.

Question seven: *What is a provincial literature?*

MR. FLETCHER: The outstanding feature of provincial literature particular to modern times is that it relates man more closely to his environment than urban and metropolitan literature—to the soil, neighbors, friends, and history. In the seventeenth century urban literature was much closer to the soil. The division between urban and provincial took place with the growth of large cities and mass production, resulting in the attempt to see man in his economic aspect entirely. I can't think of man in that way—this may be the blindness of the South. I see man culturally and morally. There is a general neglect of that now. The last great writer to deal with the urban environment in a large way was Henry James. He dealt with it in a cosmopolitan way. To be a citizen of New York was also to be a citizen of London and Paris. He wrote the epitaph to that type of literature. Since the war we have megalopolitan, not cosmopolitan, literature. I read *Manhattan Transfer* and can't remember a single incident. It seems to me a complete failure—it has no center of focus or direction. Something of the same thing has happened with the little reviews. Mr. Ford says that the little reviews are noncommercial. I could maintain a paradox that they are commercial in the sense that they deal with fashions in ideas. I have contributed to them in the past and the present, but they lack relation to their environment. They are interesting as experiments. The early little reviews performed a service for technique. I am too old for that. And I am not sure that many of them now are not imitations of megalopolitan ideas. These ideas take strange forms. Granville Hicks in his *The Great Tradition* (the best proletarian survey of American literature) says that since Appomattox literature has tended to become proletarianized. But it occurred to me that though Mr. Hicks thinks capitalism has only one direction— the proletarian revolution—he could hardly point out a single character in American fiction that is a product of the great city except in Mr. Dreiser's books. Robert Herrick has a hero in a great architect who uses poor materials and cheats. (Herrick is one of the most honest of these novelists.) Even Lewis' Babbitt is a product of the small town.

American literature began as a provincial literature, in New England. The New England writers thought they represented the whole of America. In Poe the South made a slight challenge to that supremacy, but this did not succeed. The Civil War confirmed the point that New England represented the West as well as the East. Whitman's position is strange, as Mr. Donald Davidson has pointed out in the *American Review*. Whitman thought he represented the American type. He tried to prove it by coming down this river to New Orleans *to go West*. When he sat down to write about the West, he didn't feel the bit. You get very tired of his eternal cataloging, which he thought would be evocative in its power. After the Civil War the West became economically important. I grew up under this—Twain's and Riley's homespun humor, written for the midwestern market. There was also a local color literature of the South. The Midwest seems to be very drab, and the local color school had its vogue because the Midwest hankered for something more than its drabness. Someone should write a critical survey from the modern critical point of view of the local color literature of the South. I also remember the historical romances of the eighties and nineties—*When Knighthood Was in Flower,* etc. See Mr. Canby's *The Age of Confidence.*

But slowly under midwestern influence came the drive toward naturalism. Dreiser to me is not literature at all but case history. He is a sociologist who wants to write. *The American Tragedy,* which I haven't read, is made up of newspaper reports of trials. His philosophy is pure behaviorism—instincts and reactions to them. He makes no attempt to evaluate the instincts. Mr. Faulkner, who has great creative gifts, seems to me to do the same thing—to take case histories but to relate them to environment. The same is true in urban literature—treating the Negro and the Jew in relation to oppressed areas. There is also the tendency to take neglected backgrounds, and the tendency to autobiographize one's complexes, as in Thomas Wolfe.

(I take fiction because there are one hundred readers of fiction to one of poetry. America grew up at the time when prose fiction was taking strides in England.)

Yesterday Mr. Tate said (quoting Eliot) that we at the present moment are collecting points of view. The metropolitan critics tell us what these points of view are. This is the situation the provincial critic should deal with. The large cities have become hopeless. The provincial critic has to relate points of view to his particular environment, and the task of the creator is to define the point of view that emerges from his environment and doesn't do violence to it. The critical interpretation of American life began with Van Wyck Brooks. Mr. Hicks is too abstract. He takes a thesis. The true function of the provincial critic is to check this abstraction by referring it to a larger objectivity.

(Mr. Ford begins with a discussion of American publishing conditions and problems and assails the bookstores for not knowing enough about books, authors, and publishers and, when they do not have a certain title, offering you "something just as good" instead of securing the book for you. He concludes this portion of his talk with the remark that "the commercial publishing system is such that fourteen thousand is a good sale. We might as well all give up, then, and not try to be commercial writers." He then turns to the discussion of provincial literature, offering the following observations.)

MR. FORD: 1) Provincial literature is native and of the folk, as in the mummers and troubadours.

2) Provincial literature is based on vast knowledge of your region. ("My glass is small but I drink out of my own glass.") You can't write successfully without accumulating a vast store of human instances. This gives you tranquillity.

3) But you must write with your eye on the world, which is your public. I have stood all my life for complete cosmopolitanism, but in my magazines I have always been national, with one section for British writers, one for American, etc. There is only one republic that has ever lasted—the republic of the arts, and in the long run there is no nationality in the arts. But to write successfully, you must broaden your knowledge of your home, where you live or wherever you happen to be (you needn't have been born there). I was born in London but I couldn't write a metropolitan novel. I've almost given up the novel because I don't have enough knowledge of New York.

DISCUSSION

(Mr. Ford concludes with a number of questions which he has prepared concerning the remarks of previous speakers and which precipitate a discussion, or rather a conversation—a literary chit-chat.)

MR. FORD: The phraseology of Mr. Bishop—"self-indulgence and loneliness." You have to define *loneliness*. The career of the writer is the most lonely of all careers. It is a dog's life. You know famine and cold. It is like rowing on a river in the mist—you never know whether you are retrogressing or progressing. You have no standards for measuring your work. You have friends around to praise you, but shortly you die and you never know whether you are really a great writer. You'll never know—that is real torture. Something you wrote ten minutes ago may seem great—that is the only pleasure you get.

But by *self-indulgence* I don't know what he means. Does he mean the mere joy of expressing oneself, which characterizes the writing of the young? You do not grow up as a writer until you discover you have to write for someone else, that writing is a communication with an ideal reader or class, not necessarily a large public. That becomes technique—a horrible word. It means simply how you will be able to please the ideal reader. I wrote to satisfy Conrad and he wrote for me. You get a standard from outside. If self-indulgence consists in putting in a large amount of parenthetical words, then you soon found them unnecessary and you cut them out. That seems to me to have nothing to do with loneliness. True, you do get a good deal of horror in Southern writers as an effect of loneliness.

(Mr. Bishop says it is violence—there is a lot of it in all literature but more of it in the South. Mr. Ford thinks there is bloodthirstiness in modern life. Mr. Bishop also defines self-indulgence as lingering over details, as in Joyce's *Work in Progress.*)

MR. FORD: The first thing in your writing is your subject. You must stick to it.

MR. BISHOP: You get more of this lingering over details when you lose your sense of the reader, as in the later Proust, though in his case this may be due to his illness.

MR. FORD: Dreiser, whom I admire greatly, has many sins, but that (lingering over details) is part of his mind and necessary.

MR. BISHOP: In Proust's case it seems that there was a vast exertion of the will in executing the plan of the work and then there came a reaction in the working out of the details.

MR. FORD: Proust's work is done. Let him do what he wants.

MR. BISHOP: The noncommunication of the Dadaists and the Surrealists has reached its limit. There are indications now of a swing the other way. The closed world of the writer is breaking down.

MR. FORD: The tendency is too much in the other direction. The intelligentsia I am associated with in New York are violent Communists writing propaganda.

MR. BISHOP: I think it is a reaction like ours against the glorification of sensibility in art. It is an attempt to find new artistic sensibilities.

MR. FORD: Art must be in contact with life.

MR. BISHOP: *Ulysses* is in contact with life but it is presented in such a way as to be intelligible only to a few.

MR. FORD: This brings me back to the inevitability of folk art, the only kind I am trying to write now. The magazines are taking the place of folk art. In order to have great art, you must appeal to a large number of people, as in folk art. I should like to see commercial art break down altogether.

MR. BISHOP: The Tin Pan Alley musician has taken over a great many tricks of the great musicians and has trained the ordinary person to appreciate the latter. This may occur in writing.

(Mr. Ford challenges Mr. Tate's statement that the Southern writer lives in one place and writes for another.)

MR. FORD: I profoundly disagree. That is true of every writer.

MR. TATE: New York, when it publishes, tries to transform the work. This is not true in France.

MR. FORD: What do you think New York does?

MR. TATE: It limits the choice of subjects.

MR. FORD: Under the present system we need a distributing center and New York is just as good as any, along with London and Paris. You must have a social center where you can meet your fellows in your craft. New York is such a place.

MR. FLETCHER AND MISS CAROLINE GORDON: Oh, not at all.

MR. FLETCHER: New York is just a marketplace.

MISS GORDON: The Southern writer has no chance in New York for such contact with fellows of his craft.

MR. FORD: New York overcomes the writer's loneliness. You need a provincial cosmopolitan center like Edinborough in addition to New York, but it must be cosmopolitan. You in the South now have the world at your feet. It's up to you. The North and the East are exhausted. The industrialism of the Midwest is even worse than eastern industrialism. Lenin and Stalin both think industrialism is a temporary weapon against the foe. According to a recent decree, in Russia it is no longer necessary for a writer to produce propaganda art. This is a significant development. I argued this question out with Lenin and Trotsky and they agreed with me. You have an assembly of writers here because the South is becoming a rich place. I am surprised that you had no women to address this meeting, like Caroline Gordon and Elizabeth Madox Roberts. With Miss Roberts the whole complexion of your literature changed—the local became universal.

And finally, you—the South—have the ball of the world at your feet. If you desire it the most glorious of revenges is there for your taking. You were conquered in a war; now, at peace, you are conquering the conqueror of your former conquerors. That is the *revanche noble!*

The dominance, material and figurative, of the other provinces of this continent is passing away as its equivalents are passing away all the world over. Seventy years ago you stood for the fruits of the earth and the treasures of the craftsman, means of wealth that alone can be coterminous with the life of this earth. During those seventy years of the obscuration of your traditions the industrial system rose, dominated humanity, called itself a civilization. It is now crumbling into its final decay. You, on the other hand, continued unmoved to follow out the pursuits and earnings of the husbandman—and measured by human lives, the pursuits and earnings of the husbandman constitute the only wealth that is and must be as durable as humanity itself. And you possess the richest tract of soil that the earth holds on its surface.

Your survival is therefore inevitable: nothing shall put an end to it till this planet falls back into the sun from which it issued. And if you survive, alone endowed with wealth and an undisturbed tradition, your dominance of a hemisphere is as inevitable as your survival.

So the future of the civilization of this hemisphere must lie in your hands as in other continents it will lie in the hands of men similarly minded and of similar traditions. It is for you alone to say what aspect that civilization shall assume.

POLITICS and EDUCATION

Huey P. Long
Edited by Charles East

In his Pulitzer Prize–winning biography of Huey Long, T. Harry Williams tells the story of Long marching through the streets of New Orleans at the head of the Louisiana State University band, which had become his showpiece and one of his playthings. "At a traffic light some policemen, not recognizing him, ordered the marchers to stop. Huey raised his baton imperiously. 'Stand back,' he roared. 'This is the Kingfish.' "

The Kingfish had given LSU more than a band, as he told those assembled on the campus on April 12, 1935, just five months before he was gunned down in the State Capitol. The occasion was an Italian Day luncheon in honor of Italy's ambassador to the United States, Augusto Rosso, who had been invited to visit the university as one of several events commemorating LSU's seventy-fifth anniversary. Other events included the Conference on Literature and Reading on April 10 and 11 that announced the establishment of the *Southern Review.*

Long, obviously on the defensive following criticism of his meddling in the affairs of the school, seized the occasion to charm and lecture the "school people." Robert Penn Warren, who was in the Venetian Room of Foster Hall at LSU when Long spoke, has written of the Kingfish: "At the same time that Long was a political genius, with an unwavering gaze fixed on his objective, he had many roles to play, and nobody, probably least of all Long himself, knew which was central. He was vulgarian, buffoon, clown, dude, sentimental dreamer, man of ruthless action, coward, wit, philosopher, orator." It was the only time Warren would ever see Long outside of a newsreel.

A number of visiting literary figures were at the luncheon, among them Ford Madox Ford, who would recall "the astonishing speech" in his book *Great Trade Route.* Long, he said, who earlier in the day had spoken to a gathering of upstate farmers in the dialect of the farmers ("a dialect I could not understand"), now addressed the gathering of university professors, foreign diplomats, and "the Intelligentsia of the South . . . in exactly the dialect, with the vapidity, with the images—and even some of the accent—of a Cambridge—England—Head of a College addressing his staff on a not very important occasion." Altogether, Ford thought, "a remarkable man."

What follows is an excerpt of the remarks made by Long as reported the same day in the Baton Rouge *State-Times.*

I was asked on the campus by one of your guests if I would answer a question that has been pervading the campus here. It seems many have asked when I have interfered in the operation of the university and Dr. [James Monroe] Smith has said that I haven't. I am slandered by the president when he says I did not interfere.

I want to assert that as a matter of fact I have interfered. I interfered when they were reducing salaries of teachers all over the United States and I stepped in and prevented the reductions at LSU.

Following that time we found we had several lawsuits. It is imperative to an institution that it must have a scapegoat. Whoever builds has to get licked. So we formed a little entente down here to make Dr. Smith as white as perfection and provided that if anybody had to get blacked up it would be me.

We started out here when I became governor [1928] with about $650,000 a year. The assessment of the state then was about $1,700,000,000 and the half-mill tax was yielding then about $800,000 a year, but that tax would now be giving about $650,000 a year. After you take out about $200,000 for the agricultural extension work it would leave about $450,000 [for LSU].

It is now getting about $2,700,000 a year. I interfered and gave them some more money. I am going to quit this interference at the first opportunity and give the job to Dr. Smith and let him and the others stay up nights with legislators getting the additional votes necessary to put the legislation over.

We are celebrating the seventy-fifth anniversary of the university. I have had considerable to do with only the last five years and we have done as much in that five as was done in the other seventy. You can go around and find that as much has been done in most things around here in the last five years as was done during the previous seventy. If you will come back in the next two or three years we will show you some more.

I want to give some advice to the colleges. I'm the worst politician in the United States. The way I get along with the people of this state is not by answering criticisms. I know that there are so many more that know something about themselves that they don't want told I at least get the sympathy of a large number. You will find out that you cannot do without politicians. They are a necessary evil in this day and time. You may not like getting money from one source and spending it for another. But the thing for the school people to do is that if the politicians are going to steal, make them steal for the schools.

Education comes first. That is our first business. You will find that when we had to economize—and we did economize in the operation of the governor's office, in the office of the secretary of state, and other state departments—we never economized in the schools. We raised the appropriations several hundred thousand dollars each year.

Let me assure all you good people that we have received some lessons from you and you can learn from us. I say the school teacher should get into politics. The school teacher who doesn't get into politics is standing in his own light and in the light of others.

If a war comes we train the youth in the training camps. We spare no funds in seeing that they are properly trained. We train the boys how to fight and to die but we could teach them how to live for a fifth as much. If we had a little more education, we might not need the war training.

Whenever the school people take up the fight, to fight for the principles that the man who teaches gets as much as the man who operates a slot machine and that every boy regardless of whether he is born of wealthy or poor parents has the right for education, whenever the teachers and professors have made the politicians yield the various sources of plunder, then they will have done their share in the training of youth.

The DEATH of HUEY LONG

Charles East

He was, at his death, the most powerful man in Louisiana and one of the most powerful men in the nation. He had just written a book called *My First Days in the White House,* a book intended to amuse but also to signal the ultimate reach of his ambitions, and there are those who believe that had he lived he would have challenged Franklin Roosevelt for the presidency (the book, published not long after Long's death, casts Roosevelt as secretary of the navy in the Long cabinet). There are even those who still believe, with no evidence at all, that it was Roosevelt or someone close to him who ordered Long's assassination. One of Long's most implacable opponents, Dean Emeritus (of the Tulane Law School) Cecil Morgan, a onetime state senator and Standard Oil executive, recoils at the memory of the man he calls a "power-hungry dema-gogue," and believes that Long's violent end was inevitable, given "the deep emotions of the day"—"everyone expected it, was waiting for it, knew it had to happen."

Huey Long died in the early morning hours of September 10, 1935, in a hospital room overlooking the soaring thirty-four-story State Cap-itol that he had built and that would become his monument—the building in which two days earlier he had been mortally wounded. Four days before that, the senator had come down from Washington by way of New York City, where he celebrated his forty-second birthday, and a Labor Day speaking engagement in Oklahoma City. To reporters who guessed that he had come to call yet another special session of the Louisiana legislature (the fourth of the year, and the seventh since the last regular session), the Kingfish, as Long liked to be called, was noncommittal. But the call for such a session went out on the morning of September 7, over the signature of Governor O. K. Allen, and by nightfall the legislators had gathered in Baton Rouge for the convening of the session.

As United States senator, Long in ordinary times would have had no part in the calling of the legislature or in any other state governmental matters. But these were not ordinary times, and Louisiana was, as Robert Penn Warren has noted, no ordinary place. "The shadow of the Kingfish—Satan or Savior, according to political affiliations—hung over swamps and bayous, the cane field or cotton patch . . . the new university with its football mania and operas, and the new skyscraper capitol. When the Kingfish moved abroad in the flesh of Huey P. Long, armed guards stirred too." Long had been elected governor in 1928 at the age of thirty-four, and at the midpoint of his governorship, having begun a far-reaching program that promised free textbooks for school-children, paved roads and other public improvements, as well as economic and political reform, had decided to run for the Senate. He was elected, but for almost a year and a half held onto the governorship, refusing to take his seat in the Senate until he had arranged a succession that would leave him in power. The man he chose to make governor in 1932 (Long of course had to persuade the people to ratify his choice, and he campaigned vigorously) was O. K. Allen, a friend he had brought to Baton Rouge from his home parish of Winn to be state highway commissioner. An amiable, relentlessly agreeable—some would say compliant—man, Oscar Allen understood his role and was content to play it. While Allen occupied the governor's mansion and the governor's office, Long ran the state from his office in Washington or from the apartment that he kept for himself on the twenty-fourth floor of the State Capitol.

The senator spent much of the second day of the special session, Sunday, September 8, receiving a stream of hangers-on and favor-seekers who rode up in the Capitol elevators and were ushered into his apartment by one or another of the bodyguards who attended him. When the Kingfish was in residence he wanted his friends around him, and they in turn wanted to bask in the glory of him. The House was to meet that night to consider the bills he had put before it, and shortly before it was to convene he went down to the main floor, eventually entering the House chamber in the east wing of the building. There a packed gallery awaited the arrival of the colorful senator who by 1934 had attracted a national following with his "Share Our Wealth" program. What the crowd in the gallery saw this Sunday evening was Long moving about the floor, buttonholing legislators and exchanging banter, finally coming to light in a swivel chair on the speaker's rostrum not far from Speaker Allen J. Ellender, where he was photographed by a local commercial photographer, Francis Julais, on assignment for the New

York *Times* photo syndicate. At approximately nine fifteen, as Ellender was about to gavel adjournment, Long got up and made his departure from the chamber, escorted by five bodyguards and trailed by a number of followers and well-wishers. The Kingfish never moved slowly or alone. He was usually at the head of a crowd of people, his bodyguards hurrying to keep up with him. At the center of the building he turned into the reception room of the governor's office, then moments later reappeared at the door and stepped back into the long corridor that ran east to west through the building to the rear of the main lobby. As he did so, a man in a white linen suit who was standing next to a marble column, and who until that instant had not been noticed, stepped forward with a pistol in one hand and a Panama hat in the other and fired—some said twice, some said only once. The senator gave a cry of pain and ran toward an intersecting hallway and a nearby stairwell that led to the basement floor of the building. Behind him the bodyguards, in rage and frustration, were still firing into the body of the man lying on the marble floor of the corridor.

One of those seated in the gallery overlooking the House floor has given us a description of the scene there. Robert B. Heilman, who had arrived in Baton Rouge that very week to teach on the Louisiana State University English faculty, recalls that not long after Huey strode out of a chamber still formally at business but now half-empty "there was a strange outburst of sounds in a rapid but irregular sequence. Firecrackers, I thought, puzzled. Then men came running back into the chamber below and ducking behind desks. It had to be gunfire, though to a new young Ph.D., fresh out of Harvard, this was unbelievable."

On the floor below, a Long crony who had gone to the Capitol cafeteria to buy cigars for the senator helped Long into an automobile that happened to be parked near the back entrance to the building and ordered the stunned driver to take them to Our Lady of the Lake Sanitarium, just across the lake from the Capitol. There Dr. Arthur Vidrine, a physician whom Long had named to head Charity Hospital in New Orleans and who was in Baton Rouge to lobby for appropriations for the hospital, examined the senator and found that a bullet had penetrated his upper-right abdomen and that there was a wound in his back which he concluded was the point of exit. Long would have to undergo surgery. However, Vidrine decided to wait for the arrival of two surgeons the senator had ordered summoned from New Orleans, a two-hour drive away. By one of several critical coincidences that Sunday night, one of the surgeons ran his car off the road, ended up in a ditch, and was late in reaching the hospital; the second was also delayed and was late in arriving. In the meantime, Vidrine decided that he must operate himself. Long's blood pressure was dropping and his pulse rate rising. Further delay might prove fatal. Medical opinion on the Long case is, like everything else connected with it, divided, even as to what caused the senator's death: a hemorrhaging kidney wound that had, incredibly, gone undetected during surgery; or peritonitis. Vidrine, who happened to be on the scene because of his political ties to Long, would shortly become a part of the Long legend.

The scene in the operating room is one of the spookiest in the annals of American political history, and throws back to a much earlier time in Europe when kings died in the presence of their courtiers. While Vidrine and the three Baton Rouge doctors who assisted him fought to save Long's life, they were ringed by an operating room full of political cronies and potential successors, including the governor of the state and the lieutenant governor. One of the local doctors was there to assist, but also to vouch for the anesthesiologist, who was an anti-Long and who had jokingly remarked a few days before that he would "put Huey to sleep for good" if he ever gave him an anesthetic.

Long survived the operation and lived for another twenty-eight hours, slipping in and out of consciousness, near the end fighting the oxygen tent that covered him. In the final entry on the hospital chart one of the doctors noted, "Oxygen tent discontinued as pt. [patient] grew very restless under it—delusions of photographers, etc." From time to time one of the senator's closest aides appeared at his bedside to ask Long where he had put the "deduct box"—the bank box that held funds deducted from the salaries of state employees as well as campaign contributions of other kinds. Long had deposited the funds in a Washington bank, but not long before his death had apparently moved them. As far as is known, the box was never found.

Thus the king died, whispering toward the last that he wanted to live, that there was so much left to accomplish. The masses of the plain people of the state—those who had seen Huey Long as their savior and who would name their sons for him and cast their votes for men who summoned his memory—were stricken. When the senator's body lay in state in the lobby of the Capitol, tens of thousands passed, many of them weeping. On the day of the funeral, special trains left New Orleans every half-hour on the half-hour, bringing mourners to the capital. When it became obvious that the single line moving up the Capitol steps into the lobby could not accommodate the crowd, the entire top of the massive bronze casket was removed, so that two lines could pass—one on either side. By afternoon the crowd was still pouring into the capital. "They came in flivvers spattered to the windshield with red clay from the by-roads leading to the concrete highways that made Mr. Long famous," wrote a United Press correspondent. From the west the line of cars waiting for the ferry across the Mississippi stretched miles long, despite the fact that two additional ferries had been pressed into service.

At four o'clock the doors of the Capitol were closed, and the Long family was brought in for a last look at the body. Then funeral director Merle Welsh and his assistants placed the top back on the casket, and to the muffled beat of drums the procession moved from the lobby down the broad steps to the sunken garden in front of the Capitol, where a grave had been freshly dug and where eventually a hewn granite monument topped by a bronze statue of Long would be erected.

The man lying on the marble floor of the Capitol that Sunday night was Dr. Carl Austin Weiss, twenty-nine, a Baton Rouge ear, nose, and throat specialist whose role in the shooting of Long so shocked the community that many refused—still refuse—to believe it. An intense young man who, as his mother told reporters, "took living seriously," Weiss had been valedictorian of his high-school class in a local Catholic academy and had studied medicine first at Tulane University in New Orleans and later in Vienna. Afterward he had interned at the American Hospital in Paris and at Bellevue Hospital in New York City before returning to Baton Rouge in 1932 to practice with his father. Weiss, his wife, and their three-month-old son lived in a modest bungalow almost within the shadow of the Capitol.

There is no evidence that Huey Long had ever seen Carl Weiss before the doctor stepped out from the marble column and into history. Fifty years later the mystery of what motivated Weiss remains a mystery. At least two people who knew him—both doctors—remembered that when the conversation turned to Long he had had strong feelings, and one recalled that in a casual conversation the Friday before that Sunday he had remarked that there was "no cure for Louisiana's troubles but the death of Long, the dictator." But this was a remark that any one of hundreds, even thousands, might have made in those extraordinary times in Louisiana. Hodding Carter, an anti-Long newspaper editor, later to distinguish himself as one of the most moderate of the Southern voices in the 1940s and 1950s, wrote in a 1934 editorial that the state was in "as despotic a grip as that which holds Germany" and that "there remain only the ancient methods of righting wrong." Even Julius Long, Huey's older brother, in a 1933 magazine article accused his brother of conducting "a campaign of fear, deceit, corruption . . . the like of which has never been seen before in America" and asserted that Huey Long "must be forced out of public life." Clearly Julius Long did not have assassination in mind, but the passion behind his words suggests the emotion of the times. The remark attributed to Carl Weiss, and in all likelihood coming to us not as Weiss spoke it but in the words of the person recalling it, becomes relevant only because when the smoke from the fusillade cleared that Sunday night the body on the floor of the Capitol corridor was Weiss's.

Weiss's family was never convinced that he went to the Capitol to shoot Long, and the uncertainty about precisely what happened was fueled by the fact that no autopsy was performed on Long's body and no ballistics tests were made on any of the bullets. One story that persists to this day is that the Kingfish was accidentally shot by one of his own bodyguards in the melee that followed the shot or shots fired by the doctor (a variant version theorizes that the shot from the bodyguard may not have been accidental). The generally accepted version—the one accepted by Long's biographer T. Harry Williams among others—is that Weiss went to the Capitol with the intention of killing Long and that he acted out of idealism, though perhaps also motivated at least in part by a Long bill introduced in the legislature the day before which would gerrymander Weiss's father-in-law, Judge Benjamin Pavy, an anti-Long, out of office. Williams gives little credence to the possibility that Weiss may have been part of the conspiracy referred to by Long in a speech on the floor of the United States Senate just one month before he was shot, in which he told a shocked Senate that he had evidence of a plot to kill him—and then read into the record the purported transcript of an anti-Long meeting held in a New Orleans hotel the previous July at which one of those present said, "I would draw in a lottery to go out and kill Long. It would only take one man, one gun, and one bullet." Some of those who attended the meeting in New Orleans have since denied that a murder conspiracy was hatched there, though they admit that in any gathering of those who opposed Long there were inevitably remarks made about getting rid of him.

The fact that Huey Long in effect foretold his own death one month before it occurred—the speech preserved in the pages of the *Congressional Record*—will no doubt continue to spawn the kind of conspiracy theories that typically accompany the assassination of public figures. We have not heard the last of those who believe Carl Weiss felt passionately that Long must go and that he was willing to draw straws to decide who would do it. The truth is that, fifty years later, no one can be certain beyond any reasonable doubt whether Weiss came to the Capitol that night as a loner or as a conspirator—or, as his family wondered in their search for an explanation, as a decoy, a man lured to his death and wrongly accused of being Long's assassin (though this possibility appears unlikely). Nor can one even be certain whether Long was struck by one or two bullets, or how many bullets struck Weiss (at least thirty-one, but the coroner counted only bullet *wounds*—there were sixty-one—without attempting to determine how many of the bullets entered and exited and how many remained in the body). Those close to Long, no less than the anti-Longs, feared what an investigation might uncover, and the inquiry that followed was appallingly inadequate.

The Long myth, the Long legend, did not begin with Long's death. It had its beginnings in the Kingfish himself, in the chemistry and makeup of the man: the adrenalin, the gall, the force of energy that those who came into contact with him felt. There was something about Long that defies easy explanation, some secret gift—perhaps the gift that Robert Penn Warren perceived in Willie Stark ("My study is the heart of the people") and that attracted the unabashed fascination of the American press. Writers filled newspaper columns and the columns of magazines like *Collier's* and the *Saturday Evening Post* with stories that helped to shape the legend. Huey Long was news even before he went to Washington as senator in 1932, but from that point on almost every word that he uttered, on the Senate floor or off, was reported by the newspapers and wire services. Sifting through the Long photographs and the newsreel footage, one is impressed with the charm, the magnetism of the man, but also with his resourcefulness. At moments one has the feeling that his life was in fact a series of photo opportunities, and as the cameras click or grind away the cocky smile is forever there, the thrust of the chin below, the upturned clown nose, the glint in the eyes as he leads an all-girl band in "Every Man a King" or mixes a Ramos gin fizz behind the bar at the New Yorker Hotel or rattles and roars before a microphone. "There is hardly a thing that he will not do to catch or hold a crowd's attention," said his brother Julius.

But it was Long's death, the manner of his death—even the questions that remained unanswered—that enlarged the myth, gave it a different texture, a new dimension ("The tragedy of Huey Long," wrote Hamilton Basso, "was that it lay within his ability to be a great democrat.") Long's death was the perfect ending to a novel about an uncommon man who has risen to extraordinary heights and who is seemingly unstoppable, and even before *All the King's Men* we had gotten versions of it from Adria Locke Langley (*A Lion Is in the Streets*) and from Basso (*Sun in Capricorn*). But *All the King's Men* in fact began several years earlier, as early as 1937, as a verse play that Robert Penn Warren began in Louisiana and completed on a sojourn in Italy the following year, or the year after.

Warren has written that the novel "is more realistic, discursive, and documentary in spirit (though not in fact) than the play," because when he sat down to write the novel he had left Louisiana and the world in which the story had its roots. "By now that literal, factual world was only a memory, and therefore was ready to be absorbed freely into the act of imagination." What Warren is saying—and he has put it into other words elsewhere—is that the Governor Talos of his verse play *Proud Flesh* is closer in distance and time to Huey Long, or at least to Long as he perceived him, than is the Governor Stark of *All the King's Men*. The play, like the novel, is about power, how a man "is drawn into a vacuum of power. In one sense, is a creation of history." Warren has said that his dissatisfaction with the play led him in the novel "to get some sense of the world *around* the man—the man as *seen* rather than the man as presented. The strong man should be seen through the weaknesses of others, or the needs of others, rather than taken as an abstract power presented directly. That was, I suppose, the shift of interest that made the novel."

If *All the King's Men* is about Willie Stark, it is also the story of the narrator, Jack Burden, who appears only briefly in the play, toward the end, when a newspaper reporter named Jack (no last name) comes up to his boyhood friend Dr. Keith Amos in the Capitol as Amos waits to kill Talos—Jack introduced, as Warren has explained, as a dramatic device to hold the audience in suspense before the governor appears and the doctor jerks a pistol from the pocket of his coat and lunges toward him. In the novel Dr. Amos has of course become Dr. Adam Stanton.

Warren's knowledge of Huey Long is obviously drawn from newspaper accounts and magazine articles as well as from simply living in

Louisiana during the Long era. His acquaintance with the Louisiana setting was, as a matter of fact, still forming at the time of Long's death—he had come down to join the Louisiana State University faculty only the year before, when he had not yet turned thirty. "I don't pretend that Willie Stark is Huey Long," Warren told students at a 1966 appearance at Union College. "I know Stark, but I have no idea what Long was really like. I heard him speak once at an enormous official luncheon celebrating the seventy-fifth anniversary of the founding of Louisiana State University—he had not been invited but walked in anyway, and took over, and he was very funny." Warren's recollection is accurate. Long was not invited, but showed up in place of Governor O. K. Allen.

More important than what he had read of Long, Warren had heard the Long stories—the first he tells us, when he picked up a hitchhiker on a north Louisiana road in September, 1934, on his way down to his new job at the state university. They had not gone far when the old man, one of the country folk who made up a large part of Long's constituency, began to talk about "Huey." That, says Warren, was his introduction to "the myth that was 'Huey.'" He was to hear many more Long stories. "Conversation in Louisiana always came back to the tales, to the myth." What especially interested Warren was the "strange, shifting, often ironical and sometimes irrelevant relation" of the mythical world to the factual, and his search for the truth about Long became, in time, a meditation on the dynamics of power.

Warren was not there in those last days of the Kingfish: the night the news from the Capitol crackled over the radio and from porch to porch and phone to phone across the town; the day that followed, when the Kingfish lay dying and nothing, not even his doctors or his bodyguards, could save him. The young English professor was on his way back across the country after a summer spent in the West, and he heard the news at a stop he made in Nevada. "I was in Nevada on a Monday morning getting gas at a little desert filling station when the gas attendant said, 'They shot your boy last night,' seeing my Louisiana license. And he began to call some people around . . . and said, 'I want to talk about him.' Long was billed there, you see, as somehow their friend and they wanted me to talk about him. And all the way across the continent I made a habit of stopping at the smallest places, not at big filling stations. Well, people would gather immediately around a Louisiana license and talk about Long, and I got the impression from these conversations that his power was much more diffused than I had suspected."

Warren's return to Baton Rouge was delayed by the illness of his mother in Kentucky, and he was not there for the Long funeral, though he of course read about it in the newspapers and would hear about it later from his colleagues and neighbors. When Long died, a great silence seemed to have settled on the town. "It was my only experience," recalls Robert B. Heilman, "of a situation in which . . . the whole life of a state, from its political fabric to its educational system, seemed tied to the life of one man."

When Warren returned, flowers still blanketed Long's grave on the grounds of the Capitol, where mourners—the people who had given the Kingfish his power—and the simply curious gathered. Carl Weiss's family had slipped away quietly, fearing reprisals. Soon the Long bodyguards would be heading back to their small towns, carrying their memories of the Kingfish and their relics—a folded newspaper clipping, a spent bullet picked up from the marble floor—with them. The idea of a play or book did not immediately occur to Warren. "At that time," he says, "as far as I can remember, I had no notion of writing anything based on, or suggested by, the Long regime." But it was out of his Louisiana experience that Warren later created Talos and Stark, shaped one of the great novels of our literature. We cannot read of the death of Willie Stark without remembering Huey Long and the shots that rang out that Sunday night in the State Capitol.

The
CULTURAL CONTEXT
of the
SOUTHERN REVIEW:
PROBLEMS
and
ISSUES

I.
The Twentieth-Century South
and the Image of the Writer

The POET at HOME in the SOUTH

James W. Applewhite

The Southern "climate" (in its broadest sense) may be simultaneously a sustaining earth for the Antaeus-side of personality and an isolating medium for the artist-side. For me there has never been any question of a need for, and a response to, the land and its culture. But there *has* been a question as to whether I could move sufficiently into a conscious perspective so as to see the local landscape with objectifying clarity. The danger for the artist is that of absorption into the mere intensity, the irrationality, the unconsciousness of the subject. A man up to his neck in a pond can hardly describe its geography from an aerial perspective. Perhaps that is why even major Southern writers in the past have practiced an art of musical, emotional, rhetorical intensity (from Poe to Faulkner to James Dickey) that is unable to state its premises and propositions as clearly as writing of other regions. If we cannot accept the idea that a beautiful woman, dead, is the most poetical of all subjects, then Poe cannot be said to inform us of his true subject in the way that Emerson or even Whitman does.

Poe is remarkable for the substitution of aesthetic philosophy, music, atmosphere, effect, plot ingenuity, for those intellectual underpinnings we expect in the traditional writers of earlier centuries—those before Romanticism, who wrote out of the received wisdom of the age. In Poe the ultimate subject is always irrational, inexplicable, whether a death-and-life relationship (as in "Ligeia" and "Ulalume," for example) or the self-enclosure and eventual collapse of a divided house of psyche ("The Fall of the House of Usher"). Likewise, we do not expect of Faulkner a considered philosophy to which we might, as reasoning beings, assent. That the South fell, falls, must always fall; that Caddy goes away to the Nazis, Benjy's pasture becomes a golf course, Sartoris' house a vacant shell; that spotted horses run away through the moonlight and upset buckboards of ladies; that when the Mississippi, the Old Man, rises, all goes before—these are not the elements of a conventional philosophy. We assent to Faulkner because of his emotional power, his dramatization of the intensities of our own war-wounded, outrageous South.

The Southern allegiance, even for one who has experienced it as I have, is shrouded in mystery. Certainly the means of the transmission of this exotic innoculation is beyond exposition—even to oneself. I can't recall the beginnings of my connection with broom sedge about the plowed fields and the marble headstones on rises beyond anymore than I can revisit the beginnings of my accent. I was aware from early on that the bearded grandfather in my mother's stories manipulated his double-ended knife-fork with one hand because of something called a minié ball. I remember being told that the white two-story farmhouse outside town in which my grandfather and father had been born was built "before the Civil War." But for me growing up, war was World War II and the Thunderbolts from nearby Seymour Johnson Field which practiced overhead. I was utterly astonished, as a young man, by the emotional squeeze exerted on my viscera by the image of Robert E. Lee in a brief television dramatization. I came rather late to battlefields in northern Virginia, to Donald Davidson's "Lee in the Mountains," to second-guessing the strategy at Gettysburg.

Being born and reared in a small farming community in eastern North Carolina, then, even during that era of accelerated change of which World War II was part, seems to have implied a certain innoculation by an Ur-history never fully disclosed but always hoveringly present, in the comments and asides of parents, grandparents, other relatives, and townsfolk. That irrational legacy, even from the postdepression though pre–shopping center era, was potent enough to be a mixed blessing. The social connection with an extended family sometimes seeming to include the whole town was analogous to the humid air that closed the landscape into one image. A visible water shimmer hovering over tree, field, and creek seemed to represent my connection with a larger order of things not visibly ending or beginning. Yet this atmosphere was also suffocating, a collective emotional miasma which left no space for individual speech.

I will not rehearse for this imaginative and well-informed audience the racism and sexism which automatically surrounded the automatic housing of tobacco during the homefront combat with sun-heat and fatigue during those war-era years. If I may quote the former farm-girl persona of my own "Mary Tapes":

> I hated that summertime dreading, when the heat
> Ponded up, and people were hitting or grabbing
> In their soaked-through shirts, looking drunk,

> Or asleep, or like walking underwater,
> Till you expected for their hair to float up.

Suffice it to say that such a background did not incline one toward the conscious learning, the deliberately articulate verbal skills, requisite for poetry. Certain strong bases of subject matter and emotion-charged utterance (or song) were laid, but in the absence of a superstructure which would allow those mute intensities the kind of recognition and formulation necessary to art.

Because of the enclosing Southern family, the special heaviness of our air, with that infusion of honeysuckle Quentin chokes on in *The Sound and The Fury;* because of military defeat and an introversion of intense emotion following; because of a Romantic legacy especially fostered in the South by cavalry charges, organdy dresses, moonlight on slow rivers—perhaps even because of the distillation of our land's corn into bourbon whiskey more potent by far than Keats's "draught of vintage"—for whatever reasons of social circumstance and mournfulness of mourning doves, the Southern writer has tended by birth to be isolated and almost suffocated in a specialized emotional ambience beyond rational analysis. A distance, a more reasoned component of understanding and technique, has been badly needed.

The explicit intellectuality and ironic self-analysis of modernism were surely necessary to the development of the first great generation of Southern writers: that Vanderbilt group headed by John Crowe Ransom and including Allen Tate, Robert Penn Warren, and Randall Jarrell. Great learning and an elaborately rationalized approach to art were united with the Southern passion. As with Poe, the first great Southern poet, powerful technical resources were devoted to an almost-inexpressible subject matter, rendering, instead of any clear philosophy or idea, an associated tone, landscape, atmosphere. Southern poetry in its first realization tended to emphasize the stylistic, self-referential elements of literary art, circling upon itself as in Allen Tate's refrain: "Seeing, seeing only the leaves / Flying, plunge and expire." It was this musical, evocative aspect of Southern modernism which was first able to make great verses of our land's inexplicability and tragic affect—of John Whiteside's daughter, lovers in doomed equilibrium, dead boys, Confederate infantry rising seasonally out of the earth, of a silent clawing at the floor by wolves in the next room.

The title of Tate's essay "Our Cousin, Mr. Poe" perhaps does not locate the relationship closely enough. The temptation toward a private landscape enclosed by language's formal, self-referential musicality haunts Southern poetry. Perhaps Tate should have said, "Our Common Ghost, Mr. Poe." The dual impulses (not, of course, ever entirely separate) toward openness of form, external reference, a language continuous with that "really spoken by men"; and enclosure of form, self-reference, language specialized, set apart from speech by a hypnotic music, go back ultimately to Wordsworth and Coleridge. The one leads Wordsworth toward a reasoned philosophy based on experience of nature. The other leads Coleridge toward musical encounters with the irrational. These impulses manifested themselves on our shores in Emerson and Whitman on the one hand, and Poe on the other. We Southerners have in important respects continued in the lineage of Poe. Eliot's essay "From Poe to Valéry" makes clear Poe's importance as precedent for *la poésie pure*—as theorist and practitioner of the poem concerned with itself, its own interior relationships, almost in abstraction from meaning. It is this Symbolist avoidance of direct statement that first allowed our land's irrationality a successful literary formulation.

The quintessential Southern poet is typified still by enclosure within a burden of emotion almost too intense for statement. The Southern poet has thus had to find a way out of the Gothic house of Poe by several defenses. Tate's intellectual formalism is perhaps closest to Poe. Ransom added a further distancing of irony. Robert Penn Warren opened his formal gifts to the literal distances of the American West. James Dickey, who, like Warren, has traveled widely, seems also more to imitate reality—but look (or listen) to the anapests which make his simplicity of statement hypnotic. The magnetism of Dickey's rain-enclosed mountain tent, or leaf-surrounded tree house, or boathouse at night, or vision underwater, is not wholly distinct from that of those chambers of the psyche in Poe. Notice the set-apart landscape of marsh grass, or field isolated by sun, or enclosure of screened porch in the country. Remember the Sheep Child, with all his field of memory preserved in a bottle. These barriers of screen wire or glass—between the irrationally animal and the human—are what Dickey's metaphysic strains to thrust through. This line is continued in Dave Smith, for instance.

We will remember that the idea of a poetry of objective correlatives, of emotion expressed by a formula of objects, was articulated in Eliot's essay "Hamlet and His Problems." Hamlet and his emotion beyond the fact, his essentially inexpressible burden, stand as background to this

quintessentially modernist prescription for a poetry impersonal, explicit, classicist, objective—a literary remedy Eliot the physician
forced himself to take for his own quotidian Romantic fever. Eliot's
heart as a poet, his Hamlet-like isolation in thought (as in "Prufrock"
and "Gerontion"), his grief beyond the circumstances, helped fit him as
Southern literary ancestor—as uncle of Mr. Tate.

Thus, Eliot presided over a Southern modernism which, like his own
poems, fused almost inexpressible emotion with an almost desperate
dependence on form—and on irony, on learning, on a violent union of
heterogeneous images ("Garlic and sapphires in the mud," and so on).
The "impossible union" of these "spheres of existence is actual" in his
poems—as in those of Ransom and Tate. This tension between extremes has been especially noticeable in Southern poetry—perhaps
because those qualities of rational articulation and emotional suasion
necessary to any good writing have seemed to be so separated in the
South. Whether through climate, history, or mythology, we Southerners are heir to a tradition that assigns rich feeling and expressiveness to
our region, clear rationality somewhere else. The poetic world of
Wallace Stevens, for example, revolves between poles of clear-sighted
snowman among New England conifers and "Donna, donna, dark" on
Florida's "venereal soil."

The extremes *Northern* and *Southern* seem even to have the same
values in other languages. Rousseau's *Essay on the Origin of Languages,* as
analyzed by Derrida in *Of Grammatology,* posits a Southern origin for a
primal, spoken, vowel-laden, richly accentuated language of emotional
expression. Northern, written, consonantal articulation developed later
and is associated with a thought impelled by need, and with repression.
In Rousseau's mythic South, "language is instituted but still remains
pure song." Derrida's deconstruction of this essay as historical explanation leaves still a richly metaphoric account of the two contrary states of
the human soul in words. Recent evidence from psycholinguistics
suggests that Rousseau's South would be better read as earliest childhood. The child's first words are expressive of affect, are socially
communicative, and are perhaps not wholly distinct from the tone-
inflected questions, recognitions, rejoicings, and sorrowings expressed
through nonsense sounds. Language at first is a calling or a playing, a
repetitive, self-reflexive syllable-music; the infant is our first Poe, absorbed in the song of *la poésie pure.*

As Derrida's analysis implies, Rousseau's account of the later fall into consonantal clarity, articulation, writing, repression, is a psychological rather than a geographical story. We each have Rousseau's South and North within us. But perhaps those of us born in the American South have had this Southern pole of the psyche (and of language) especially reinforced by early verbal and climatic surroundings, by a sweeter, more potable atmosphere, by an especially oral tradition of language. Perhaps we Southerners, Oedipal intensities extended by honeysuckle to the landscape, are simply more in love with our origins than others. To alter Donald Hall's phrase, we have a sweeter residual milk on the tongue. It often turns to poison as we sip, of course, but the impulse to pay homage to a land as rich and as irrational as the unconscious pysche produces poets who are innately musical, oral poets, poets who want to sing speech and to rock the listener in the cradle of stories whose rhythms are a hypnotism. This has been a problem and an imprison- ment, a reinforcement of an outmoded Romanticism, as well as a deep strength. The need is to escape into articulate, self-acknowledging speech, while retaining the formative music.

The Southern poet may require an intellectual distance, but this direction away or "upward" is often disguised within a landscape explo- ration inward, or downward, toward merger. This impulse toward total involvement (or immersion) is perhaps best epitomized by the South- ern lineage of underwater poems, from Robert Penn Warren's "Bearded Oaks" ("how subtle and marine" as "The layered light / Above them swims") to James Dickey's "The Lifeguard" and "Rootlight" to my own "The Capsized Boat" to Fred Chappell's "Cleaning the Well" to Richard Tillinghast's "The Knife" to David Bottoms' "Under the Boathouse" to Betty Adcock's "Walking Out." While not quite so flagrantly frequent as the Southern encounters with serpents, these and the many similar trips under the river or pond's skin or down the well are perhaps tropes for the poet's subjection by birth to an enveloping irrationality.

Salvations from these threatening baptisms are various. Warren es- capes his oceanlike deeps through a metaphysical irony, an energy of intellect. Bottoms seems saved from the rusted fishing hook (which seems, thankfully, to have no postlapsarian ancestry) in part by the shower of plastic knives and forks dropped from the dock by his frantic wife. Is this salvation by shopping center—by the homogenization of the South? Along with our omnipresent media, lowered airfares, the literary penchants for workshops and conferences, I sense on the part of the younger Southern poets a new capability for plain statement.

Perhaps it is hard, these days, even to *find* those swimming holes in intellectual backwaters as of old. Richard Tillinghast, up in Michigan by way of Sewanee and Harvard, wonders whether the South we write about really exists anymore. Well, the river, ponds, and marshes are still there. I remain undecided as to whether we are continuing to conceptualize and articulate more fully and originally the nature of the conflict symbolized by threatened entrapment underwater.

Some geographical approximation to an abstract North / South duality of articulation and expression seems to have been graphed out in the careers and works of our region's mightiest poets. A. R. Ammons has left the South, in body and in diction. His musings along the New Jersey shoreline of Corson's Inlet or at home now in Ithaca have about them a rather scientific detachment and Emersonian rationality. When Ammons animates a daily speech with a fervor not merely intellectual, we have the genuine article—artistic language made new as Pound told us to make it new. But the Southern poet out of the South, as Ammons sometimes demonstrates, runs the risk of losing passion in abstraction (or detachment). Charles Wright, Donald Justice, and Dave Smith, like Dickey earlier, have recently moved back to the South.

Robert Penn Warren has mastered such emotional and spatial distances, such experiences of landscape in the South, the American West, and abroad, as to make us feel both the passion of the Southerner and the wisdom of the philosopher. Like Eliot our honorary Southerner, our adoptive father, Warren reunites the meditative intellect able to roam over the known cosmos with the Southerner's devout involvement in place. With his passion and his intellect, he seems to live both in and out of the South. One of the most irrationally haunting images in all poetry is the blood-suffused face of the hanged woman in Warren's *Audubon: A Vision.* It is described by the immaculate craftsman who killed birds to paint their beauty. With Warren and the others I have mentioned, Southern poetry has escaped any earlier provincialism and has become the dominant poetry of our time.

One may be forgiven for wishing for oneself some analogous escape—not from feeling, but into understanding. My current admiration and wonder are evoked by the younger Southern poets who have escaped song into speech—have defied the flaming word of our irrational past for a current precision. I offer you a recent poem by a North Carolina poet, Robert Morgan, friend and younger colleague of Ammons at Cornell.

The Gift of Tongues

The whole church got hot and vivid
with the rush of unhuman chatter
above the congregation,
and I saw my father looking at
the altar as though electrocuted.
It was a voice I'd never heard
but knew as from other centuries.
It was the voice of awful fire.
"What's he saying?" Ronald hissed
and jabbed my arm. "Probably Hebrew."
The preacher called out another
hymn, and the glissade came again,
high syllables not from my father's
lips but elsewhere, the flare of
higher language, sentences of light.
And we sang and sang again, but
no one rose as if from sleep to
be interpreter, explain the writing
on the air that still shone there like
blindness. None volunteered a gloss
or translation or receiver
of the message. My hands hurt
when pulled from the pew's varnish
they'd gripped and sweated so. Later,
standing under the high and plain-
singing pines on the mountain I clenched
my jaws like pliers, holding in
and savoring the gift of silence.

This genetic father who spoke in tongues is mightily reminiscent of earlier Southern poets like Dickey. They too have wished to allow themselves to be so electrocuted by the dynamism of a speech (or song) from beyond the rational consciousness.

Yet we are now well into the workshop era, and for reasons of practicality the ethos of writing seminars tends to be Imagist rather than Symbolist, speech instead of music. Like Morgan, an impressive group of younger poets in (and of) the South have learned to speak extremely well, including Dave Smith, David Bottoms, Richard Tillinghast, Betty Adcock, and Gibbons Ruark. The poet of my own generation who for me rises triumphantly above the dualities of speech and song is my old friend from undergraduate days at Duke, Fred Chappell.

If I may once more, as in the beginning, use myself as example of the poet at home, I would like to compare with Morgan's my own earlier account of a language beyond the personal: that poetic gift of tongues (we Southerners are all influenced by the church and by the Bible). I made of the uninterpretable language which is sometimes mysteriously given to us a single golden word. I imagined an illuminated manuscript wherein the text in the center was simply overlaid scenes of my life there in conscious vision. About the edges of the page were intertwined the characters of this single word. Perhaps I sought to control this language of fire seen only in peripheral vision by confining it to the boundaries of a text. But nevertheless I felt committed to its numinous syllables.

Bordering Manuscript

I am alert to these letters in extraordinary numbers: perhaps
from grass heavy-headed with seed, flickering a's and r's
under pressure of sun that I recognize as holy and intended—
while a bird of indecipherable mind is scrolling margins of air.
A gold, illegible word rests on the left hand of vision.
Illusions of its spelling leaf from the lacquer of hedges past
exits of buildings. Women removed across hundred-foot stretches
of chained grass evoke vowels with their liftings of hair,
but let me confess: the name could be a man's as well as a woman's.
People printed with my children and wife in the foreground, though
accurate and clear, seem from a sufficient, forgetful distance
to twine into the gigantic characters which fit no speech.
Places redolent with heat and resinous pines of meetings
perhaps ten years ago form amber in retrospect.
The puzzle I see has thousands of pieces, each poor day
hiding its two or one. Had I all the days permanently together,
I could assemble the jig-sawed chips in a lifetime. This thought
chills me close to a water-like stillness, tea-colored and brackish
with vacations on rivers, as if a plane of focus shimmering behind
the tear in a photograph, or body of air from all fields
inhabiting a music. Behind my lips, tipping my unknown
tongue, she waits in her surface, her name my speech's mistress.

I recall writing this poem parked in a wooded hollow behind the ball diamond on Duke University's west campus. That location, quiet then in the summer, seemed to symbolize, with the familiar foliage and atmosphere and contrasting academic architecture, a combination I was desperately seeking. The campuses (and all they represent) of schools such as Louisiana State University, Vanderbilt, Sewanee, Duke, the universities at Chapel Hill and at Greensboro, and now many others, are of crucial importance in allowing the poet to be at home in the South. They offer whatever hope there is of seeing, still, past the Kudzu, used-car lots, fundamentalist congregations, and slumber of Sunday-noon dinners, that rare smoke of the soul's fire rising beyond the pines. They symbolize the structures of understanding necessary to make of our intensities something other than sound and fury—to sing ourselves a speech resembling consolation, understanding.

SOUTHERN WRITERS in SPIRITUAL EXILE

Walter Sullivan

As has already been mentioned in these proceedings, we are gathered here fifty years after a similar conference held in this city in 1935 to discuss Southern letters. In reading over the record of that meeting— or that part of the record which was published in the spring, 1985, issue of the *Southern Review*—I was struck by the fact that the participants had little if anything to say about why the South was in the midst of a literary renascence. As I recall, hard things were said about university administrators and even harder things about publishers, most of which, I am sorry to tell you, might justly be repeated today. But there was scant discussion of literary theory, because, after all, those participants were producing the work, writing the poetry and fiction which was to be the stuff of the renascence; and a movement can hardly be dissected and subjected to theory until it is over, or until a significant phase of the movement is complete.

Whether or not the renascence ended after World War II, the theorizing about it began then, and the most commonly accepted theory of why the South had produced, and to some degree was still producing, great literature was basically agrarian. The logic went like this: life lived on the farm is more authentic than life lived in the city, because the rural experience teaches the nature of reality. To take the argument on its most basic level, in the city one is insulated from the elements. Those who work the land learn from the weather. Though, according to the agrarian theory, farmers are the most contented of people, conditions never suit them. It either doesn't rain or rains too much. The spring is too cold or comes too soon. Mules are contrary and tractors break down. This is only the beginning of a litany of troubles that any experienced farmer has on the tip of his tongue. But these very vicissitudes contribute to bucolic fulfillment. The agrarian sees how things work. He knows nature and therefore knows reality firsthand in a way that the city dweller can never know it.

What I like most about this theory leads me to a question that I have been pondering and attempting to write about for many years. In 1970 I published in the *Southern Review* an essay entitled "Death by Melancholy," in which I attempted to trace the loss of a sense of the transcendent in modern society and the effect that this loss had on literature, particularly that of the South. I began then, as now, with agrarianism because it has always seemed to me that the most telling argument to be offered in behalf of rural life is that it develops a sense of piety. Southern religion was thought to be connected with, perhaps an outgrowth of, the Southern experience of planting and harvesting. It was, Allen Tate maintained, the wrong religion, Protestant when it should have been Catholic, but however that may be, it served Southern writers very well. It was so much a part of the culture that it was taken for granted. Most of the poems produced during the high renascence were secular in theme, as were almost all the novels. Frequently, no character in a piece of fiction ever entered a church or claimed a religious affiliation or referred to God except to swear. But there were enough church scenes and enough prayers said in the novels, and sufficient references to Scripture in the poetry, to demonstrate that both Southern writers and their readers were aware that the renascence was rooted in a Christian ambience.

Now, what happens when the Christian ambience ceases to exist? My argument in "Death by Melancholy" was that society develops an impulse toward self-destruction, a death wish which manifests itself paradoxically in a frenzied worship of life. In the late sixties, when I was developing this theory, we had freed ourselves from old behavioral restraints which were religious in origin and replaced our lost belief with a new freedom, as we termed it, to make love with anyone at any time in any way under any circumstances. This had many ramifications, of course. The unrestrained pursuit of physical satisfactions leads to the abuse of almost everything, but of most importance, free love imperils the family as an organizing institution of society and as a central force in maintaining and conveying a sense of the sacred. Also, since the young and the beautiful are thought to be the best lovers, our understanding of the rhythms of human existence was distorted by the advent of a cult of perpetual youth as evidenced by the building of thousands of health clubs; the enrichment of the man who invented the Nautilus, who, incidentally, has had many wives, each younger than the one previous; the publication of innumerable diet books (I will not adduce as evidence pro or con the unhappy end of Dr. Tarnower); the sale of hundreds of millions of jogging costumes; and the full employment of legions of plastic surgeons. In such a society, no pleasures are reserved for old age, and since there is no way to win at time's game, we became, as we aged, a people of sorrows; our lives were bereft of meaning and our very efforts to live forever and to stay young forever were symptoms of a moral sickness that propelled us toward death. So went my argument in 1970.

But times change, and with the end of the Vietnam War and the reassessment of the implications of our involvement which followed, there has been in our society a moral as well as a political disengagement. A few protesters are still left, a few voices are still raised in behalf of this or that cause, but most people, young and old alike, are tending to their own affairs. Religious and political leaders who urge us to work for social reforms are left with diminished followings. I suspect that one reason for our moral indifference is our loss of a belief in absolutes. Bereft of commonly held first principles, almost any intelligent and articulate person can take either side of almost any issue and compose an argument as convincing and logical as his counterpart on the other side, but not more so. This state of ethical confusion issues into the moral detachment of which I speak, and this has great consequences for literature and for those who write it.

Literature ought to mean something; novels and stories and poems ought to be informed with a view of reality, with some kind of belief in, or at least attitude toward, the human condition and the truths which underlie it. I am not thinking of programmatic literature, of works that set out to prove a preconceived theme. Writing is a process of discovery, a way for the author to determine in essence who he is and what he thinks: writers start with questions, not answers. A writer of fiction will begin with a concept of a character about whom he wants to know more, or with a situation which he wants to pursue, with what James called the "germ" of the story. But to find out who he is and what he thinks, the writer has to be somebody and think something, and herein, in my judgment, lies the modern difficulty. To write a Christian novel, said Jacques Maritain, you should be a Christian and write the best novel you can write. I would add, follow the same directions for a Jewish novel or a Muslim novel, or an atheistic or an existential or any other kind of novel, but whatever kind of novel or story you are going to write, you have to be something first and to have, in a rudimentary form at least, developed your own sense of values. To put this another way, literature is a moral art in the sense that it pursues images and sequences which are morally significant, and moral disengagement on the part of the author will impoverish it.

Let me offer an example. Flannery O'Connor and Bobbie Ann Mason have similar styles and write about similar people. O'Connor's involvement with the grotesque was greater than Mason's, but Mason has the same ear for dialogue, the same eye for detail that O'Connor had, and she is interested in the same kind of people. Her talent, her technical virtuosity seem to me to be equal to those of O'Connor except that O'Connor came first. The difference between them is one of moral commitment and religious belief. O'Connor's work is too familiar to require exegesis. We need think only of her stories and novels, of the religious imagery that permeates them, of the Christian rituals which appear in them, and of Christian doctrine which is at the heart of every significant scene. There are pictures of Christ and images of the Holy Spirit and peacocks and lambs and visions of ghostly processions into heaven. There are baptisms and last rites, sermons and symbolic fires, and these set the tone for a religious vision that informs all the events and characters in the O'Connor canon. Take away the Christian intention from O'Connor's fiction and you have left a human menagerie, a collection of hollow-headed and willful people who are largely unsympathetic. Or, we are left with a body of literature that except for its heavier emphasis on violence is similar to the fiction of Bobbie Ann Mason.

For the two authors, even the characters' names seem to have been drawn from the same sources. In Mason's "Shiloh," there are Leroy and Norma Jean and Norma Jean's mother, Mabel. Leroy is a truck driver incapacitated by a wreck, Norma Jean sells cosmetics at the Rexall drugstore, and Mabel works in an upholstery shop and spends her free time visiting her daughter, giving free advice and snooping around the premises. The story is about the death of love, the disintegration of a marriage, which in the first place was nourished by Leroy's long absences as he drove his truck around the country. Forced to be with her husband for an extended period, Norma Jean falls out of love.

What we have here is a kind of no-fault fiction. People come together, pair off, get married, then get divorced, but no serious commitment is made at the wedding and nothing of enduring value is lost when the marriage fails. Deprived of its sacramental quality, literature ceases to be art and becomes artifice. In a morally detached world, neither

Leroy and Norma Jean nor their marriage has any significance beyond the clever surface details and the ingenious dialogue which Mason is able to conjure up. Norma Jean lifts weights, studies English composition, plays an electric organ; Leroy builds model houses with Popsicle sticks, watches television, smokes pot. The text is peppered with brand names of products; the titles of songs and movies and TV programs; the nomenclature of the lower middle class.

Mabel calls a dachshund a "datsun," and tells how it chewed off a baby's leg. Both of his wife and strangers, Leroy asks, "What do you think?" but the question is rhetorical: he seeks no opinion, has no specific topic in mind. Norma Jean, chagrined to have been caught smoking by her mother, says: "She don't know the meaning of the word knock. . . . It's a wonder she hadn't caught me years ago." Mabel urges Norma Jean and Leroy to visit the battlefield at Shiloh. She suggests that Norma Jean might join the United Daughters of the Confederacy. But the past means nothing to any of Mason's characters. Shiloh, Mabel thinks, is a place to repair her daughter's dying marriage, but at Shiloh, where the cemetery reminds Leroy of a subdivision site, the marriage and the story come to an end. Whatever meaning is here is on the surface. Unlike the fiction of O'Connor, in which underlying meanings are significant and the vision apocalyptic, in Mason, everything is on the surface: what you see is what you get.

When the commonly held sense of the sacred is lost, you can shout as Flannery O'Connor did, but you have to have something to shout about, and therein lies the difficulty. If you are devout, as Flannery was, you can work out of your own sense of the divine, but if you do not have the sacred within yourself, your work is in jeopardy because society will no longer furnish it for you. Or at least this was what I thought when I wrote "Death by Melancholy" those many years ago. I am not prepared yet to abandon that position, but I should like to modify it. Until the recent past, the basic question which most writers asked themselves— and which admits of innumerable variations—was, "How do you feel about God?" You could be for God, against God, disgusted with God, indifferent to God: you could believe or not believe; but the act of asking the question established a connection, no matter how tenuous, between the writer and the spiritual dimension which has informed Western literature for thousands of years. A conscious decision not to believe is in a way an act of devotion: to take the time to ask the question is to recognize the importance of what is being asked about. Now, in our state of moral detachment, we are no longer asking the question. Caught up in material concerns, in hedonistic and acquisitive impulses, we have transferred our faith to secular millenialism—which is a form of gnosticism. In spite of the failure throughout history of every human scheme devised to bring about the enduring happiness of mankind, we as writers and intellectuals place our trust in social programs and political action without reference to whether there is a divine element in the circumstances under which we live. But this is another subject and must be reserved for another time. The point I wish to make here is that those writers who continue to ask about the existence and nature of the transcendent are better writers than those who do not.

One of the most prominent novelists to emerge in the last twenty-five years is Cormac McCarthy. Though one suspects he is an ex–altar boy, he was done with God before he ever put pen to paper, and he writes as if he has taken the advice of Flannery O'Connor's Misfit to do as much meanness as he can. From the opening scene in *The Orchard Keeper*, in which Kenneth Rattner is shoplifting, to the murder of the Kid in a Texas outhouse, which is the final action of *Blood Meridian*, McCarthy has compiled a 1,491-page catalog of viciousness unequaled by any other author I have read. No paraphrase does justice to the original, but McCarthy's fiction is particularly difficult to recount or describe. The mention of a head severed, a skull broken, an eye gouged out, a corpse violated, hardly hints at the intensity of such actions as they are rendered by McCarthy. His ear for dialogue, his eye for detail are the best; though he occasionally overwrites, his prose is sharp and charged with energy; though his structure is weak, his narrative sequences are filled with movement and stunning imagery. He writes like a fallen angel, lavishing on the most depraved of human actions his brilliant style, his consummate technique.

McCarthy's theme is survival, or more than that, the celebration of the strong and the clever who live at the expense of others by cruelty and deception. In his moral economy, the only virtue is the ability to endure. His vision is fragmented, but there is something healthy in it. That aspect of the world that he has chosen to explore is firmly rooted in reality. What he sees, he sees clearly, and above all, he still knows the proper question to ask. At the end of *Blood Meridian*, the sole survivor of a large band of cutthroats is a hairless giant, a peerless fighter and self-taught scholar called the judge. Here is the final paragraph of the narrative. The scene is a Texas saloon.

> And they are dancing, the broad floor slamming under the jackboots and the fiddlers grinning hideously over their canted pieces. Towering over them all is the judge and he is naked dancing, his small feet lively and quick and now in doubletime and bowing to the ladies, huge and pale and hairless, like an enormous infant. He never sleeps, he says. He says he'll never die. He bows to the fiddlers and sashays backwards and throws back his head and laughs deep in his throat and he is a great favorite, the judge. He wafts his hat and the lunar dome of his skull passes palely under the lamps and he swings about and takes possession of one of the fiddles and he pirouettes and makes a pass, two passes, dancing and fiddling at once. His feet are light and nimble. He never sleeps. He says that he will never die. He dances in light and in shadow and he is a great favorite. He never sleeps, the judge. He is dancing, dancing. He says he will never die.

I cannot resist mentioning two other works in which the image of the dance has been used in a religious context: Eliot's "Burnt Norton," and Charles Williams' *The Greater Trumps*. I do not mean to imply that McCarthy's image is comparable to those of Williams and Eliot or that good and evil coalesce in McCarthy's novel. But evil can exist only as a defect of the good. It is a reversal, a denial, a parody, but always it is a defect. For example, there is no way to understand what a lie is unless first we have a concept of the truth, of which a lie is a defect. If truth should cease to exist, then the idea of a lie would be meaningless and would die with the death of truth. We can only destroy what has been created; we can only steal what a moral system has declared to be the property of another. Because evil is dependent for its existence on its opposite, it always implies the opposite, which is good.

McCarthy's judge is a parody of God—he is naked like the God of the Sistine Chapel, he is a great favorite, he never sleeps, he will never die. This parody must take seriously the idea of God or it has no significance. Thus it thrusts us into a world where the possibility of the transcendent is valid. Though approached from a different angle, it is the same world in which the characters of Flannery O'Connor live their lives. I prefer O'Connor's vision to that of McCarthy, but I prefer McCarthy's work to that of the legion of writers, Southern and otherwise, who ignore the question of the existence of the sacred or who do not know that there is such a question to be asked. To reject God is to remain in touch with reality in all its dimensions.

What, then, of the southern writer in exile? For him or her the dilemma is not whether to remain in the South, but rather how to remain in touch with the sense of piety that informs the best southern writing. I am afraid that in what I have already said, I have made the task seem easier than it is. When Andre Maurois, a good writer and a devout man, learned of Maritain's prescription for creating a Christian novel, he threw up his hands in hopeless dismay because, he thought, Maritain's advice would be impossible to follow. Doubtless Maurois was being overscrupulous, but faith is a gift and not everyone receives it.

It is well enough to say, as I have said, that in a world bereft of the sacred, the writer must furnish the sense of piety that society once furnished for him. But this leaves writers who do not have such a sense in a lurch, and I have no notion of how they can pull themselves out of it. More to my point is the fate of those who include a sense of the sacred in their work and offer it to a world which in general does not share their vision. As we know, Flannery O'Connor shouted and drew in bold lines, but since her death an industry has arisen, the concern of which is to prove that she was not a Christian writer. Those Southern writers who are endowed with less talent than Flannery, those who speak with a softer voice and draw in thinner lines, are mostly doomed to wander the world like latter-day Prufrocks, not refuted or even criticized, but ignored, dismissed by publisher and public alike with ironic but tolerant smiles as anachronisms, representatives of an age and a philosophy which have been invalidated by modern ontologies.

But where in this gloomy scheme, you might ask, do we fit Eudora Welty and Walker Percy and Elizabeth Spencer, three of the distinguished southern writers of fiction who are a part of this conference? It is not coincidence, I think, that they all were raised in Mississippi, which has remained southern as long as or longer than any other state and which endowed them with the southern sense of the sacred. They have by right of birth what is no longer available. For them, the problem is solved, but it remains for those born in other places and in other times. It is presumptuous for me to give anyone advice, but I must do so to be true to my topic. I think southern writers in exile from the spirit of the contemporary world should seek in their work the sacred at the expense of the South.

This seems, as I say it, heresy, particularly to those of us who have been raised on the work of the giants of the southern renascence and who have seen the South as the most fertile of all fields for literary endeavor. But with its sense of piety gone, the South of the renascence must be recreated, and there is a danger in our seeking out for our fiction details that are specifically southern. I must be very careful here. Writers—at least writers of fiction—begin with the concrete, not with the abstract. Faulkner began with what he saw and heard, with what his senses told him, and in the shaping of details and sequences he discovered the southern piety that underlay them. My contention is that under present circumstances, with the sense of the sacred gone, the shaping of details that are specifically southern will lead the writer to think he has done what Faulkner did, and he will not have done so. Rather, he will have created work similar to that of Bobbie Ann Mason, whose stories are southern all right, but as I have tried to demonstrate are bereft of piety and of meaning. The only way to recreate a South that is hospitable to the production of great literature is to recapture the sacred. I think, paradoxically perhaps, that the best way to do this is to seek the transcendent outside the ambience of southern imagery be- cause the images of the South, familiar and beloved as they are, tempt us to believe that we have not lost our piety. I do not mean that we must stop writing about the South forever. But we are writing about it badly now. Whether we recognize it or not, our spiritual diaspora has begun. It can end only with a rejuvenation of the spirit.

Robert Penn Warren and Cleanth Brooks

Lewis P. Simpson

Donald E. Stanford and Eudora Welty

James Olney and Robert Penn Warren

Thomas Cutrer, Robert B. Heilman, and William C. Havard

Eleanor Clark and Walter Sullivan

Walker Percy

Elizabeth Spencer, James Applewhite, and Jo Gulledge

Ernest Gaines

Eudora Welty

Cecil G. Taylor, Tinkham Brooks, Cleanth Brooks, and George Core

Fred Hobson   Ronald Schuchard

Steve Lewis, Gloria Naylor, and Susan Mann

Evelyn Heck, Robert Heck, and Maryanna Stanford

Charles East and Eudora Welty

William C. Havard, Robbie Phillabaum, Louis D. Rubin, Jr., and
Leslie Phillabaum

Daniel Littlefield, Anthony Barthelemy, and Houston A. Baker, Jr.

The HOME VOICE in a FOREIGN LAND

Elizabeth Spencer

I have lived in Canada for some years now, specifically in Montreal, an old city dating back to the days of trappers, explorers, and missionaries, come to create New France, "la nouvelle France." Some of my American friends seem yet to have no idea where Montreal is, and casually mention that I meet them for lunch when they are in Toronto (some four hundred miles west), or ask if I often go to Calgary or Halifax, two even more remote places. As you here know, I am sure, Montreal is directly north of New York City, about two hundred miles north of Albany.

When I first went there, it did trouble me quite a bit to be a Southern writer so far out of the South. It is true my husband and I had lived in Italy for a few years, but I think there we always had the temporary feelings of being sojourners; the move to Canada had all the indications of being a permanent one. My husband is English, but partly Canadian —I had barely escaped having to take up residence in the British Isles, a farther remove than I care to think about.

Writers strongly identified with a place, as at that time I had become with Mississippi, are naturally dependent on the place to furnish them much in the way of character, story, landscape, incident, and above all speech. (In other words, just about everything.) How was I to continue to write anything in a landscape that was gray, if not actually white, six months in the year (those "fields of snowy white" definitely did not refer to the cotton crop), in company that praised or remarked on my accent, mainly because, as they said, "they'd never heard anything like it"—well, maybe at the cinema.

I did feel wobbly at first, maybe even a little desperate. I tried to write something with a Canadian setting, but found myself rather hopeless at it. Not even introducing an officer of the Royal Canadian Mounted Police—one of those "Mounties," you know—was any help. For one thing, I'd never met any, and when I did, I had to learn they didn't necessarily go around in scarlet coats looking handsome.

But moves are stimulating just the same, and I kept thinking of one story after another that I wanted to write down, mostly set in the South or in Italy, where we had come from recently. Memory, at this time, proved my great source. I've wondered since if it isn't the source of more writing than we can imagine. Time is always passing life into memory whether we stay right where we are or not. Our heads are storehouses absolutely filled with memory; you've only to shake this store a little and you can probably remember what you wore to school on your first day, or the smell of your new book satchel. You can remember, once you start trying, how your mother beat eggs to make cake batter, and how your grandfather cut a plug of chewing tobacco, first taking off the little red star or brown mule with the point of his penknife for you to play with (but not to put in your mouth), and how your father's label on his after-dinner cigar became a ring for your finger.

Once I began to try, things came first in a trickle, then a flood, and all—here is the most important thing about memory—with the most uncanny accuracy, as true as old photographs. I don't mean that memory is good at communicating facts like the third of June or the tenth of July, or whether your party was for your ninth or twelfth birthday; but only that memory is sensually accurate, showing you not the exact hour but the precise cast of light and the quality of the weather, recalling the step of someone approaching on the walk, letting you all but taste once more your homemade birthday cake—coconut, with white icing. In Greek myth, I am told, Memory was the mother of all the Muses. There must be a powerful reason why this was so.

There are all kinds of separation. I've been talking up to now just about geography, the simplest kind, the separation of distance. Modern literature, however, is so full of writers who for one reason or another have put distance between themselves and where they were born and raised that the condition has attracted a lot of names to itself: *expatriate,* for instance, or graver still, *exile.* We think of the days of Hemingway and the many in his time who went to Paris. Before that, we recall, were Eliot and Pound, and earlier still, Henry James. One has to suppose that every case is different and that there is no one word that will cover us all. Back in the early days of my own work's being published, an editor who took me to lunch in New York wanted to know why so many Southern writers lived outside the South. The number who did was noticeable even then. I remember remarking that these same writers, though they might live far away, were still identifiably Southern and in most cases had kept on writing fiction set in the South. James did not continue to write about Boston, nor Hemingway the north woods. So why was that? The only conclusion is that there must be something powerful here that won't let us go and that we keep holding on to.

I take *exile* to mean that somebody chased you out; *expatriate* to mean that you left because you didn't want to stay. There are other words, like *alien, alienation, separation, displaced person,* or just plain *absence.* Alienation is something you can feel toward the people you live with, eat with, and talk to everyday. In that sense you don't have to go anywhere to feel cut off, and so I suppose there is such a thing as "spiritual exile," which you might, heaven help you, feel if you stayed right at home. But in this case, I guess you couldn't really call it home. Far better then to go elsewhere, go north—Maine or Connecticut—and write "down home" fiction, because then you might finally discover what home is. We recall that famous New England definition: "Home is where when you have to go there / They have to take you in." You may have hoped for a warmer view of things in the friendly, good ole South, but wound up getting kicked out the back door. Such cases, I hope, are rare.

Language! What are you going to do without the constant stream of talk around you, all set to the rhythms and nuances and social gradations you have known since you were a child? On the other hand, you have to realize, that if you try to reproduce local speech too relentlessly, you may wind up being locally interesting and nothing more. Eudora Welty in *The Ponder Heart* carries us along with no one but Edna Earle Ponder speaking for an entire novel; but I have a feeling that it takes Miss Welty to do this without any risk of monotony. The wonderful Uncle Remus stories of Joel Chandler Harris are read very seldom today, I believe, because the dialect, accurately recorded though it was, prohibits its finding many readers. For fun I sometimes read a page or two from it to my students in Montreal. They can hardly catch a word—I might as well be speaking medieval Chinese.

In dilemmas caused by the absence of your mother tongue, it is just as well to get to know your grandmother. Loving one in no way stops your loving the other; in fact, they get on very well together. A student of mine recently went to New York to interview Anthony Burgess for a Montreal paper. Burgess is quoted as follows: "What I hold onto with every breath of my being is the supremacy of the English language. I think our greatest achievement was to spread the language, and burnish it, and enrich it. We've got the greatest instrument that's ever been known."

This is worth thinking about. Language itself is an instrument of expression, and our own—eloquent, lyrical, witty, elegant, coarse, musical, precise, and powerful—what else?—offers infinite possibilities to the writer. It has been put to the use of many dissimilar cultures; it can live through and endure the onslaughts of journalese and bureaucratese; it retains, like a great stream, its own central force, identifiable as itself from the mid–seventeenth century onwards.

Mavis Gallant, a Canadian writer of English parentage, brought up with both French and English in Montreal, now lives in Paris and frequently sets her stories in that city. But she also writes about the French and the English in Montreal in the days when she lived there. Her triumph is to render these different locales in an English prose style that is a joy to read in itself, so crafted and suited to her as to seem a natural part of her, though there is nothing in it that has to remain hers alone, that the reader cannot share. One feels that she could, if she wished, do far more with the speech patterns of the Quebecois in the 1930s or with the curious modern-day expressions of Parisians, but she touches these areas lightly, though always with accuracy.

Nadine Gordimer, the wonderful South African novelist and short-story writer, has not strayed but stayed at home. She too, if she chose, could spin out the numerous local dialects and languages she must have encountered from the days of her childhood in a gold-mining community onwards; but it is our grandmother's broad back—the English language—which is carrying her stories to us.

Some writers have seemed to have had such a quarrel with English that they have set about overriding and overruling the language with a language of their own. We think of Joyce and Faulkner here, of course, and then we must genuflect. But I personally don't have a quarrel like that with my grandmother. I think of Jane Austen, of Hampshire, England; of Elizabeth Bowen, of Cork County, Ireland; of Katherine Anne Porter, of Texas, U.S.A.—no less individual and unique as writers because they also knew and loved the language and used it with passion and delight. I don't see anything wrong with that.

Nevertheless, I have to say that when I sometimes telephone to a student I have not spoken to in recent months, in Montreal, a city of one and a half million people, and not even having given my name, I hear the patter of little feet and a voice crying, "Mommy! It's E-liz-a-beth!" I'm sort of pleased. You never lose your native voice, I guess, especially if you're from Mississippi, and I think that's a good thing.

The AFRO-AMERICAN WRITER and the SOUTH

Panelists:
Daniel C. Littlefield, Moderator
Houston A. Baker, Jr.
Henry Louis Gates, Jr.
Gloria Naylor

DANIEL LITTLEFIELD.   The civil rights movement of the 1960s focused public attention and interest on all aspects of black American life and culture. Black literary expression was no exception, and it has gained and continues to enjoy increasing public attention. The context of interest, however, conditions the reception and sometimes modifies the perception of black writing. Before and after the 1960s, the literature of black Americans was frequently dismissed as protest writing and given short shrift by those who, if they considered it at all, placed it in a special category and gave it severely circumscribed notice. Even the provincial dignity generally accorded to ethnic literature was frequently denied black literature. It was, like American society, largely segregated, and the mind-set that society reflected changed even more slowly than the environment of which it was a part. This fact was as true for scholars and literary critics as it was for the reading public. There have been, of course, earlier periods during which black literary creativity broke through the restraints of indifference and hostility to impress itself upon the American consciousness, but this more positive reception was nearly always tempered by some kind of social or political crusade: the autobiographical writings of westernized Africans as part of the struggle against the eighteenth-century slave trade; the nineteenth-century slave narratives as part of the Abolitionist movement. Even the outpouring of artistic expression that flourished during the decade of the 1920s, the so-called Harlem Renaissance, was made possible as much by new fads and fashions convulsing American life as by newly evinced black pride. But between these periods, and indeed throughout most of American history, there has been a continuous black literary ferment. Normally ignored, it increasingly has made its presence known in the twentieth century. Examples are to be found in such people as W. E. B. Du Bois, James Weldon Johnson, Richard Wright, Ralph Ellison, Gwendolyn Brooks, Chester Himes, James Baldwin, and Lorraine Hansberry, to name a few. Indeed, since the 1970s black artists, literary and otherwise, have had greater access to the public, and black scholars have enjoyed greater access to and influence upon academia. The subsequent range, variety, and quality of black literary expression have increased dramatically as blacks attempt to define and shape their own unique voice in American letters. Some have suggested indeed that the most interesting American writing today, particularly among women, has been created by black artists.

Our panelists are all distinguished representatives of current Afro-American literary enterprise, creative and interpretive. Houston A. Baker, Jr., Albert M. Greenfield Professor of Human Relations at the University of Pennsylvania, is the author of *Blues, Ideology, and Afro-American Literature: A Vernacular Theory* and *Blues Journeys Home,* his third volume of poetry. Henry Louis Gates, Jr., professor of English and comparative literature and Africana studies at Cornell, is author of *The Signifying Monkey* and *Figures in Black.* Gloria Naylor is a writer and lives in New York City. Her first book, *The Women of Brewster Place,* won the American Book Award in 1983. Another of her recent novels is *Linden Hills.* Our topic this morning is "Afro-American Writing and the South." We are going to begin our discussion by getting the panelists to react to the topic. Then we will take questions from the audience. I would like to begin the discussion by taking up something Houston introduced in discussion yesterday. Richard Wright in 1940 said:

> Early American writers, Henry James and Nathaniel Hawthorne, com-
> plained bitterly about the bleakness and flatness of the American scene.
> But I think that if they were alive, they'd feel at home in modern
> America. True, we have no great church in America; our national
> traditions are still of such a sort that we are not wont to brag of them;
> and we have no army that's above the level of mercenary fighters; we
> have no group acceptable to the whole of our country upholding certain
> humane values; we have no rich symbols, no colorful rituals. We have
> only a money-grubbing, industrial civilization. But we do have in the
> Negro the embodiment of a past tragic enough to appease the spiritual
> hunger of even a James; and we have in the oppression of the Negro a
> shadow athwart our national life dense and heavy enough to satisfy even
> the gloomy broodings of a Hawthorne. And if Poe were alive, he would
> not have to invent horror: horror would invent him.

What I would like to ask our panelists to react to is this question of horror. What would you say about the image and influence of the South on Afro-American writing? Has it been one primarily of horror?

GLORIA NAYLOR.   Well, I guess I'll start, and my first reaction is, "Oh, my God, no!" But we will have to break this down, because I hope we won't in this discussion fall into the problem of looking at black writers, even the black writers from the South, as a monolithic unit. You will have to dissect them by generations, often by their initial classes to see their reaction to the Southern experience. And you will have to separate them by gender because that is leading me up to my answer. I have found that with the black woman writer, both those who have traveled back in their literary imagination to the South, or those like Alice Walker and Zora Neale Hurston who may have been born in the South, they did not encapsulate the social situation via horror into their literary imagination. They stayed more within an interior world where they took what was uniquely theirs in that community, and they spun a tradition out of that. I don't want to generalize, but I find somehow with male writers from the South there is more of a delineation of what was going on in the social circumstances. The man would have, given the patriarchal nature of our society, pitted himself and his malehood against the outside society. The female did not. She, because of our social circumstances, found her actualization through other ways, her creativity through other ways. So, no, I would say, they are not all tales of horror. We will take the most recent masterpiece that has come from a Southern writer, Alice Walker's *The Color Purple*. The problems in that book are very *personal* problems for those protagonists, and Walker tries very hard to deal out of that woman's humanity and to get her past that. Now we understand what the outside influences were. But for other writers, that may not be the case, and maybe my two colleagues will talk about Richard Wright.

HENRY LOUIS GATES, JR.   Houston, I defer to you.

HOUSTON A. BAKER, JR.   Well, I don't particularly want to talk about Richard Wright. I do want to respond to the question in a kind of right or left oblique way. I suppose what I want to say about Wright's essay is that it is in harmony with a kind of model, or problematic—if you are a poststructuralist—that is interesting to me now, and it raises a set of questions that might be posed about an entire expressive culture called "Afro-American Expressive Culture." The model for me is one that emphasizes, to quote from a Gates essay, the phrase, "If you are black, you believe not your eyes, but your ears." It carries me to the image in a Ralph Ellison essay where he and his brother had gone hunting, and they found themselves walking in an unfamiliar field on a winter day during the depression. They looked up, and all at once they saw charging across the stubbled and harvested field toward them with shotgun in hand and muzzle down, gesturing in frantic and excited ways, a white man dressed in farm clothes. And he kept running toward them. A cold sweat broke out, and each of the young black men leveled his shotgun at a vital spot of this white man. When he got within a foot of them, he stopped, breaking out into his own sweat as he realized that one shotgun—probably a Remington—was pointed right at his belly and the other was aimed at his head. Then they said, "What do you want?" And he said: "This is, this is Mr. Johnson's field, and y'all can't come in this field and hunt like this. It ain't my field, but y'all niggers can't come in." Ellison points out that it wasn't even his [the white man's] field and that what he [the white man] had misunderstood in this situation was the potency of gesture, that is, what he had misunderstood was how easily the visible could be mistaken. But when he came close enough, and they could exchange, and the sounds were there, then they could have rational discourse. Now, Ellison is answering Irving Howe. And what Ellison is saying is that when Howe waves his arms around in sociological ways and talks about protest literature—no matter what the implicit intention of Howe might be—that he has threatened us in vital ways because he has cut us off from an ideational base. He hasn't *heard* our sound. He hasn't *listened* to us. And it seems to me that what Wright did in his essay was to continue a tradition of sounding, and sounding is important in our culture. Gates can talk about that too: signifying, sounding on the resoundingness of the sounds of Afro-America. I would like to suggest quickly here that the locus, the Southern locus, is extraordinarily important, not only for a problematic or a model that emphasizes the sound of Afro-American culture, but for an interpretation of an enterprise, like, for example, the Harlem Renaissance. The Harlem Renaissance, you see, is that "outpouring" that has been written about by blacks and whites in almost exclusively one way, as a failure. The dominant question surrounding the Harlem Renaissance is, "Why did the Harlem Renaissance fail?" Now, I can't imagine a group of white scholars addressing themselves to the question, "Why did expressionism fail?" "Why was Irish modernism a failure?" But nonetheless, this has been the problematic which argues for a kind of disciplinary power-tripping on the part of historians. Now you might go to Nathan Huggins and say: "Nathan, write a book showing why the Harlem Renaissance failed. Use the best disciplinary tools. You'll render a service to history, to your race and to yourself."

GATES.   "And we will pay you a lot of money."

BAKER.   "Yes, we will pay you a lot of money, give you a chair." We are talking here about power and the way these things are done. But it is asinine for a group of scholars of the culture themselves to accept that. The new problematic then talks about a dramatic success of *a sound* that begins, perhaps, on Southern turf. You know when people go, "Ain't no hammer, sounds like mine babe, ain't no hammer, strikes like mine," that's the kind of sound and the kind of base, it seems to me, that carries a type of energy that allows a Booker T. Washington to say: "They think we sound like minstrels. They think we are all chicken-stealing darkies. They don't know our power." Okay, so what Washington does is to master that minstrel form. Right in the middle of his Atlanta compromise speech, he says, "Starting some thirty years ago with ownership here and there in a few quilts and pumpkins and chickens—gathered from miscellaneous sources." This is scandalous, utter *scandal* in the French Derridian sense of that term. I mean it scandalizes that situation, that we would have a chicken-stealing darkie here in the first speech delivered in the South by a black man called a national leader. That imagery begins in fact in his narrative [*Up from Slavery*], where on page three, he says: "My first memory of my mother is her awaking us late in the night. She had cooked a chicken, and she had called us to come and eat it. Where she got the chicken I don't know, but I suspect that it came from our owner's store." So on page three of *Up from Slavery,* we have the mother as chicken-stealing darkie. Right in the middle of the Atlanta speech, we have the chicken-stealing darkie. Now, what that leads to in the narrative is an embedded document that reads as follows: "I shall be glad to assume the expenses of the library building to the sum of six million dollars and whatever other expenses you may incur. I commend you once again on your noble work. Signed Andrew Carnegie." Washington knew exactly what he was doing, what kind of sound was expected. What he does is to get inside that sound, inside that minstrel mask, and master it with a sound that is quite different.

Why does one talk about Washington this way? Well, obviously because Washington is usually characterized in terms of "Booker T. and W. E. B. [Du Bois]." Was he an accommodationist, or whatever? But structurally, out of two hundred pages of Washington's *Up from Slavery,* forty pages are devoted to public speaking, specifically chapters thirteen through fifteen. I call, therefore, Washington's *Up from Slavery,* which has a Southern locale, a speaking manual. It is a book of strategies: how you can *sound* on white folks, build libraries, and advance what Washington wanted, a skills center in the South. In contrast to that in the Southern landscape is, of course, W. E. B. Du Bois. W. E. B. Du Bois is traditionally viewed as the person who stands utterly outside the Washingtonian realm. He has very little to do with the South. New England is his locus. But when we see a review a couple of weeks ago in the New York *Times* written by Nathan Irving Huggins—who else?— on Aptheker's new volume of essays, we find Du Bois writing in 1887 an essay called "An Open Letter to the People of the South." And one of the quotations that was in the review from that letter was directed toward black people, Negroes. He said most of you are quite, by your own designing and absence of responsibility, ignorant. 1887, right? And then, he appeals to the whites of the South to look to their own self-interest and to take what Du Bois advocates at one point in *The Souls of Black Folk:* a responsible leadership position. I mean in *The Souls of Black Folk* he said: "I hold it to be true that an underdeveloped nation should have its stronger surrounding people to control it. If that were true in the South now, I wouldn't have to do anything else. But the best whites are not in charge. The crackers are in charge. So you know, we have to do something on our own here." But he says that in *The Souls of Black Folk.* But the sound of Du Bois is the sound of the spirituals. I mean if you look structurally at Du Bois' text, what you see at the beginning of every chapter is what would now be called, of course, a displacement or a deconstruction of Western expressive culture by the spirituals. Alright, I mean he will put Swinburne up there at the top, and then right under it comes the spiritual; I mean it wipes out Swinburne and Byron. Du Bois does this until the point in chapter fourteen where the entire text, that is narrative or expository, gives way to song, and what appear are the words and the score of "Let Us Cheer the Weary Traveler." And this is Du Bois' millennial apocalyptic vision.

If Washington's narrative is a speaking manual advocating a strategy of the mastery of form, what Du Bois' *The Souls of Black Folk* is, is a singing book which deals with the deformation of mastery, as it were. Now I would like to suggest that those two discursive strategies capture a sense of the sound of Afro-American culture that carried into the Harlem Renaissance in a book like *The New Negro.* And there Afro-American discursive culture comes to a kind of fullness that discounts, takes away, renders utterly ridiculous, all notions that the Harlem Renaissance was or could be considered a failure. *The New Negro,* it seems to me, also discounts the traditional and very stupid notions that black writers have one tonality. I mean the second most insulting thing to William Dean Howells' assertion that the race moves between humor and pathos which expresses the stops of the range of the Negro imagination, is the assumption that anger somehow is either good or bad. You know if you are going to talk about black people you have to call that word somehow: "Are you one of those *angry* ones or not?" Right? So, I mean I think that's fairly insulting to a rich discursive history.

And what I would say is yes, the horror is certainly there, but it is not a Kurtzian horror. And what Wright knows is that it is not a Poe horror. I think what he is doing in that essay, in a sense, fits along the pole of the deformation of mastery because what he is setting forth, in a Duboisian way, is an analysis of the contemporary world. That essay moves out to Russia; it moves out to China. He says look at the condition of our world today—for this conference, the *modern* world. And if you would find a metaphor for that *modern* world, if you would understand the power nexus that gave birth to the horror that is today's wasteland, look—as my friend Carl Wagner was saying just before this session—look to the Negro. Look to the Afro-American. Look to the sounds and those discursive strategies, and I think you get a quite different sense of "the modern" from the one that traditionally comes to us only in the voice and sound of Anglo-American, British, or Irish *men*. I think the modernism that is encoded, that is set forth by those people, and that is commented upon by their critics—like Lionel Trilling—is hopelessly bourgeois and undeniably and unequivocally optically white and has very little to do, it seems to me, with an explanation of what we might want to talk about as the modern condition. I mean that anyone like D. H. Lawrence could put that passage in the mouth of Birkin in *Women in Love,* about African statues and the disintegration of the African to the point of a beetle. And this is what we want. That anyone like Eugene O'Neill could write a wonderful kind of epigraph at the end of his list of dramatis personae that says, "On an island in the Caribbean as yet uncivilized by white Marines," and then put all those psychosurreal trappings at the end of *The Emperor Jones.* That anyone like Fitzgerald could have blacks driving across a bridge in a white chauffeured limousine rolling the yolks of their eyes up in haughty rivalry. "I laughed," says Nick Carraway. I mean this is utter and total bullshit; it has absolutely nothing to do with the genuine authentic sound, I would say, of the modern world. It has to do with the malaise and the trouble of

Anglo-American, British, and Irish men. I think that they are captured very well in Tom Buchanan saying, "Civilization is done for, you know!" while drinking a corky but rather impressive claret on a lavish Long Island estate to which he has brought a string of polo ponies. And continuing, he says, "I've gotten to be a terrible pessimist." But, who has he been reading? He says, "I've been reading this fellow Goddard." He means, of course, [Theodore Lothrop] Stoddard [*Racial Realities in Europe*].

I mean it's all a bookish decline, falling towers of civilization that has a repertoire of cultural images and riches behind it which we shore against our ruin. But again, when Lionel Trilling says, "I have great reverence for this, because it teaches us to ask questions like, 'Am I happy? How's my family life? Do my friends like me?' " You know, you think that in the largest geographies of the world the single most pressing question is, "Where do I find water, wood, and food enough to make it through *this* day?" So I mean that there is a very different sense of the modern that comes, it seems to me, when one listens to the sound of Afro-American culture. And it does proceed out of a horror, but not the one, certainly, of Conrad, who never lets his Africans speak except to say in guttural minstrel syllables, "Mistah Kurtz—he dead." There it is. A little bit about Southern locus. The important thing of course is that Booker T. Washington and Du Bois knew that they have to look at the South in order to come forward with strategies of address to an oppressive culture.

GATES.   Now, how do I follow that? Thanks a lot, Houston.

BAKER.   Easily, easily, easily. No problem.

GATES.   Gloria and Houston have raised very interesting questions in response to Richard Wright's essay. The essay, first of all, strikes me as an echo, indeed an ironic echo, of Henry James's catalog of the absences of all that makes culture "culture" when he described what was lacking in America, and why he fled to England. And it certainly echoes T. S. Eliot's sentiments as well. Wright's signifying trick, of course, is to make the black person the ultimate saving grace of an American culture which is a desert, a wasteland. And it is a very curious gesture for him to do that. He hoped that by making this statement he could transform the way in which great artists in America, his contemporaries, viewed the Negro. These artists themselves would transform the use of the black as the ultimate figure of negation and absence, which has a long history in Western literature, and make the black the metaphor of possibility, of

hope, of presence, etc. Unfortunately, Richard Wright's contemporaries did not heed his call, and we continue to be figures of absence in
the literature created still largely by white people in the United States.
But, it seems to me that what both Houston and Gloria have touched
upon is that there are three problems here. First, we are talking about
black people as subjects and objects—that is one way to put it—in
literature. And, second, we are talking about the white South as a
metaphor of oppression, of horror, of tribulation, and of trial in the
literature and culture of black people. Third, we are also talking about
another South—the black South—in other sorts of works, such as
those Gloria identified as part of the black women's tradition, in which
the South is a kind of nesting ground, a place to which we turn from the
inside to create our fictional worlds.

You see, in so much of black literature, particularly the literature of
black men, the South was a place, of course, from which to flee. One of
the most fundamental motifs in black literature is the migration from
the South to the North, and it occurs across generic categories. It
occurs certainly in autobiography, and most certainly in fiction. The
plot starts in the South and ends up in the North. And until very
recently, this motif has been fairly fixed. So I have to confess, when I was
asked to speak here and to think about the relationship between black
literature and Southern literature, I agreed because I wanted to see my
good friends on this panel. I agreed because I wanted to hear the
distinguished people whom we've already heard read and whom we
will continue to hear read. I agreed because James Olney is a dear
friend. And I agreed because I happen to like LSU and Baton Rouge. But
I was not sure what I would say about this problematical relationship
because of this fact that the South was a place from which we fled, and
because in a real sense all black Americans are "Southern." Let me
explain what I mean through an anecdote.

A few years ago, John Oliver Killens sent me a letter—John Oliver
Killens, of course you all know, is a great novelist. Killens lives in
Brooklyn but is indeed from the South. Well, he sent a letter and asked
me if I would serve as a consultant to an anthology that the New
American Library would be publishing on Southern black literature.
Since I always wanted to meet John, I hopped on the train from New
Haven and went to New York. (I made him take me to my favorite
Indian restaurant.) But the reason I went was to find out what he
defined as "Southern" black literature, A, and B, why he was so con-

cerned with doing this. We had a very pleasant lunch. We talked about terms and responsibilities and editorial collaboration. Then I said, "Well, who would you include?" And he said, "Well, it is obvious." I said, "Well, do we have that many black Southern writers?" I didn't know if he was defining this as people who wrote about the South, people from the South, people who passed through the South or what. He said, "Well, there are Charles Chesnutt and Richard Wright." I said, "Yes. What about Ellison?" He said, "Well, he's from the territory, and it's sort of Southern, so we could include him." And I said, "What about Ishmael Reed?" And he said, "Well, he was born in Memphis or Nashville; I think we can include him, too." So I said, "Uhm? What about Toni Morrison?" And he said, "Well, where was she born?" I said, "Lorain, Ohio." He said, "Well, she suffered a lot of discrimination, so we could include her." I had just had the pleasure of meeting Gloria Naylor in graduate school at Yale, and so I said, "What about Gloria Naylor?" And he said, "Well, wasn't she born in Brooklyn?" I said, "Yes, but she's fond of saying she was conceived in Mississippi." He said, "We can include her, too!"

I did not collaborate with John on the anthology, but I think it is a most important anthology. However, what that conversation and what this discussion has suggested to me is the curious relationship between regionalism, on one hand, and black literature, on the other. Contemporaneous with the larger discussions in American letters of regionalism—in the nineteenth century, initially, then with the growth of the Southern Agrarian movement in this century, which has been very problematical for black writers and for black scholars, incidentally—black people responded to notions of regionalism by declaring implicitly and then later explicitly that *blackness* itself was a *region,* and that our literature cohered in the same way that a regional literature would cohere. Ironically, however, our region transcended mere geography, because to be black in the South and to be black in the North was fundamentally a similar condition experienced within a unified culture. Subsequent writers such as Ernest Gaines and Alice Walker and others have now turned to the South, it seems to me, to wipe out the history of Confederate romances and the plantation novel—to name two specific subgenres in which black people are symbols of horror, symbols of terror, symbols of the ultimate negated other. They have returned to create worlds grounded in the South, grounded in traditional values, echoing that traditional black voice that Houston Baker so brilliantly just evoked. And I think that this is a very important moment in our letters because of these things.

NAYLOR.   I'm so glad that you brought that up because last night when I was trying to think of modern black writers who would fit into having contributed to a Southern literature, via the whole definition that has been kicked around at this conference there are none until you begin to talk about young people whom I can name but whom you might not know; they are in their twenties and are mostly poets. There is a woman named Nikky Finney. There's Brenda Marie Osbey, another poet who is now coming out. These young people who were born in this part of the world stayed here. They absorbed the culture. But for the majority of the so-called established black writers, it has been a literature of exile. And when they return to the South in their work, they will either return in the vein of Richard Wright, as was brought up, aligning him with T. S. Eliot and that whole imagery of a wasteland, of being an exile. Or they will return romantically and incorporate a sense of nostalgia about this region. But actually to do what the few like Ernest Gaines or Lucille Clifton have done, to live it out and to work it out in all its complexities, could not exist for most established black writers because they were not here. Myself for an example, yes, I was conceived in Robinsonville, Mississippi, and my parents made sure I would not be born in Robinsonville, Mississippi. Yet, you can change your geographical location without changing your milieu. So I grew up with the foods of the South, with the behavioral codes of the South, with the cadences and speech of the South. By the time my parents had really become New Yorkers, we were in our twenties, and we had left home.

Now all of this informed the kind of individual I am, and while my work evidences this dual sensibility, the Southern elements in it are nostalgic, romantic. And the hard reality is that I could not have nurtured a creative consciousness had my folks remained where they were. One reason is the basic factor of access to books. In the years I would have been coming up in the South, blacks were barred from using the public libraries. And whether or not I would have had the resourcefulness of Richard Wright, who in *Black Boy* tells of forging his employer's signature on a pass to get reading material from the library, cannot be known. But it is impossible to think of myself as ever writing if I first did not have the opportunity to read. But even when you go beyond access to just the books themselves, there is a need for potential writers to have reification of that desire within their community, a creative environment to breathe in and give back to, which could not have existed for me in Robinsonville, Mississippi, before the 1970s. It is very different now for the younger black writer. They will give you your Southern literature in all of its richness.

BAKER.   I feel some of the same things that Skip [Gates] has pointed out about being here. And one of the joys of being here is being with Skip and Gloria. Gloria and I have not been together as much as Skip and I have been together, but the time that Gloria and I were together we had a really heady and awfully good conversation. I think one of the things that is important when we sit together in a place like this is that we do break boundaries, and I think that one of the traditional boundaries that holds us in check and partially in fee and in bondage is a boundary called "the written word." It is not that there was not Southern black expressiveness that was manifold and of a character that we would call, using sort of sports terminology, "world class" as early as the seventeenth century. It is true you didn't have people writing heroic couplets or Restoration verse, but you certainly had people carrying a sound from Africa that was impressive, that established a kind of resource, that resonates throughout the writing of our best literary artists, as it were. I mean I would shudder to think of the black fiction writer, playwright, poet who said, "I really try to sound like Faulkner," you know. Or, "I really model my work on James Joyce a lot." Or, "I want to sound like Conrad." It seems to me that what you are doing if you are an African in America, in these hemispheres, is always an act of what Gloria describes and what is captured by a person like Richard Price as *marronage*. You know who the Maroons were, right? Maroons were the people who said: "We can't deal with this. I don't work good for other people. I need to go to the mountains and set up an African community." And this happened all over the new world.

Richard Price has a book called *Maroon Societies: Rebel Slave Communities in America*. It seems to me that that definition of *marronage* is the kind of fleeing that one does, but you do it in order to set up your own African identity on these shores. In a quote from Price's book, he says that the Maroons were able to fight because they were mobile. They were guerrilla warriors and so forth, fighting only when and where they chose, depending on reliable intelligence networks among non-Maroons, both slaves and white settlers, and often communicating by horns. And often communicating by horns, and often communicating by horns. Yes, by horns. Now it seems to me that the sound that comes out of that image is the sound of *marronage,* and if you look at it, it is a deeply African sound. Look at Alain Locke's *The New Negro.* The subtitle of the book is *An Interpretation.* Exegesis, hermeneutics. All right, we will interpret. We will deal. By the way, the paperback from Atheneum by which many of us came to *The New Negro* doesn't have the subtitle of the book. It's been dropped, which says something about the publishing industry, right? The book is filled with African masks and photographs, a whole leitmotif, also dropped from the paperback edition of *The New Negro,* twenty-two color genre studies, portraits of African types dropped. The frontispiece of that book is called "Brown Madonna." *The New Negro, An Interpretation,* the frontispiece of "Brown Madonna," black woman, baby in hand, says something about the sound of *marronage.* Two million people fled the South in five years, established a Northern camp, communicated by horns, pushed the sound through, did it in African ways. But the only way we can see this is to break down boundaries that separate expressive products into "Is it a poem? Is it a novel? Is it really a play? Would Shakespeare have called this a play?" I mean, let's think about this one. "Would not Dr. Johnson have said that this was a mixing, a horrible mixing of genres?" Well, I'm suggesting that the sound that moves through as Afro-American expression, as African expression, as *marronage* on these shores is only now beginning to be attended to in analytical, communal . . .

GATES.   And creative . . .

BAKER.   *And* creative ways.

GATES.   I think Ernie Gaines put his finger on that when he made the joke about multiple points of view and said, "I didn't get this from Faulkner, Faulkner got it from me." I am perfectly prepared to believe Ernie. But we must move to a time when black writers are welcomed back to the South, and I mean welcomed back to the South in the most sophisticated sense of welcoming back. When white writers learn to turn to black writers to learn how to use language, how to create a world of the South, how to evoke what it felt like, what it feels like, to be here. I was touched last night when Eudora Welty said—she's one of my favorite writers, incidentally—that she will never forget the feeling of having her very first short story accepted for publication by the *Southern Review.* Until now, what black writer could ever have shared that feeling through the pages of the *Southern Review?* It's time for the complexity of our experiences, our personal experiences and our literary experiences, to come to bear upon each other in a mutual way of influence so that Faulkners do learn to use multiple points of view from Ernest Gaines and not merely, as we pretend to presume, the other way around.

NAYLOR.   Well, to answer your question, this black writer had that experience with the fiftieth-anniversary issue, and that's due a lot to the masterminding of James Olney, and hopefully that is going to be the vanguard of this sensitivity and complexity that Skip [Gates] was talking about, because we all stand to gain by that as Americans—and now I am getting up on my bandwagon. But, I truly do believe that I could not write if I did not hope, and if I did not believe that the greatness of our society lies in our complexity and our differences. And I am a staunch opponent of people talking about all becoming one sort of amalgamous American, and I say, no. We each have something unique to give, but we have to finally understand that the different gifts are *equal* gifts, and we haven't done that yet in this country, but this is a beginning. I came here today because of James Olney and because of the *Southern Review* and what it has represented in the past, what it represents now, and the wonderful potential that is awaiting that journal and awaiting this region.

BAKER.   It is important, of course, to say that on the down side of that, one brings a special relationship to the Agrarians and the Fugitives if one hears the following anecdote before being told that they are the *classics* of a certain era. It seems that a person from Vanderbilt who was a bit ahead of his time—as he found out—invited Langston Hughes and James Weldon Johnson to a party at Vanderbilt and invited the Vanderbilt English department faculty. Allen Tate instantly wrote to his colleagues and said: "Did you know that Hughes is a Negro? I personally plan not to attend." And he didn't. So, this really does condition one's view of the Fugitives and the Agrarians and other movements in literature. When Hughes, you see, at this time was a person who traveled to Cuba, and within two weeks of his visit there Nicolas Guillen had turned his entire orientation away from a literate poetry to write folk poetry. Hughes was translating Chilean poets at the time, and they were writing to him, and he was in correspondence with them. Hughes had been to France and England and was in correspondence with British and French poets at the time. Hughes was the most international and perhaps well-recognized writer by a global community in the late 1920s and into the 1930s. And these people refused to go to a party with him.

They should have gotten down on their *knees* to be near that man. That is the down side of the region. I'm sorry. I'm sure that has changed here.

GATES. Why don't we take questions?

BAKER. Yes, why don't we? After all of that there have got to be some questions.

QUESTIONER FROM THE AUDIENCE. Does the United Kingdom's treatment of its black authors in the Commonwealth set a model for the United States?

BAKER. Well, now it would be important for you to specify areas and domains of inquiry. What do you have in mind?

QUESTIONER. The West Indies and the countries of former British West Africa.

BAKER. A model in terms of writers, is this what you have in mind? I can talk about it.

GATES. Sure, go ahead.

BAKER. Well it seems to me that a person like Edward Braithwaite, for example, has won the highest awards conferred by the United Kingdom, and he is on Caedmon Records and is frequently looked to as a person you want to greet with the cameras as soon as he gets off the plane for the latest visit. You can stretch it out to people like Derek Walcott and Andrew Salkey. It seems to me that the motion of Caribbean culture in Britain is often more accepted and relished than it [Caribbean culture] is in the Caribbean itself. I mean there is an irony to this, you understand. When you come in and you colonize people and you say, "British is all good; everything else, forget it." You know, "Give up your indigenous religion" and all that. So, you have the irony, of course, of a University of the West Indies, which said until fairly recently: "We don't want any Caribbean literaturist out here. And Eddie Braithwaite is a historian, so we don't really want him, though he is a great poet, to teach Caribbean literature in our *English* department." But, in Britain, he is lionized; he's celebrated. You have people coming to hear him read and so forth. I think that the kind of Americas' approach is one that is of interest, particularly in terms of that image that I mentioned earlier too in terms of *marronage*. And certainly Eddie has done a lot with the Maroons in Jamaica and the kind of indigenous religions that are there. I suspect if one is talking about the Antilles— and there are people here certainly far more qualified to talk about this than I—one thinks of the Parisian response to people from Guadeloupe and the whole negritude group. The curious thing is that the metropolitan or the metropole's relationship to those bodies of expression is often more enthusiastic than the indigenous response which is not true, certainly, in America. I mean, New York doesn't want to hear it, you know; and they don't know who Eddie Braithwaite is. I mean he gets off of a plane with almost total anonymity there.

GATES.   What is interesting about your question is that there is, I think, a difference in the response of various white cultures to black writers. I was trying to think as Houston spoke of what the difference could be, and the difference, I think, is in regard to, and *for*, language use. If the negritude writers could use French in a certain way, with certain levels of sophistication, if a Chinua Achebe or a Wole Soyinka and a Derek Walcott can use language in certain sophisticated ways (which, I have to admit, had to be consistent with someone else's taste within the metropole), then these people could be citizens of the Republic of Literature. We've never had—perhaps until recently, but we can all argue about this—that sort of open avenue into the Republic of American Letters. And it has to do with differences in a culture's regard for language use, a certain understanding of language, the so-called purity of language, about which Americans, I think, continue to be insecure, but about which English people and French people seem to be much less insecure and far more arrogant. And I think that our alternative voices, to use the metaphor that Houston has used so well this morning, have been the discordant note in the American symphony.

BAKER.   Let me say just a quick word or two. It is important, I think, in terms of those writers like Hughes and Sterling Brown and others to point out that when asked, "Who were your models?" Edward Braithwaite will say, "I had to go to Uncle Tom as my image of the subservient Jamaican, because in our written traditions there was no equivalent." When Leopold Senghor was asked, he said, "I turned to Langston Hughes, of course, and to Sterling Brown and others." Here again the internationalism of a Hughes, for example, is something that has yet to be dealt with. Fortunately, Arnold Rampersad has written a brilliant biography of Langston Hughes, and it will be out from Oxford in months. We can all read the first nine hundred pages of his first volume. Then we will get a sense of the international in American letters at a period when people were going into exile but weren't having dramatic impact, as far as I can see, on the countries to which they went. They were carrying those countries back and saying, "This is much better than America, y'all." Well, black writers were going out and saying, you know, we have a message for the world, okay, for Africa, for the Antilles, and so forth.

QUESTIONER.   In that case the South African black writers are predicting what will be.

BAKER.   Thank you, yes, for that addition.

QUESTIONER FROM THE AUDIENCE.   When Afro-Americans first came to this country, the first Western text that they confronted, absorbed, and really made their own was the Bible. The Bible, of course, is the text that Pound wanted excluded from the canon of literature entirely. But yet in trying to sort out the African roots of black writing in America from other sources, the Bible is still incredibly influential in Afro-American discourse today. Do you feel a need to reexamine the relationship to the Bible, or do you think it will continue to be an important literary text in the black tradition?

BAKER.   We turn to the writer to answer that.

NAYLOR.   The Bible is going to remain an important literary text in the entire Western tradition. We have seen elements of its influence in all of our traditional literature. And for the black American, to the extent that we are part of Western culture that will remain true. But, there are also influences with perhaps even a greater historical tie than the Judeo-Christian Bible for black writers, and those were the things that these two gentlemen were talking about. That which was not written down, that which could be heard, and which could be spoken; and all you are seeing now are constant revisions, revisions, and more revisions, building on the oral tradition—for lack of a better phrase for it. And I definitely don't think that will ever phase out.

BAKER.   You know one of the things that Gates would say if he were talking now (he will agree with me, you watch), he would say that black people came as interpreters, that they were always sort of between the spaces and intertextually involved with the Bible, and that what they did was to signify on, to trope, to come out with their own sounds on the Bible. So you can read Ezekiel and then what you have is, "Ezekiel saw the wheel way up in the middle of the air." And people say, "Where is that in the Bible?" And they say, "It's in the book." And so you go and check it out, and if you don't see it, then you don't see, as Mr. Gaines pointed out. Right? You ain't never heard, okay. And I've read the book, and they are right. You know, it's there, but so that what happens is that you reach a point, a kind of ironic point where a friend of mine who is a

Renaissance literature scholar told me about three years ago, that his next book was going to be *The Afro-American Influence on John Milton.* So, there is that change that one gets, in a sense, a revised version of the text. There's the aphorism that I am sure the gentleman out there knows: "When the white men came *we* had the land and *they* had the Bible. When they left. . . ."

QUESTIONER FROM THE AUDIENCE.   Can you think of any recent white writers or critics who do with some success write about different cultures? Are there any like Russell Banks, who tries to span two or more cultures in his book *Continental Drift?*

NAYLOR.   No, I haven't read that so I can't address that question myself.

BAKER.   I haven't either.

NAYLOR.   He asked about Russell Banks's *Continental Drift,* which tried to span three or four different cultures, but I guess the question in general was: "How do we feel about other American writers and the way they look at the black experience? Are there any others who do see?"

BAKER.   I think it would be presumptuous of me as a black person to try and talk about it.

GATES.   Now, *that*'s signifying. That's signifying. Go ahead, brother.

NAYLOR.   What I want to mention is John Irving's latest work, *The Cider House Rules;* for anyone who doesn't know it, black characters play a central part in that. I think, just speaking as a writer, that anyone's psyche and life is your territory, if you choose to delve into that. Most American writers deal with Americans. I think lately because we perhaps have American writers who may know other Americans as human beings versus types, who might live in another neighborhood, or someone who has come to them through their schoolbooks, that you will get more complex pictures. If your question is implying can only a black writer write about black people in that way—now I think Houston will fight with me—but I say, no. I can write your life if I took enough time because that is my talent. And I give the right of that talent to other writers too. Often where we have had bad portrayals of other Americans, it's through that individual writer's ignorance or laziness about the world around him.

GATES.   Or desires.

NAYLOR.   Yes, exactly, but I didn't want to give them mal-intent, but yes.

GATES.   Oh, you have to sometime.

NAYLOR.   Sometimes it is just deliberate mal-intent, but I choose not to think that way. But yes, it's true.

GATES.   Because Gloria's nice, that is why we put her in the middle.

BAKER.   I think that one of the things that Skip [Gates] brought up was the question of regionalism, and I think of two people. Joe Porter is now at Duke, but I met him at Virginia, and I first read his short stories in Virginia, and they are about Kentucky and the mountains of Kentucky. I have also read Breece Pancake. And it may be something about the short story and its relation to the commercial nexus that produces it. If one thinks of Miss Welty's short stories, for example, or some of Faulkner's short fiction—as opposed to the one that features the dim-witted Dilsey. But, if you think of the shorter, punchier, more artistic sorts of expressive forms, then I would say that there is often an intensity of the impact of some of those works on me. And again the reason I say this is not to denigrate an entire canon. I don't throw that out lightly; I do think that Dilsey is dim-witted. I think she meddles in everybody's business and that her sound is nothing like Afro-American sound and that sermon at the end of the book is a parody and a travesty and has very little to do with Reverend Daniels in Detroit today or people I go to hear in Philadelphia or that I heard in my youth. But on the other hand, it seems to me that what Faulkner does in *Absalom, Absalom,* the kind of moral engagement of that text speaks to me, and I think it can speak to all black people. I think it is a hard and costly book and a great book that Faulkner produced in *Absalom, Absalom.* So I think if we reinstate, in a sense, regionalism, as the South—I grew up in Kentucky—so that those stories of Porter and Pancake speak to me in special ways. The interesting thing that Gloria pointed out at the beginning, and that was my point—often it is totally lost, you know. "Boy," I go home and tell my wife, "I really made a good point there, you know, nobody understood"—that was my point about anger, and Gloria's was stated much more clearly. We are not monolithic. I mean, the first law is that we are extraordinarily complex, which is why we can serve metaphorically for the entire American condition and the modern condition. So that to assume that no person who was not descended from Africa could speak to the multiplicity of our desires, strivings, longings, and complexities is *racism,* in a word.

NAYLOR.   For the artist, at the base of any depiction will lie those primal elements. How do I as a female get into a male character, which I had to do in my last book. I began to go toward the least common denominators. What do these young men feel that I feel? I start with pain, move up to joy, then love, then aspiration, and then slowly as you begin to ascend it gets more complex, and you start to think about the way social pressures might apply to different things. But, yes, underneath it all is that. And Houston is right. To assume that John Irving could not have written about those black migrant workers would have been racist. To assume that Toni Morrison could not write well about her white couple in *Tar Baby* carries definite cultural arrogance. And also we are just talented people as writers, and the world is your notebook. You look at it, and you can take it apart, if you give yourself enough time and put enough work into it.

GATES.   Amen. Could I just say one more thing, and then you ask your question. I think Pancake is a perfect example of what we are talking about, for James Alan McPherson, you remember, writes the preface of the book because they had a formal relationship. And Pancake's understanding of language, at least as I understand it, was very much informed by James Alan McPherson's use of language. Now that is influence in the way that I am talking about influence.

BAKER.   Good point.

GATES.   This is such a complex issue. It's a complete reversal of what happened in the past, you know. You would write a book and then look for the smartest, biggest, or most successful white man generally, or white woman, to write your introduction, to write your preface. It's a convention in black letters that began with the slave narratives for all sorts of different reasons, but the convention continued. For McPherson to be authenticating, as it were, a white writer, is remarkable. It is a wonderful moment. And, of course, in literary criticism there are a number of white critics of black literature—not the least of whom is James Olney—who are superb critics by everyone's estimation. Critics are either good or bad, not black or white. So that is my response to that.

QUESTIONER FROM THE AUDIENCE.   You have been talking about sound as being very important. It seems to me that the song is not considered a literary genre. It seems to me, however, that songs are the most important literary genre of youth and of my youth. I think it is clearly a Southern genre. What about the song in Afro-American literature?

BAKER.   Well, it seems to me that if you think of the beat movement, for example, and you think of this sound that is always behind that, it is the sound of bebop. And it is the sound of avant-garde jazz then, since we have had, you know, manifold movements. But, you know the interesting thing, of course, is that Hughes—again Hughes, always Hughes—had done readings to jazz in the 1940s, before there was a beat movement. And so there's this sort of return movement on the part of a group that became the avant-garde group of American poetry, Ginsberg, Gary Snyder, and so forth, who said, "Well, you know what we want to do is capture a sound of America." And often that sound was a sound that would begin with that same thing, you know: "Ain't no hammer in this land." The sound comes through field cries and hollers into the blues, transforms itself into a blues revolution in the 1920s with Mamie Smith's recording of "The Crazy Blues," an event that in 1925 is probably far more significant to a lot of folks than Joyce's publication of 1922, and comes through into modern jazz as it were. So I think that a sounding in terms of music-words, of free flow.

You look at journals, for example; I mean that whole school of *Alcheringa*, for example—an alcheringa is a board that is used in Australia to teach children the tribal cultural lore. But it moves in a free-form kind of way. And so this journal *Alcheringa* where people say what we must do is get back to the voice, we must get back to a spoken vernacular. I would call it sound, and I would say that that achievement has been something that has always marked in very specific ways Afro-American expressive culture. I mean if people could not connect to whom you thought you were speaking, then they would look at you as Mr. Gaines says, and say, "You don't hear, and you don't see." You know, you might be talking your best like John in "Of the Coming of John" at the end of Du Bois' *The Souls of Black Folk*. He's been to college and everything, and he gets up before the congregation. And when he finishes his talk, an ole brother jumps up fuming, you know, just stands there shaking for about two minutes to gather the audience. And then he storms down the aisle and gets behind the pulpit and condemns John, scandalizes his name, calls him everything but a child of God. And John walks out and says, "I thought I was talking good." Something is wrong here. So that I would suggest that in Afro-American culture, partially because of not seeing—I mean in a linear written way—sounding is the law. And in 80 percent of the world's geographies today most of the information is not passed by written forms. We are talking oral cultures. So that I mean to suggest that the sound of spoken vernacular, voice song, music, is vital and perhaps more important for large segments of the world's populations than sightings.

LITTLEFIELD.   Our time is about up. Thank you all for coming; it has been very stimulating.

II.
Culture and Publishing
in the South

SOUTHERN CULTURE:
A PERSONAL MEDITATION

William C. Havard

My paternal grandfather was born in 1850 and died in 1942. This bare-bones biographical notation is not entered out of genetic pride; an individual's life-span is too contingent a matter to risk challenging fate in that way. It is intended instead to lead into a brief comment on a feature of Southern cultural distinctiveness so frequently evoked in recent years that by now it threatens to become a cliché. I refer to the idea of history and memory as the touchstone of the moral ethos of the traditional South. The point is that my grandfather did live a long life, and in doing so constituted for me the longest link in a chain of living memory stretching across a considerable span of the history of the American Republic.

Although by no means a notable figure in even a small segment of that history, and not having a retroactive claim to notability by producing descendants of note, he may nonetheless be taken as a representative figure of his time and place. Certainly he is one of the very few persons that I knew well enough at an early age to draw on in memory to try to understand the influences on the formation of my elementary historical consciousness. Naturally I was not aware at the time that I was storing up a host of perceptions and limited or confused cognitive responses to them that would be sorted out over time as clues to the conduct of my life within the natural and social environment in which I have lived. Eventually, as my scholarly vocation pushed me deeper into a concern for the nature of the cultural and political identity of the South and of myself as a Southerner, these memories gave me an experiential basis against which my reading of history could be tested in the effort to sort out the truths from the misperceptions and falsehoods advanced by the romantics and the realists, the modernists and the traditionalists, and such labels as creative writers, literary and social critics, and a host of other intellectual types employ in an attempt to explain this still enigmatic region.

I have said that "Pappy," as he was familiarly known to his grandchildren, was a representative figure for his time and place and had no special claim to a place in recorded history, but neither was he a "common" man if one means by that designation something of the order of the modern mass man—dependent for his livelihood on the powerful, impersonal forces of a national and even international marketplace, a consumer whose desires for the acquisition of external goods are first ascertained by market research surveys and then stimulated to excess by continuing sales promotion campaigns on the part of a multitude of manipulative hucksters—a nonparticipating spectator of life whose "leisure" is occupied by alternations between electronic waves of romantic fantasy and live athletic contests that induce vicarious triumphs of the will to power through identification with the violent forces in action on the field. But here I am anticipating the move from the traditional South to the "modern" or latest "new" South, about which I am supposed to say something.

To return then to Pappy: over his long and active life his geographical mobility was quite limited, and the scattered population that inhabited the three or four Mississippi counties in which he moved probably restricted the number of persons he knew directly to a few hundred, no more than half of whom could he have known well enough to make reliable judgments on their characters, personalities, and capabilities. Yet he lived, as nearly as I can discern, a pretty full life. Although never a man of means, he was independent, roughly self-sufficient, hardworking, a man of his word, and, by consensus of the neighbors, honest to a fault. He worked his own land, raised seven of nine children to adulthood, and when my grandmother, who was twenty years younger than he, died and his sons all proposed to try what was then called "public work" (meaning any kind of employment other than farming your own or rented land), he sold up and went to live with his daughter. In a society in which the home place and the workplace were not separated one did not retire. Useful, personally satisfying, and appreciated things could still be found to do around an economically self-sufficient household.

My aunt was married to a reasonably prosperous farmer who carried on most of the direction of the farm operations propped up in a large bed in a huge back room with twelve-foot ceilings and a six-foot fireplace in his plain, rambling, and somewhat shabby old house. That old house could, and nearly always did, accommodate a considerable number of relatives in residence as well as the immediate family. In addition, one never knew for certain how many more members of the family, along with friends and more distant relatives, might appear for meals, especially on Sundays and holidays, including preachers who happened to be riding circuit to the local churches. Hospitality in rural Mississippi in my youth tended to run in the ecumenical direction. The semi-invalid status of my uncle by marriage was attributed to his having been gassed in the trench warfare of 1918, but he was known in the locality as a resourceful hunter of the plentiful native species of game and birds, and a remarkably fine shot. He was a man whose powers of recuperation were almost unlimited during the hunting seasons. He also managed to drive to Natchez frequently to conduct business, and to get back and forth to the dining room between meals to carry out his duties as a justice of the peace, although he often took his own meals in his bed-sitting-room.

During the depression some twelve to fourteen families lived on the place, about half of whom were black and half white. Some were members of the family who had taken up public work after 1918 and fallen back on subsistence farming to tide them over when the crash came. Southerners of all social strata had been accustomed at best to being semidepressed since the 1860s (for that read "poor" in varying degrees, from too poor to paint and too proud to whitewash all the way to *dirt* poor). Many of those who had begun the migration in the 1920s to the jobs in the cities and towns appeared less devastated by the depression losses of savings and jobs than people elsewhere. They at least had a secondary occupation to return to, and dependable family and community support to fall back on in furnishing them the land and basic supplies necessary to go back to farming. I do not remember that the white tenant families and the black ones on the place lived very differently so far as economic conditions were concerned, and these were somewhat better than the general run of households in the Deep South because the farm was better cared for than most individually owned marginal farms or larger tenant-worked ones.

The contacts between blacks and whites, although governed by the sometimes blunt and threatening, sometimes subtle and compromising order of segregation, were sustained and usually personally amiable. They worked the fields together, hunted and fished together, exchanged or shared certain kinds of produce, and helped one another out in various ways in times of need. They mingled under many circumstances, but did not really socialize across racial lines; and although blacks could work for whites for pay, whites worked with blacks only out of compassion.

Perhaps an illustration from another source may make the complexities a little less obscure. When I was about four years old my family was visiting at another place that belonged to relatives on my mother's side of the family. I was playing in the yard with the other children when Uncle Bud, the titular head of a household that was run completely by his wife, Aunt Tete (my maternal grandmother's oldest sister), walked slowly around the house, aged, bent, leaning heavily on his sturdy walking stick, and looking like a bearded ghost of the Confederate past. I don't think Uncle Bud was quite old enough to have been a Confederate veteran, but the few that I had seen in person, as well as those I had encountered in picture books, all looked like him. Just then a mild commotion took place on the steps leading to the ground from the kitchen, which was connected to the main house by a short walkway as a fire-protection measure (the arrangement also kept the house free of the kitchen heat while cooking in the summer). The stir was caused by a frail, ancient black woman, scurrying (as nearly as she could) down the steep, slightly rickety steps shouting, "Bud!" As the old man turned and cupped his ear with his hand, she gave a peremptory order for him to go in the house, where they were ready to eat. It was the first time I had ever heard a black person address a white adult by his or her first name, let alone issue an order to someone not of his or her own color in the manner of a top sergeant. My mother solved the problem for me: Aunt Jule had been born into slavery, and in her teens had served as a nurse to Uncle Bud while he was a toddler. They had lived their whole lives on the place and had reverted to their original statuses in their waning days.

Although my first memories of Pappy were at my aunt's, the times I remember best were those years when he was in his eighties and I was in my preteen and early teen years and he came to Baton Rouge for an annual extended visit. In some ways grandparents and grandchildren were closer than parents and children in my youth. The authority relation did not get in the way across two generational lines; and grandparents were less occupied than parents with the recurring business of ordinary life, so they could spare more time for sharing with grandchildren their reflections on the essentials. Pappy was a good companion. He was a fascinating storyteller—his memory was excellent although I am sure that like all good storytellers he embellished some of his tales; he had a lively sense of humor; and after I had reached an appropriate age, he was remarkably frank. Among his senses only his vision was defective (some alleged that his sense of hearing was keener than it should have been), and his mind remained clear and his speech coherent until the day of his death. He undoubtedly knew in his youth some people who had been born in the late eighteenth century. He remembered the Civil War well, had two brothers who had served in the Confederate army, told about running a few messages and hiding animals and other valuables from possible enemy raiders, and witnessed the financial ruin of some of the considerable number of wealthy families of Natchez. His experience of great change, both immediate and secondhand, stretched over nearly the whole of the nineteenth century and almost half of the twentieth.

He told me that he learned to play the fiddle on an instrument made out of a gourd, and when he was ninety, I heard him play some old-fashioned reels and hoedowns on a friend's violin. My friends enjoyed his visits as much as I, and the owner of the violin happily acknowledged the fact that the sounds Pappy evoked were improvements on his own screechy attempts at producing a melody. The lyrics to some of the old tunes tended to be scatological.

Pappy's political interests, like those of many rural Mississippians, were largely confined to county courthouse concerns, and he was conscientious about jury duty. Early in this century he owned a pair of mules that he whimsically named Vardaman and Bilbo. I never was sure what this christening symbolized, but it was in keeping with his lively satirical sense. He was not a regular churchgoing man, but he once told me that he had read the King James Bible from Genesis through Revelation at least four times. He also read the Natchez *Democrat* regularly and other newspapers as well, among them possibly the Woodville *Republican* (circulation two thousand), founded in 1826 and today reckoned to be the oldest newspaper in continuous circulation in the state. My other grandfather continued to subscribe to the latter paper throughout his life, even though he moved to Baton Rouge in the 1920s. The name of the Woodville paper was another of those longtime puzzles that I solved for myself when I read enough history to learn that the Jeffersonians were originally called Republicans, and the paper was thus named for the party of Jefferson and not that of Lincoln.

Since Pappy was never patronizing or didactic, I was influenced by him only by way of suggestion and precept. But I did absorb enough from him and others of his type to become one of those Southern boys who would stand in imagination with Faulkner's Chick Mallison looking across the field at Gettysburg on that bright day in July just before the charge and momentarily renew the faith that the South of the fathers might still be saved. I never had to be persuaded that the rural life was not only the preferred way—that was taken for granted—but I was also sure that it was the life that was most conducive to proper moral development under the tutelage of family, church, and other institutions of the local community whose most respected members were schoolteachers and evangelical Christian ministers. John Taylor of Caroline and Thomas Jefferson remained alive in the agrarian ethos of the South, although one doubts that they were much read by either the farmers or the politicians for their advice on the conduct of the good life by way of the practice of sound husbandry or for their wisdom and experiences in the arts of statesmanship. Thus, although I never really lived in the country and would have been hard pressed to make a decent living farming, I still identify more with that mode of life and with the places I associate with it than I do with the culture of the cities, large and small, in which I have lived most of my life. One or two of Mr. Jefferson's "academical villages" constitute the exceptions.

It follows, then, that my attitude toward the modern, or "new," South is that it has become, or is ever more rapidly becoming, almost exactly what the Vanderbilt Agrarians in 1930 anticipated it would be if the region finally capitulated to the imperatives of the urban-industrial order—a materialistic society whose human relations are based almost entirely on the cash nexus (today it might more properly be called the credit nexus), an industrial economy based on production that is an infinite series in which work is pursued in order to secure the means to consume the massive quantities of things produced with the aid of constantly changing techniques of applied science, a mass-based urban culture engaged in a constant war of conquest against nature to keep the machines fed with raw materials and driven by powerful natural energy sources. Thus it is that Atlanta is now known as the Yankee capital of the South, and Houston may be pointed to as the embodiment of Lewis Mumford's idea of the paleotechnic city, one laid out on a linear basis in which the streets are adapted to endless growth in all four directions to accommodate the pressure for more industries producing ever increasing goods and services. And one need take only a quick look at smaller, growing cities such as Nashville and Charlotte to catch a glimpse of the Atlantas, Houstons, and Dallases of the near future, even as the local civic leaders strive to reassure us that "we don't want to be another Atlanta or Houston." So-called progress is on an uncontrolled rampage, and the markets are glutted as the machines (including not least the artificial-intelligence ones) are in control of man rather than man in control of the machines. And we are already referring to "machine intelligence," leaving the notion of artifice out of the formulation altogether. Even as we characterize the machine in animistic language, we dehumanize man and society by machine programming of virtually all of man's activities, especially his work, his education (now more often referred to as "training"), his leisure activities, and his most impressive human invention—language. Even though my grandfather lived into the age of the automobile, radio, airplane, mechanized farming, and many of the other modern "miracles," he missed out on television, nuclear power, suburbia and its essential adjuncts—the Chaplinesque supermarket and its manic automotive setting, the shopping center.

Although the South began a serious effort to align its attachment to the myth of the romantic Old South with the industrial thrust of modern America in Henry Grady's time, and has intermittently worked the New South theme ever since, it was not until the end of World War II that the success of that effort began to show up in the demographic statistics by which such "developmental" changes are measured. But the more difficult problem is how to assess the changes in moral, political, and cultural values that have occurred since 1945. Suffice it to say that for all the changes in social circumstances and all the wars and revolutions that he witnessed at first hand and from afar, the traditional South my grandfather inhabited remained to the end of his days more continuous with the past and thus more nearly a part of a coherent history of a society than the South we inhabit today. As Andrew Lytle put it not long ago with reference to his birth in 1902, "I opened my eyes on a world closer to the Eleventh Century than it is to that of my grandchildren."

I have said little about the Louisiana, the town (as it was then) of Baton Rouge, or the LSU I knew during the 1930s and early 1940s, leaving those things to the others on this panel whose assignments are closer to that scene than is mine. And as far as the *contemporary* local scene is concerned, I am geographically too far out of touch to have anything useful to say about it. But since this literary conference is supposed to be, at least in part, a reprise on the themes of the 1935 one, I would like to speak briefly to the ways in which reading, writing, and literature in the South have been and are being affected by the changes I have been talking about. And that will necessarily mean touching on the nature of higher education, since the colleges and universities are the main repositories of the literary tradition of a society as well as being one among several types of institutional centers for alteration of that heritage.

One of the canards against the South in which I grew up was that it had no reading public. It may be that the South did not have a book- and magazine-*buying* public—a condition largely attributable to the region's economic condition—and it certainly had a higher proportion of illiterates than most other areas of the country, but it did not lack a reading public, or rather reading publics. In the absence of an intense group of readers it is difficult to imagine the Southern Literary Renascence taking place, just as it is difficult to divorce that remarkable flowering of talent from the classical tradition in the "Academies" and in some of the Southern universities. I frequently canvass my students about their reading habits in high school and college, and the response is pretty thin. I recently discovered in one of my classes a young man who had read *Tom Brown's School Days* and some of the other books that were standard fare in my high-school days, and I have slowly come to the conclusion that my introduction to literature in high school must have been better than I had previously thought and was almost certainly better across the board than that available today. And I am sure that this was the case with what went on in the university then as compared with now because I took freshman composition from Bob Heilman and the sophomore survey course in English literature with Tommy Kirby. In the former course we read at least a book a week over a greater number of weeks than the semester extends now, ranging through all the genre from the epic (we read the *Iliad*) to the modern novel (Aldous Huxley's *Point Counter-Point* is the one I recall as the final assignment). What is more, we wrote at least one essay each week by contrast with the five per semester that seems standard today. And we did it for two semesters rather than a single one. Good literature is apparently being displaced by the products of mediocre to bad electronic media—a sort of reverse cultural Gresham's law.

But I see a far more serious problem emerging that affects not only the prospects of offering a coherent humanistic education in the contemporary university but the very idea of a university as Cardinal Newman understood it. With the "modernization" of the South has come a consolidation of economic power in the region that represents a local recurrence of the national Gilded Age and has produced what may be a new social class, one that resembles the late-nineteenth-century "Lords of Creation" that Frederick Lewis Allen wrote about a number of years ago. In some respects the people who constitute this small but increasingly dominant social class exhibit the merged characteristics of Matthew Arnold's Barbarians and Philistines adapted to the American setting. Look at the "power structure" in any of the larger New South metropolitan centers and you are likely to find a half-dozen to a dozen major corporate executives holding interests in, and seats on, the boards of large financial, manufacturing, and service companies. The directorates are interlocking, and the conglomerates expand until they resemble the holding company Samuel Insull created in the 1930s—they become so complex that even their creators do not understand them.

Although making money was the initial object of the members of this recently risen class that now dominates the metropolitan South, sheer personal power soon became the unacknowledged goal, and nothing eludes their control. Universities are particularly appealing objects of their interference, and places on the boards (especially of the more prestigious private ones) are much in demand by these provincial giants of industry and finance who see the industrial corporation as the model for all organized forms of human activity. As the new Southern class consolidates its position of power, it seeks managers as heads of educational institutions, and a marriage of convenience is contracted in which the university helps meet its constantly rising costs by a partnership with business in which grants and contracts for technical services to the local corporations become key to the financial management of the university. Thus Stanford's relation to Silicone Valley and Harvard's and MIT's to the R. and D. establishments along Route 128, the circumferential route around Boston, are frequently cited as the arrangement best suited to the development of the local university. More often than not, however, the university becomes less a partner in the new business than one of the subsidiary corporations of the conglomerate. President Eisenhower's warning against the military-industrial complex needs reissuing in a form to assure that the university does not lose control over its own purpose, which includes preserving and transmitting to succeeding generations our civilizational heritage, humanizing the professions, taming and cultivating the Barbarians, and providing the Philistines an opportunity to refine their tastes other than for possessions and domination. And when one considers the great contributions of the South and the Southerner to the Western literary heritage over the past fifty years and contrasts it with the attitudes one hears expressed by the preponderance of the New South class on the partnership between the university and business in making the world over through the growth of "high tech"–based industry and on the need for "training" specialists to fill the manpower and womanpower requirements to carry technical progress to perfection, the urgency of such a warning becomes all the more imperative. Perhaps we should paraphrase one of my favorite aphorists and parabolists, Andrew Lytle, who said, "A farm is not a place for growing wealthy, it is a place to grow corn," by saying that a university is not a place for being managed, it is a place for being educated.

In 1935, when that strange concatenation of events that Thomas W. Cutrer has described in *Parnassus on the Mississippi* was leading to the founding of the *Southern Review* and the establishment of a university press at LSU, neither the standing of the literary and other arts nor the economic and political circumstances in the South looked promising for launching a regional venture in literary creativity. To be sure, in the case of great art, the spirit bloweth where it listeth, and we know little about the circumstances under which art flourishes in a given time and place. The depression had become a worldwide one (in those days Europe and the North American continent were what was connoted when we referred to a social phenomenon as worldwide), and World War II was shaping up as the Western democracies, seemingly already well on the way to cultural deracination, were trying to muster the will, if not yet the physical resources, to resist the newest and most deadly form of tyranny devised by man—totalitarianism—then in full poisonous bloom in the dual form of the Nazi regime in Germany and the Communist one in the Soviet Union.

The 1935 Southern Literary Conference was planned and the *Southern Review* was launched on little more than a hope that something might be done about the state of letters in the South and Southwest. The questions that were addressed by the participants were large ones, and they were knowingly asked in an atmosphere in which few people inside the South apparently had the interest, and fewer still the resources, to support even modest efforts at doing something about the problems. And in New York, the center of American literary culture, as well as other places where there might be an interest in American letters, the South was still looked on as Mencken's cultural wasteland—a void without readers, let alone writers with talent and commitment, publishers, editors, critics of discernment, and universities or other cosmopolitan areas that might furnish centers that would draw aspiring writers into communities of letters that might nourish a literary culture.

In retrospect, of course, we can see that much was going on of which New York was unaware or at best only opaquely aware—a situation that is more common than the reverse when one stands beyond the narcissistic circles of the New York literary set and tries to assess who the true provincials are. The cultural alienation of the American men and women of letters growing out of the disillusioning forces of World War l and its catastrophic political and economic aftermath resulted in such phenomena as the Paris exiles and later the much publicized 1935 American Writers' Congress, which met in New York in April, and its expanded version, the First International Congress of Writing in Defense of Culture, which met in Paris in June. Both the American and the international congresses were more political than they were literary; indeed one might describe them, respectively, as efforts of the American and the Euro-American "Republics of Letters" to establish leftist united literary fronts. Even the exclusion of nonleftist writers from these meetings did not prevent political ideology from dominating literary topics in the discussions. The most telling expression of the triumph of ideology over the moral and aesthetic values among the dominant members of the national and international literary community is the justification for their actions most often heard from participants who later broke their ties with Marxism: "We didn't think we had any choice," an explanation I was surprised to hear, almost in passing, from an unexpected source quite recently.

Although little public notice was taken of the Southern Writers' Conference either in or out of the South, it had its own effects, which can be felt in the spirit of our commemoration event fifty years later. It is no exaggeration to suggest that it provided the impetus for a new stage of the Southern Literary Renascence, one which would continue and expand the influence for at least another generation, during which the Renascence would become the most creative phenomenon in the history of the literary arts in America. But just as there was a lag in the recognition of how far the South already had moved beyond the critical applicability of Mencken's description in "The Sahara of the Bozart" by the end of the 1920s, so it was not until after the end of World War II that that second (or perhaps third) phase of the Renascence was recognized as such. What had begun in Nashville with the formation of that small literary community of the Fugitives, and then the Agrarians, continuing the pursuit of their individual literary interests in combination with the philosophical quest for understanding the cultural conditions necessary for the production of a great literature, and abetted by a few independents, most notably Faulkner, was to continue with the establishment and early recognition of the *Southern Review* and the things that were eventually associated with that bold venture. In the larger sense (and in cooperation with others here and abroad) these activities included the transformation of the method of teaching literature in the colleges and universities throughout the country, the development of a school of criticism that was dominant for at least two decades after it was perceived as such, and the recognition of universities (even provincial ones) as places which could (in some cases at least) provide congenial atmospheres for writers to earn their livings by teaching writing while having some time to write. In the best of such circumstances they would also have access to good critics, editors, and publishers, both of books and quality "little" magazines. Some of the best of the latter were developed in Southern universities and now provide models for what university-based publishing of the highest quality can be.

Early in the first session of the 1935 Southern Writer's Conference John Peale Bishop made a somewhat convoluted appeal to the idea that a traditional culture (that is, one that is a result of the historical experience by which a society has achieved a sense of its own common life) is the only type whose self-interpretation is grounded in shared practice, purpose, and meaning. He then defined a decadent society as "one that has lost its sense of form in which to live. . . . The ultimate point of social decadence is reached when it [a society] has lost its sense of life and substitutes for it abstractions or nothing." In this brief argument Bishop pursues too many themes, is too diffuse in his rhetorical appeals, and throws out too many allusions in the modernist literary manner to permit a commentator the indulgence required for the close exegesis its rich content deserves. But Bishop does indicate that without a reading public of his own the writer lacks a "corrective," and thus much of Southern writing is directed to an outside public rather than to one within the society—a condition that makes for judgments by standards outside the writer's experience with his own society, and that is an unfair standard. It was a New York standard that led to the expectation that you get in every book about the South "decadence" and "degeneration." In a subtly ironic twist Bishop notes that since everything is upside-down, and there is decay everywhere, the New York judgment involves a substitution of abstractions for an understanding of the Southern writer's way of treating the subject from within. The implication is clearly that the very abstraction imposed on Southern writers as a condition of publication is a reflection on the actual decadence and hypocrisy of New York as the literary center of America.

In a summary comment following this statement, Allen Tate capped Bishop's multileveled analysis of the interplay between writer and audience and of the cognitive difficulties involved in the interpenetration of a culture by a literature written from inside another distinctive one when he noted that since the eighteenth century there has been only one public left—"the general public—which must buy the book as a commodity."

The identification of the book as nothing more than a commodity harks back, not only to what Bishop meant when he spoke in that strained language about a decadent society being one that has lost its sense of a form in which to live, but also to the whole of what the Fugitives and Agrarians were about when they levied their philosophical attack against a modern society that was out of order by reason of its inversion of a classical hierarchy of goods in which the lesser (that is, external) order of things prevailed over the higher things of the mind and spirit.

In order to consider the implications of the book becoming a commodity, one needs to have some concept of the place of literature (as well as the arts generally) in the society about whose historical culture we are concerned. What is the function of literature in interpreting the historical existence of a society and in establishing and maintaining the moral ethos through which that society possesses its sense of the form in which it lives and attempts to fulfill its purpose or purposes? If the book becomes a commodity, the symbolic meaning attached to the "word" as the carrier of the moral and aesthetic truth is lost as the determining standard by which we distinguish literature from anything else that appears in print and can be marketed at a return exceeding the cost of production.

In 1935 there were still signs that publishers and others involved in the production of books and magazines (writers, editors, publishers, critics, and distributors) had a sense that their respective functions involved commitment to a good in itself because a great piece of literature is a higher good than the material product (the external object) in which that thing of the mind and spirit is embodied, although in the ideal condition the physical object would be in design and workmanship worthy of the quality of its essential content. Obviously, in a market economy (and especially one in the midst of depression), one must give attention to the economics of publishing (in a mercantilist system or in a collectivist economy it is likely that the financial support for literature and the other arts will be dependent on a patronage arrangement or on a government agency, and those conditions present their own problems regarding who determines who and what gets published). But in 1935 most of the publishers who were regarded as quality trade publishers were located in New York and Boston, and many of the firms were family owned and were run by members of the family under the family name. Publishers naturally wanted to sell books, but they also wanted to carry a distinctive list that they could be proud of, and do well by their authors both economically and in terms of editorial and other assistance needed to produce the best book possible out of the materials at hand, while avoiding efforts to interfere with the author's intentions.

My favorite example of the individual publisher who most nearly approximated the motivation and mode of operation roughly characterized here is Alfred Knopf, who was obviously active in every aspect of the firm he headed, and he exhibited these identifying traits most conspicuously in the production of his list of books on the South, the most notable of which are Wilbur J. Cash's *Mind of the South,* William Alexander Percy's *Lanterns on the Levee,* James McBride Dabbs's *The Southern Heritage,* James Weldon Johnson's *The Autobiography of an Ex-Coloured Man,* and V. O. Key, Jr.'s *Southern Politics.* In the case of Cash, it is not too much to say that the one book he had in him almost certainly would never have come out had Knopf not been personally involved as discoverer, encourager, pusher, editor-critic, promoter (and who knows what else) in the commitment to that book and that author. *The Mind of the South,* together with the other books on this list, constitutes a small library of indispensable reading for anyone who wishes to understand Southern culture through the first half of the twentieth century. And at no point can I discern any tampering with the literary integrity of any of these writers, and especially any effort to employ the old, generally recognized practice of shaping the work of Southern writers to pander to ready-made audiences outside the South, whether of a moonlight and magnolia inclination or one motivated by a taste for degradation and mindless violence.

As we are all too aware, commercial publishers (and I am still speaking here of those publishing houses with reputations for contributions to the higher culture in America) have over the past twenty-five or thirty years moved steadily away from operating under the rarely articulated but often practiced ethic suggested in the preceding comments, to the industrial ethical mode outlined in the earlier description of the new social class in the major metropolitan centers of the region. Not that the South has gone very far in developing a visible growth of major publishing enterprises (except in certain special areas, such as religious publishing houses); the Northeast remains dominant in that respect, as it does in magazine publishing and certain of the ancillary activities connected with the literary life in this country. The one exception is that the largest (or second-largest) wholesale book distributor in the country is located in the South and is a subsidiary of an engineering and development corporation. We are talking rather about the industrial mode in general, to which the South is basically a newcomer, but as such is striving so hard to outstrip the old industrial order that the practices, as well as many of the social effects, are to be observed in exaggerated form in the region.

In publishing today, not only are few of the old-style family operations still functioning independently, but very few publishing ventures in general are managed by executives who are engaged exclusively in publishing. The growth in corporate scale through mergers, takeovers, vertical and horizontal diversification, interlocking directorates, and so on, has helped create financial holding companies the like of which were rare even in the days of the antitrust drive at the turn of the century. A publishing division (subsidiary corporation) of a corporation whose name implies that it is in some area of communications may in itself be in legal thralldom (or in the act of becoming so) to some complex financial corporate structure whose financial decisions are the real determinants of the substantive decisions about what is produced, and about how the company operates in acquisitions, production, and marketing, with the cardinal rule being the brassy cliché about the main focus being on the "bottom line."

It is impossible in an essay of this length to cover everything one would like, but one reference and an example or two cannot be resisted. Some five years ago, while the Internal Revenue Service was busily applying a recent Supreme Court ruling that permitted the application of an inventory tax to the backlist of books on publishers' shelves, Mary Lee Settle published an impressive article in the *Virginia Quarterly Review* which was cogently entitled "Works of Art or Power Tools." That article elaborates the themes I have suggested here (and several more) about the way the changes in the organization and operation of the publishing business have affected all aspects of writing and publishing. Most noteworthy in this respect are the effect on the creative process and the quality of literature produced and available for choice among individual readers.

Two recent examples illustrate how far we have slid toward cultural decadence (in the name of progress, of course) in only five years. The first is from a story in the "Books" section of *Time*, dated August 26, 1985, dealing with the new methods of acquisitions (and indirectly with the latest trends in the type of material that interests publishers with lots of money and a keen eye for the "bottom line"). Specifically, the story is about the recent $2,000,000 advance by Harper and Row (once Harper and Brothers) to David Stockman for the former budget director's projected book *The Triumph of Politics*. Little elaboration is required. Several other big political "name recognition" figures with manuscripts at the million-dollar-advance level are discussed (with photographs), and high-bid "success story" authors in a number of other occupations are mentioned, including that ubiquitous example of the inflated Horatio Alger story among the industrial set, Mr. Lee Iacocca. Handsome contracts are even being let to the better known of the ghost writers collaborating with the go-for-broke publishers producing these masterpieces, so we may expect a few of the ghosts eventually to write their own stories about how they became rich and famous writing in the name of the rich and famous.

My second example has to do with current book-marketing techniques, and is drawn from that fey, self-consciously stylized revival, *Vanity Fair*, now specializing in the scandals of the dessicated lesser aristocracy, the extravagant diversions of the new rich, and the mind-deadening escapism of the mod set. In the October, 1985, issue, the "Book Marks" department of that magazine discussed the efforts of publishing (a business not known for its financial acumen, according to the author) to give a new look to literature. A prime example is Random

House's Vintage Contemporaries line, launched in 1984: "The covers exude a uniformly hip, Art Deco aura: bright colors, blocky print, a geometric logo." The senior editor responsible for this new mass-directed line explained the cover designs by saying that he told the art director to make the covers look like record albums, to which the author of the *Vanity Fair* article responds, "That casual suggestion was a stroke of marketing genius."

Penguin's new Contemporary American Fiction list similarly tries to reflect the contents of the novels in the images projected by its covers, and *Vanity Fair*'s designated bookman finds much to delight him in the way "something playful and campy in these images . . . evokes a whole era. They speak to a generation brought up on rock music, old movies, and a heavy dose of hallucinogens." When one learns that books have to be bootlegged by major publishers to today's reader under covers disguised as record albums, one does not have to read further in "Book Marks" to know how the contents of today's American novels are shaped and what really sets the standards of taste in all art forms. The cultural decadence is too much in evidence. And the term *contemporary* has become implicitly synonymous with *progressive,* at last displacing *modern,* which has already had too long a history.

BOOK PUBLISHING in the SOUTH; or,
The VARIETY of SNAKES in IRELAND

Louis D. Rubin, Jr.

If we wish to understand the situation of the book publisher in the South, we might consider the case of the late Dr. William A. Caruthers. He was born in Lexington, Virginia, in 1802, grew up there, attended Washington College, studied medicine, then moved to New York City and set out to write fiction. His first two novels were published by Harper and Brothers, were widely and favorably reviewed, and attracted much attention. In the late 1830s he moved down to Savannah, Georgia, where he wrote a third novel, *The Knights of the Horse-Shoe: A Traditionary Tale of the Cocked-Hat Gentry in the Old Dominion.* We do not know why Harper and Brothers declined to publish it; the assumption is that the financial panic of 1837 had so reduced the market for fiction that the Harpers were afraid to risk it. For whatever reason, in 1845 Dr. Caruthers chose to publish his new novel in Wetumpka, Alabama, with a press owned by a man named Charles Yancey. Although it was the best of Dr. Caruthers' books, it received only one review and four brief notices, and found its way into but very few bookshops; and in effect that was the end of Dr. Caruthers' career as a published novelist. He died the year following.

The literary career of William A. Caruthers could be considered almost a capsule version of the perils of publishing books south of what used to be called the Smith and Wesson line. During the approximately 140 years that followed the publication of *The Knights of the Horse-Shoe,* the place for a Southern novelist to send his books if he or she desired to have them reviewed, sold, and read has been to the Northeast, principally to New York City.

Even before Dr. Caruthers' day Southern authors were complaining about this situation. Not only did they have to get their books accepted by a Northern editor to get them properly distributed in bookstores and read, but the Southern newspapers, magazines, and bookstores would not pay sufficient attention to their books *unless* they were published elsewhere than in the South, and readers would not buy them unless published elsewhere. In short, to be considered as an important writer *in* the South, you had to be published *outside* the South.

Much ink and frustration have been expended on the question of why this was so. Why were there no Southern publishing houses, and no reading audience to support them in the South? It was said that successful book publishing and authorship required the existence of large cities, with their literary coteries and communities; and in the South there were none. Southerners did not read books to any important extent. The institution of slavery before the Civil War, and after it the institution of white supremacy and racial segregation, inhibited the resident Southern author from undertaking any kind of serious literary dissection of his own community, and should he try it, the only place he could get the book published was in New York.

All these elements, and others, played their part. The result, which was certainly true a hundred years after Dr. Caruthers, in the late 1940s when I began reviewing books, was the following set of circumstances.

First, for a Southern writer to be considered a full-fledged professional author in the South, it was mandatory that his books not be published at home.

Second, except for scholarly publishing by university presses, the only books published in the South other than those of a vanity-press nature were cookbooks and works of local history, generally of very indifferent quality, or else books of quaint local color designed for the tourist trade, and these books were available only in the immediate locality of publication.

Third, any Southern author who wrote a book depicting the South in other than self-congratulatory terms, especially in matters regarding race relations, and published that book with a reputable New York trade house, was open to attack by local newspapers and ostracized for having sold out for Northern gold. But contrariwise, any ambitious Southern publishing house quixotically attempting to venture beyond cookbooks and local history by publishing serious literary work was ignored.

Fourth, not only was being published in New York the mark of literary fame in the South, but being favorably reviewed in the Northern press and in the national media, which emanated from New York, was considered by the Southern press and by Southern bookstores to be proof of merit and the occasion for editorial congratulation, interviews, and prominent bookstore displays. (But if the book in question was critical of the South, then what was achieved locally was not fame but notoriety.)

Fifth, Southern bookstores took their merchandising lead and cues almost entirely from New York City. Except for occasional books by local authors, usually from socially prominent families, they followed the best-seller lists uncritically, and any book prominently featured in the national media was at once accorded star treatment in window displays, book-and-author luncheons, and the like.

And sixth, the same newspapers that on their editorial pages excoriated the Northern-based mass media for maligning the South; attacked book reviews in the Northern press for praising books that depicted Southern life critically; and lamented the South's subservience to uninformed Northern opinion, accepted no institutional responsibility whatever in matters of literature and culture. They were unwilling to spend any money to speak of to publish book pages that might offer any real critical leadership or sophisticated literary guidance for their own readers. Either they published only "canned" syndicated reviews, or else they featured a book page that was usually edited by an overworked news-staff member along with a full burden of other duties. The books on that page were reviewed mainly by reporters on the newspaper staff or by local citizens who received no payment for their reviews other than getting to keep the book. Such reviewing was of a quality ranging from mediocre to ludicrous. Moreover, most of the play on such book pages was given to books from the New York houses, while locally published books were either ignored or else—particularly if the author was socially important—given uncritical praise.

What I have just described is the picture of a colonial cultural situation, and just as for generations after the Civil War the South was economically and politically in a colonial relationship to the Northeast, so in literature and culture it has long known colonial subservience. Its relation to the Northeast in literature has been much like that of Ireland to London in the late nineteenth and early twentieth centuries, or for that matter like the relationship of the cultural life of the early American Republic to that of England in the 1780s, 1790s, and 1800s. As Sidney Smith declared in the early nineteenth century, in the four corners of the world who reads an American book? The same could as appropriately be said about the South in the 1940s and 1950s: from Boston to Seattle, from Washington to San Francisco, who reads a book published in the South other than by a university press?

Let it be remembered, however, when we contemplate the low esteem which books published in the South enjoyed in the South, as against the prestige accorded those books published elsewhere, that there was considerable reason for it. Except for scholarly books, cookbooks, and the like, almost all the works of fiction, poetry, and other subjects published in the South *were* inferior stuff. I search my memory in vain for a single book of fiction, poetry, or nonacademic history—other than narrow local history—published in the Southern states from, say, 1930 to 1960 that is of any literary or historical importance. You could usually spot the locally published product immediately, just by looking at the amateurish dust jacket—if indeed it even had a dust jacket. During the 1950s and 1960s, I served as book editor for two Southern newspapers. When a book from a Southern publisher arrived, it was almost always a little local affair, written so unprofessionally that I dared not send it out to anyone to review. If the author was a local citizen, we would publish a few paragraphs announcing its existence and describing its subject, with no critical commentary whatever.

The situation, of course, was the result of 150 and more years of American history. It was the product of an agricultural economy, slavery, a century of poverty and of economic bondage to the Northeast; and these manifested themselves in the form of the absence of cities, a high rate of illiteracy, inferior schools, poorly endowed and poorly supported colleges and universities, inferior libraries, a low per capita income, a subsistence economy with little money left over for the arts, and so on. The result was the virtual absence of a sophisticated, informed reading audience.

That such a situation was not without its social and spiritual advantages as well, I do not question—and we have the existence of two generations of the literature of the twentieth-century Southern Renascence to demonstrate that. But it produced the anomaly, in the year 1930, of a group of Southern writers and scholars producing a symposium, entitled *I'll Take My Stand,* calling upon the South to hold fast to its own intellectual and cultural tradition and, in order for that book to be published and reviewed, having to send it to New York City.

As we know from the literature of the Southern Literary Renascence of the 1920s and thereafter, the publishing houses of the Northeast have by no means been unwilling to publish books by Southern authors. Yet the need to publish one's books elsewhere, and the dependence upon New York City and the rest of the Northeast, posed difficulties for the

Southern writer that were very real. What got published and what did not too often depended upon extraliterary considerations, and these were, and still are, based upon the prevalent attitudes toward the South in New York.

During the years immediately following the close of the Civil War, for example, it was enormously difficult for any Southern author to get published—and for understandable reasons, since the writer had recently been The Enemy. But during the late 1870s, the 1880s and into the 1890s, the writer of Southern local color who could illuminate the more exotic surfaces of Southern life or voice the legend of the Lost Cause was warmly welcomed. Then, in the mid-1890s, critical fashions changed, and local color was out. Critical realism was wanted for the more sophisticated audience, and costume romance for the popular reader; and if the Southern author wished to get published and reviewed, those were the acceptable modes.

After World War I, in the 1920s, the desired modes were either exotic romance featuring blacks as primitives, or else fiction that emphasized squalor and violence. In the 1930s a Southern author who could display the sufferings of the downtrodden rural masses or else deal romantically with the old plantations or the Civil War—preferably both—became valuable literary property in Manhattan.

From the mid-1940s well into the 1950s, for complex reasons, almost any well-written fiction dealing with the South was sure of a hearing. I am not sure just why this was so, but that was what happened. Beginning in the late 1950s, however, new Southern fiction that did not focus upon racial issues began to have rough going. In the 1960s the Vietnam imbroglio gave rise to the New Left, which, though it may have enjoyed comparatively little vogue in the South, was enthusiastically welcomed in New York. A more hostile climate for new Southern authors could not be imagined. Fiction had to be "relevant," the milieu had to be urban, and depictions of family life in a small city or community that wasn't torn with social upheaval—which Southern communities tended for the most part not to be, once the civil rights issue was settled—were considered escapist or nostalgic. The other reigning fashion was the antinovel, or the novel of the absurd, with its emphasis upon the impossibility of representing real life or finding meaning in one's social experience; and most of the Southern writers, being by nature storytellers whose milieu was the family and the community, were almost completely out of it.

I saw this graphically illustrated in the late 1960s, when I was a regional judge for a competition being sponsored by the Book of the Month Club, whereby young writers in colleges submitted portfolios of their work in the hope of winning attractive fellowships. The manuscripts I read were submitted from colleges and universities from New Jersey to Florida, along the seaboard. What I discovered was that almost unerringly students from the Northeast, whether attending college there or in the South, were writing mostly psychological fiction demonstrating the absurdity or hopelessness of ever finding meaning in existence, while students from the South, no matter whether they were in college in the South or in Maryland, New Jersey, Pennsylvania, or Delaware, were still telling stories. The novel might have been dead, but the young Southerners hadn't heard about it yet. The division bore no relationship whatever to the merits of the manuscripts they had submitted; there was good and poor work of both kinds. Yet it was true in almost every instance that the Southern-born applicants were telling stories, while the Northern-born applicants were wrestling with problems of meaning and society.

Now in recent years something has happened, and the Southern novel has apparently once again become popular in New York. One could get metaphysical or sociological about this and grope for reasons, but the point is, for whatever reasons, good or bad, for better or for worse, that for more than a century the Southern writer's work has been viewed in New York publishing circles and in the national media as an entity. Despite the individual differences between the various Southern authors, there is believed to be a product known as Southern writing. A young novelist from, say, Ohio or Vermont who submits a manuscript to a New York publishing house isn't thought of as something known as a Midwestern or a New England novelist. But a young novelist from North Carolina or Mississippi is inevitably viewed as a Southern writer who is engaged in making conscious use of regional material.

The limitation here can best be depicted by an anecdote, which happens to be true. Several years ago two of my former students published new novels with the same New York house. Both are women, but beyond that their work is very different in nature. Both happened to have rape scenes in their novels. The one whose novel was due to appear several months after the other's received a telephone call from her editor asking her to remove the episode, because the other one's novel had a rape scene. What this indicates is that despite what seems to me the obvious and vast differences between the fiction of these two young women, in New York they were considered much more alike than different, because they were both Southern authors. Only one Southern rape scene was appropriate for the publishing house's list that season!

Now I think there are good reasons for viewing Southern writing as an entity importantly set apart from other American writing. But the disadvantage of this, from the writer's standpoint, is that the individual author's publishing prospects and critical reception have been at the mercy of trends, vogues, and fashions that are out of the writer's control, involving politics and other matters, and having little or nothing to do with the literary merits of the writer's work. However one might agree or disagree with the extraliterary criteria being used at a given time, it is nonetheless true that the writers who must depend upon such auspices for getting published and reviewed are handicapped by being viewed en masse, and being judged by editors and reviewers whose ideas about the good, the true, and the beautiful are in certain important ways distanced from their own. (One might add that the same has been true for black American writers; they have had for generations to deal with editors and a reading audience which have certain set ideas and attitudes about what black writing *ought* to be, and which are only the more limiting for being unconsciously held.)

Several years ago, having spent more than a quarter-century teaching the writing of fiction and encouraging talented students, most of them Southern, to pursue literary careers, I found myself getting so irked at the difficulties that good young Southern authors habitually encountered in getting their work published that I attempted, on however small a scale, to do something about the problem by establishing a small but full-fledged trade publishing house in North Carolina. It seemed to me that most of the handicaps that historically had made it difficult to publish books in the South were now significantly reduced. No longer was the South poverty-stricken. No longer was it without numerous large cities. No longer were its schools inferior. Many of its colleges and universities were among the leading institutions of higher education in the world. It had good public libraries. No longer did the racial situation exercise a demand for orthodoxy upon the writer.

There existed in the South now, I felt, a large potential audience of informed, sophisticated readers, sufficient to provide a foundation for critical and commercial success. Moreover, the economics of the met-

ropolitan publishing industry were such that there would be considerable financial and editorial advantage in *not* operating a trade publishing
house in New York.

To achieve our objectives, my associates and I felt it important that
our publishing house must be national rather than regional in philosophy and function. Because of our own literary associations, it was not
only unavoidable but indeed desirable that many of our books would
have a Southern identity, but we would by no means restrict our books
to Southern authorship or Southern subject matter. What we wanted,
and what we believed was commercially and literarily feasible, was a
small but genuinely national publishing house, operating not in New
York or Boston but in Chapel Hill, North Carolina.

It is still too early to tell whether our experiment will turn out
successfully. We have been heartened, however, by the reception our
books have received, and have discovered that the national media have
been quite generous in reviewing our books. Indeed, what we have
found is that many persons in the New York publishing industry, far
from resenting us, have been pulling for us to succeed. There have been
disappointments, including the rediscovery that in many Southern
cities and in many Southern newspapers the long-established colonial
mentality is not dead, and the assumption remains that if a book is
published in North Carolina rather than in Boston or New York it is
probably not worth noticing. Even so, we have received considerable
recognition the country over, and this has already enabled us to do what
we wanted most to do: launch the literary careers of several talented
young Southern authors upon the national literary scene.

In 1935 Allen Tate deposed as follows:

> The exact degree of immediate satisfaction that Southern publication
> would bring to its authors I cannot predict. It, too, would be the system
> of the cash nexus; and the Southern publisher would be a capitalist
> plutocrat not noticeably different from his colleague in the North. Like
> his Northern friend he would, for a few years at least, sell the Southern
> article mostly north of the border. Until he could be backed by a
> powerful Southern press he would need the support of the New York
> journals for his authors, if he expected them to be read at home. I
> suppose the benefit of a Southern system would lie chiefly in this: that
> the Southern writer would not have to run the New York gauntlet,
> from which he emerges with a good understanding of what he can and
> cannot do.

From my brief experience I would have to say that Tate's diagnosis remains fairly accurate after a half-century of great change in the South. I trust, however, that we have shown that what Tate calls the "Southern article" *can* be sold south as well as north of the border. Other than that, however, and the sad fact that I am still waiting to become a plutocrat, it does appear possible to publish good books in the South nowadays.

There are those, of course, who would say that the South has now become so much like the rest of the country, and that so little of what was distinctive about the South still remains, that it no longer matters. If there is no longer anything meaningful about the South in terms of affording an identity, then the term "Southern writer" can have only an antiquarian significance. To paraphrase Jonathan Swift's quatrain:

> Behold this proof that now comes forth
> of one man's sad affliction
> Now that the South's become the North
> He publishes Southern fiction.

Needless to say, I do not share the viewpoint. For myself, I am quite happy not to be defending certain institutions that in the 1930s were still thought in need of defense, and I do not think their departure has weakened the South. On the contrary, we have only been strengthened by their removal. As for what constitutes the entity known as the South today as in the past, I believe there is still much to cherish. Meanwhile, we are looking for a few good cookbooks.

UNIVERSITY-PRESS PUBLISHING in the SOUTH

L. E. Phillabaum

One of the participants in the original Southern Writers' Conference was the thirty-year-old managing editor of the *Virginia Quarterly Review,* Lambert Davis. Shortly after the conference, Davis succeeded Stringfellow Barr as editor of *VQR* and within five years had gone on to New York and trade publishing. Initially the New York editor for Bobbs-Merrill, he subsequently joined Harcourt-Brace, and it was there that he served as Robert Penn Warren's editor for *All the King's Men.*

Lest this story appear to have no relevance, I must explain that when I went to the University of North Carolina Press as editor-in-chief in 1963, the director who hired me and gave me my first real break in publishing was Lambert Davis. He is one of the two finest editors I have ever been associated with, and it is literally impossible for me to discern how much of what I know about editing and publishing I learned from him—it is unquestionably a large percentage. Now, fifty years later, I am honored to be participating in the reprise of that first conference, and I feel in some ways a sense of symmetry, a closing of the circle, that gives me a particular personal satisfaction.

Lambert Davis was director of the University of North Carolina Press for twenty-two years, from 1948 to 1970. The press at Chapel Hill had been the premier scholarly publisher in the South during the thirties and forties, and it certainly continued to flourish during his directorship, although most Southern university presses had been established before he left New York. The first was founded at Duke, which at the time was Trinity College, in 1921. North Carolina was established in 1922, and there was then a thirteen-year hiatus before another Southern university press came into being, this one on the banks of the Mississippi in Louisiana the year of the Southern Writers' Conference (although the LSU Press imprint had appeared as early as 1931). It is somewhat ironic that at the conference Davis commented that the economic poverty and physical isolation of the South had been massive deterrents to the success of the *Virginia Quarterly Review,* and

W. T. Couch, who was then director of the University of North Carolina Press, said that "the general lack of interest in books and the feeling that the intellectual life is of no importance" made the South a poor risk for a publisher.

Between the time of the conference—held during the depths of the Depression, when the Roosevelt administration referred to the South as the nation's number-one economic problem—and the end of World War II, six more presses were founded, and there were university publishers in every Southern state except Virginia, Mississippi, and Arkansas. For the most part, these were small operations in the late forties, with largely apprentice staffs.

The decade of the fifties was essentially a period of consolidation, but with Sputnik came a new awareness of the importance of higher education and university-sponsored research. Presses as well as their parent institutions were the beneficiaries. Nationally, university press title output increased significantly, as did the size of staffs and sales revenues. The sixties were in many ways golden years for university press publishing, although only one new press was established in the South, the University Press of Virginia in 1963, the first state consortium press.

The war in Viet Nam and policy changes at the national level brought an end to the largesse. I need not recite the events of that unhappy era. For a multitude of reasons, aid to higher eduction was substantially reduced, library sales diminished, subsidies were cut. We soon found ourselves with warehouses full of books that nobody wanted—or nobody could afford to buy—and with shrinking budgets.

The decade of the seventies was ushered in with the central focus of the annual meeting of the Association of American University Presses being "the crisis in scholarly publishing." The 1971 meeting was dubbed "son of crisis," and by 1972 we had accepted the reality of "the crisis as chronic condition." During the first half of the decade, increases in new-title output by university presses—which had been proceeding apace—came to a virtual standstill and, among Southern presses, decreased by nearly 10 percent. Two Southern presses—Vanderbilt and Miami—were so adversely affected by the changing fortunes of higher education that they were forced to discontinue operations. Ironically, Mississippi founded a press in 1971, in the midst of all this chaos and adversity.

The year 1976 proved to be the nadir, and the rest of the decade saw only modest changes, both nationally and in the South, as we learned to deal with life's new realities. The year 1980 was pivotal, with new-title output jumping a surprising 18 percent nationally and 26 percent in the South. The increases since that time have been far less dramatic, averaging about 3 percent a year, and in fact 1984 saw a 4 percent decline.

The past ten years have, in many ways, been encouraging ones for university presses in the South. New-title output has increased by 36 percent, compared to a national gain of 31, although virtually all of that increase was achieved between 1975 and 1980. I cannot state precisely what the increase has been in terms of dollar and unit sales because such statistics are not gathered on a geographic basis. I think it safe to assume, however, that over the ten-year period both are substantially ahead. During the past five years, however, both curves must be significantly flatter, since on a national level new-title output has increased by 7½ percent, which has generated a 24 percent increase in sales revenues but only a one-half percent increase in the number of books sold. Interpolating those national figures to the South would suggest an increase in dollar sales during the past five years of less than 5 percent and a decrease in the number of books sold of between 5 and 10 percent. My seat-of-the-pants guesstimate is that our unit sales are probably a bit better than that since, as a group, we have tended toward lower prices for our books than national averages, which would mean more copies sold for the same revenue produced.

Statistically, therefore, Southern presses appear to have performed creditably during the past ten years, at least as well as presses nationally. The past five years, however, have indicated a leveling off, though this is not necessarily an ominous sign if the presses, overall, are of viable size, and there has clearly been progress in this direction. In 1980, of the eleven presses active in the South, three reported publishing fewer than 20 titles and two others published only 21 apiece. The largest number of books published by a single press was 83 and the second largest 61. In 1984 only one press (excluding Arkansas, which is brand new) reported publishing fewer than 20 new books during the year, but the high total was down to 56. The average number of new titles issued per press in both years was 35, but the discrepancy between largest and smallest had shrunk from 69 in 1980 to 39 in 1984. In other words, in the rather short period of five years, the profile of university press publishing in the South changed quite dramatically. The largest are no longer quite so large, the smallest neither so small nor so prevalent, and the average of

35 new titles a year is a far more accurate representation of the kind of presses that exist in the region.

Statistics are, of course, not the only way to judge a publishing house, but their indication that we now have more presses in the South of respectable size is borne out by my admittedly subjective observation that these presses are also more professionally staffed and better managed than at any time in the past. It is simply true that any press staffed for and successfully publishing 35 to 40 new titles a year is better able to support a strong acquisitions program and secure higher-quality manuscripts than is a press publishing fewer than 20 books. Overall, then, university press publishing in the South is, by any measure, stronger now than ever before.

In 1982, when I addressed the Radcliffe Publishing Procedures Course, I stated that I anticipated a continued decentralization of publishing, with increasing strength flowing to regional publishers, both trade and university press. I was speaking, in that context, of employment opportunities, but nonetheless I feel this trend will continue, as is demonstrated by the statistics I have quoted and by the participation in this conference of Louis Rubin, president of a vigorous Southern trade publishing house that was no more than a gleam in his eye when I talked to the class at Radcliffe.

No great prescience was required to discern this emerging pattern. It has come about, in no small part, because of changes in those impediments to success articulated by Lambert Davis fifty years ago. The South as a region simply is no longer poverty stricken, and with the advent of jet propulsion, the interstate highway system, and television, it is no longer physically isolated. And if Bill Couch's reference to "the general lack of interest in books and the feeling that the intellectual life is of no importance" continues to strike too familiar a chord, I can assure you it is by no means a tune unique to this region. Clearly, the South is a more hospitable climate for a publisher now than it has ever been.

But we must not grow sanguine. The fortunes of university presses, in the country as a whole as well as in the South, are inextricably entwined with the fortunes of higher education. Not only are we the publishers *of* universities, we are also the publishers *for* universities. Two of our major markets are university libraries and university faculties, neither of which are likely to see a significant increase in disposable income over the next several years. Therefore, unless we drastically reorient our programs, we can anticipate only modest increases in revenue. And there are very real limits to how much we can alter our editorial mix toward the end of increasing revenues without losing our identities as university presses and failing to do the job for which we were created.

University presses *are* important, and I would submit that regional university presses are especially important. We have published many books of major significance to our states, our regions, and the nation as a whole. It would be a shame if the financial support for such presses were so drastically reduced that we could no longer effectively meet our responsibilities. But the question of our prosperity or, indeed, our survival is linked to a question of far greater moment. University presses will falter only if the universities that nurture us are placed under such financial stress that the choices they must make are not how best they can fulfill their missions but rather what elements of those missions they must totally abandon. If we permit our institutions of higher learning to be reduced to such a condition, it will be not merely a shame, but a tragedy.

The LITERARY QUARTERLY in the SOUTH

George Core

The profession of letters in the South existed long before the literary quarterly in the South, but that profession's fortunes have risen considerably since the South has had solidly established and reasonably well-supported quarterlies, some of which have been associated with university presses and nearly all of which have been sponsored by colleges. I would not be so foolish or self-aggrandizing as to argue that Southern literature since, let us say, about 1920 has depended upon quarterlies in our region; that would be manifestly absurd. But I would aver that the rise of literary quarterlies in the South—and the rise of university presses—has helped the native writer establish himself in the region and in the larger world not only of the nation as a whole but of the Republic of Letters.

In the early days of what we now confidently call the Southern Literary Renascence—as though it were planned with all the foresight and craft that medical science now can provide would-be parents—the writers got along with almost nothing in the way of regional publishing outlets. When the *Virginia Quarterly Review* was founded in 1925, only the *Sewanee Review* and the *South Atlantic Quarterly*—among quarterlies with literary pretensions that are now still extant—were in existence; and neither magazine was very lively. By early 1926 three of the South's best literary magazines of then recent vintage—the *Fugitive*, in Nashville; the *Reviewer*, in Richmond; and the *Double Dealer*, in New Orleans—were as dead as the passenger pigeon and the dodo. The quarterlies that I have mentioned—the *Sewanee Review*, the *South Atlantic Quarterly*, and the *Virginia Quarterly*—were general magazines of discussion and politics as well as literature. There wasn't a first-rate literary quarterly in the South, and there would not be for another ten years until the *Southern Review* was founded. In the present company it seems superfluous for me to recount that magazine's history.

The *Southern Review* was modeled partly on the *Dial* and *Hound and Horn*, both defunct by 1935, as was *Smart Set;* it was also influenced by

Eliot's *Criterion* and Leavis' *Scrutiny* in England, both going concerns in 1935. At the time the literary situation in the South so far as publishing was concerned was gloomy, to say the least. On the other hand, by 1935 not only were the Fugitives and Agrarians established writers but so too were Faulkner, Wolfe, and a good many other Southerners of notable talent and ability. It is not too much to say that a large percentage of these writers earned national reputations before they were heard of locally or regionally. Through the agency of the *Southern Review*, Southern writers began to secure local and regional reputations at the same time the *Southern Review* was making a national and international reputation. In 1939 John Crowe Ransom, now happily working in Ohio, founded the *Kenyon Review*, a magazine that would depend largely on Southerners like himself and would continue the *Southern Review's* program in large part after that magazine's demise in 1942. The same was true of the revamped and revitalized *Sewanee Review* under Andrew Lytle and Allen Tate after 1942, which became largely—rather than partly or incidentally—literary in complexion and followed the general directions of the *Southern Review* and the *Kenyon Review.*

Tate had already drawn a blueprint for all three magazines in "The Function of the Critical Quarterly," which was published in the *Southern Review* in winter, 1936. There Tate describes what the critical performance of the quarterly should entail, and he says that it "lies no more in the critical essays than in the 'creative' department; good creative work is a criticism of the second rate; and the critical department ought to be run for the protection of that which in itself is the end of criticism." Criticism in this sense, he makes plain, joins literature in a common cause—to reveal "the meaning of experience, what is and has been."

John Donald Wade would found the *Georgia Review* in 1946, and Thomas Carter *Shenandoah* in 1955. These are the best of the region's minor quarterlies. I use the adjective *minor* as a term not of depreciation but of description: both magazines have regularly published lively poetry and fiction, but neither has had a real and continuing critical program, even the *Georgia Review* of late—unless we except its gaudy phase in the mid–1970s as the *Yale Reserve Review.* Tate declares:

> The critical program must have an objective, and not be contented with partial glimpses or mere reports or points of view. The reader needs more than the mere news that a given point of view exists; he must be initiated into the point of view, saturated with it. The critical program must, then, supply its readers with coherent standards of taste and

examples of taste in operation, not mere statements about taste. Mere reporting enjoins the editor to glance at all points of view. The reader gets a "digest" of opinion, not critical thought; he is encouraged to sample everything and to experience nothing.

It is easy to perceive how Tate's principles were applied by Brooks and Warren, Ransom, Tate, John Palmer, and Monroe Spears at the quarterlies in question—and by Frederick Morgan at the *Hudson Review.* The critical programs of these magazines, even over a long period, are easily discernible. At their best, as in the case of Brooks and Warren's *Southern Review,* these magazines make intellectual history while publishing literature and criticism.

The minor quarterly, as Monroe Spears has observed, stands between the little magazine, with its emphasis on experimentation in fiction and poetry, and the major quarterly, which is devoted largely to criticism through its essays and reviews and which has a critical program that to a considerable extent is even reflected in the fiction and poetry it publishes. By Spears's definition even the *Paris Review,* one of the nation's best-known and most popular quarterlies, is minor, as is *Grand Street,* a good quarterly recently founded in New York City. As Spears points out, such quarterlies carry on the best tradition of the little magazines by extending "special hospitality to experimentation and innovation"; and generally "they publish more fiction and poetry than criticism, and tend to concentrate on new and younger writers." They also are often irreverent: "Any tendency of the major quarterlies to take themselves too solemnly has been promptly ridiculed, and in this as well as in other respects the smaller quarterlies have served as valuable correctives to the larger."

The recent history of the *Kenyon Review,* in both its original and its new series, offers a striking example of how a quarterly can move from being major, as it was run under Ransom, to minor, as it was edited by Robie Macauley and then coedited by George Lanning and Ellington White, all three of whom cut back drastically on formal criticism and published a considerable amount of fiction and poetry together with the kind of reports and digests of opinion that Tate deplored. In the new series, begun in 1978 under the editorial direction of Frederick Turner and Ronald Sharp, the *Kenyon Review* was encouraging innovation and urging its writers to provide copy on everything from cooking to gerontology. The result, whether the editors knew it or not, was a minor quarterly; and one never knew what to expect in the magazine because there was no critical program and little apparent continuity of purpose otherwise. Now, under the leadership of Galbraith Crump and Philip Church, the *Kenyon Review* is being edited along the lines laid down by Ransom; and if it continues to expand in size and to carry out—through the increasing publication of critical articles and reviews—what has been done in outline over the past year and more, it will become a major quarterly as Tate and Spears define that term.

It is too bad that our terms—*little magazine, minor quarterly, major quarterly*—seem to carry a certain invidiousness.[1] Anyone reading Spears's "The Present Function of Literary Quarterlies" will immediately perceive that he is not stacking the deck for the major quarterlies and against the other forms of periodicals. In any case, it should by now be clear, a major quarterly can be a dull and pretentious compendium of stuffy and arch criticism that also includes belletristic fiction and poetry, while at the same time a minor quarterly can publish lively fiction and poetry and good occasional reporting on the literary scene here and abroad. The anthology celebrating the first thirty-five years of *Shenandoah,* chiefly edited by James Boatwright during that time, shows how good the minor quarterly can be—and how essential.[2]

The first series of the *Southern Review,* as has been plain for at least three decades, is the archetypal modern literary quarterly in the United States, as Ford Madox Ford's *English Review* is the archetypal modern British literary magazine. That Ford contributed work to the *Southern Review* and influenced and supported many of the principals in the story that I am recounting is more than pleasantly fortuitous circumstance: it has historic rightness and significance. The immortal soul of Ford may

1. In "The Function of the Academic Critical Quarterly," *Mississippi Quarterly,* XXIV (Spring, 1970), James Colvert, then editor of the *Georgia Review,* makes similar distinctions. Of the little magazine, he writes that its function "is to chart avant-garde movements, to promote radical experimentation in fiction and poetry, to rescue unknown writers from obscurity, and in all this to lay the groundwork for radical creative departures into the future." He adds, "Dispassionate criticism may find much in them of value besides their raucous enthusiasm and ritual irreverence." In contrast, he sees the proper function of the "relatively ordinary academic quarterly" (which in Spears's terms constitutes one form of the minor quarterly) to be "wholeheartedly academic" and "to extend to its readers the best that is being thought and said in the university community."

2. Monroe Spears, "The Present Function of Literary Quarterlies," *Texas Quarterly,* I (Spring, 1960), republished in revised form in *Sewanee Review,* XC (Spring, 1987). See *Shenandoah,* XXX, Nos. 2–3 (1984), a double issue presenting a large selection of fiction, poetry, essays, and reviews from that magazine's first thirty-five years. See also the spring and fall issues of the *Georgia Review,* XL (1986), fiction and poetry retrospectives from that quarterly. My "Procrustes' Bed" in the *Sewanee Review,* XCIV (Fall, 1986), is a response to these anniversary numbers and to retrospective issues of the *Yale Review* and special issues of the *Southern Review* published in 1985 and 1986.

be in heaven, as Robert Lowell once wrote in a memorable poem; but his mortal spirit is with us here now—and not only through his influence on Southern writers and editors from Tate onward.

The critical quarterly as we now know it was largely founded in response to modernism—to the work of writers like Ford, Yeats, Pound, Eliot, and Joyce. At first, magazines such as Ford's *English Review* and his *Transatlantic Review* were intended primarily to provide outlets for fiction and poetry; then increasingly the emphasis turned to criticism—a criticism that would explain the obscure and pithy indirections of the modernist manner and style by penetrating its masks, illuminating its shadowed modes, and translating its muted voices.

The major American literary quarterlies since 1935—the *Southern, Kenyon, Sewanee,* and *Hudson* reviews—therefore have existed largely to explain modern literature, while at the same time publishing fiction and poetry that for twenty years or more have been characterized mainly by the feeble term *postmodern.* In general, the last two to three decades have seen the steady rise of a madly overproductive writing and publishing establishment in the United States, especially of the little-magazine subestablishment, with 1,200 or more periodicals and thousands of contributors, many of whom are ill read and some of whom are barely literate by any reasonable definition. Bad "literature"—which is by no means entirely popular literature written for the mass market—is threatening serious and good literature. In the meantime, the man of letters and the informed general reader have become threatened species, but the national endowments and the other foundations, not to mention the academy, have done little or nothing to save either from extinction. The patronage of the foundations and the universities has too often involved subsidizing mediocre to wretched work and rewarding cronyism, logrolling, and backscratching.

There are more writers than ever—and fewer serious readers (a serious reader is one who doesn't let a day pass without devouring something in print besides the newspaper); and many of these writers expect to feed at the public trough while turning out work that is deplorable. A large percentage of those self-styled writers, who aren't good enough to be hacks, are siphoning off most of the funds intended for genuine artists. In part this is the unfortunate legacy of the second- and third-rate writing programs throughout the country. Here is democracy with a vengeance—something uncomfortably close to a democracy of letters, and a democracy of letters in this country would mean the nation has achieved postliteracy.

Such are some aspects of what Lewis P. Simpson has called a falling off from the literary intelligence and a failing of the Republic of Letters.[3] The literary quarterly in its corporate entity—that is, in the collective image represented by its editors, authors, and readers— must be devoted to various fictions, including the continuity of literature as the essence of culture and civilization and the continuation of the Republic of Letters (itself a construct or image that is more fictive than real). As the century goes on, those of us in the literary world who have committed ourselves to these and other fictions may be doing so with more desperation than our forerunners—may seem to be, in the humorous formulation of A. J. Liebling, so many monkeys clinging to a raft, a raft in seas that are becoming choppy and menacing. The seas will be constituted of the rising tide of periodicals and books being published in the United States and abroad. In this country alone, thousands of newspapers and magazines are published regularly—and well over forty thousand new books and reprints annually.

The sense of well-being that any editor of any literary quarterly feels in these circumstances must spring largely from his institution's backing. Since World War II the academic community has experienced halcyon times for the most part, with the result that in the South and elsewhere most responsible literary quarterlies and scholarly journals have received continuing support while many new academic periodicals devoted to literature and literary scholarship have been founded, including many good ones such as the *Hollins Critic,* the *Southern Poetry Review,* the *Southern Literary Journal,* and the *Mississippi Quarterly.* The major and minor literary quarterlies in the South are receiving strong support. But anyone who has looked at the historical record knows that magazines, especially little magazines and quarterlies, are threatened perennially with extinction, sometimes for reasons that are frivolous or the next thing to it.

Among the many paradoxes and ironies involving the literary marketplace today is the necessarily increasing support of sponsoring institutions for presses and periodicals at a time when subscribers are remaining

3. In "The *Southern Review* and Post-Southern American Letters," *Tri-Quarterly,* XLIII (Fall, 1978), Simpson writes of the new *Southern Review* (and by extension of the *Sewanee Review* and perhaps other related quarterlies): "We have said, if mostly by inference, that the sixties and seventies are not a time of literary origination but a time of falling off from the literary intelligence. We have said, if only by implication, that the falling off from the literary establishment . . . has left a vacuum. . . . In the late twentieth century the best news the literary journal can report from the failing Republic of Letters is the feasibility of its restoration and perpetuation. . . . But it must be admitted that the restorationist motive is haunted by the suspicion of its mere redundancy."

constant in number or tailing off slightly—in part, admittedly, because there are so many periodicals available. The circulation of quarterlies is affected by factors other than the mere laziness of readers: one of them is the revolution in photocopying. Another is that more and more readers of the academic persuasion increasingly are discounting the importance of what appears in magazines and mainly are considering what appears in books. Such comical locutions as the "book-related article" show an indifference to—if not an outright hostility toward—periodical literature. From this benighted standpoint—that of the academic drudge laboring in the bomb shelter of the ivory tower—Pound's formulation of what constitutes literature must now be altered to this dreary formula: Literature is the news that achieves publication in book form—never mind whether it remains news or not.

This condescending attitude toward periodicals, including quarterlies, is shared by book publishers, especially trade houses, who evidence an increasingly patronizing attitude toward quarterlies, seeing them as mere farm teams for the big leagues of Madison Avenue. The truth is that without quarterlies many good writers would be in deep trouble—and that their troubles in turn would adversely affect the serious literary programs at the best trade houses, such as Farrar, Straus & Giroux; Random House; and Viking. But many people at these publishing houses are ignorant of the contribution made to letters by quarterlies, even as they are ignorant of how literature differs from the ordinary commodity. This especially applies to the reprint houses, which are often nothing more than parasites feeding ravenously off the periodical press and paying little or nothing for the feast.

Despite the fact that we may be living in both a post-Christian and a postliterate age, an age in which mass culture threatens to overwhelm what has constituted Western civilization for hundreds of years, I will not announce the end of high civilization, even though when the last dingdong of doom sounds most people may be reading Silhouette romances or watching "Miami Vice." I remain moderately hopeful that the future of literature, like the future of civilization as a whole, is not behind us; and I believe that literary quarterlies will continue to play a major role in maintaining cultural values, so long as their harried editors do not experience a failure of nerve—a failure that usually results in a redefined moribund magazine with pernicious anemia or in its near cousin, the defunct magazine. In such circumstances the editor may be very nearly paralyzed by the sense of what Tate calls the "modern divorce of action from intelligence." Only a strong sense of being a part of the historical order of letters—not of being caught in the present-day or future turmoil of literary and cultural disorder—will save him or her. The editor must recognize that at any given time the expansion or contraction of first-rate literature depends upon the ratio of social and creative pressures of the moment and that no editor can do much to alter either force or bring them into productive balance. The editor can respond to each pressure or to both without allowing the quarterly to lose its definition, focus, and momentum. That editor, as Tate has argued, must remember that he "owes his first duty to his critical principles, his sense of the moral and intellectual order upon which society ought to rest, whether or not society at the moment has an interest in such an order or is even aware of a need for it."

In an age of continuing creative contraction and of almost unbridled critical expansion and consolidation, the literary quarterly should play much the same role that it has since the great artists of high modernism experienced their salad days while forging a great literature.[4] Today there are many signs of hope—among them the liveliness and energy and strength of letters in general, especially the personal essay and other modes outside fiction, poetry, drama, and criticism. We need not decide that the rough beast of the cultural apocalypse is now slouching toward Bethlehem; nor need we despair so long as there are a few good writers to write good literature and a few good magazines to publish them—in and out of the South.

4. To what extent the major quarterly has succeeded in the 1960s and 1970s and can be successful for the rest of the century remains to be seen. Lewis Simpson suggests that we may be moving into a nonliterary world—"an age so possessed by history as process that it has no past." He continues: "If so, there is no need for literary journals. There is no news from the nonexistent Republic of Letters." James Colvert believes that great quarterlies "rise with great literary movements, or even in some cases set them in motion. . . . Such quarterlies occur at special historical moments when radical changes in the operation of the critical intelligence are germinating, and when men of unusual abilities are on the scene to command and shape them." As of 1969 he seemed to think that the last great quarterly in these terms was Ransom's *Kenyon Review.*

My projecting glass is clouded, and the vision that it yields of the future is dark. I would hazard the observation that, with the passing of the survivors of modernism now in their seventies and eighties who are still making a substantial contribution to quarterlies, especially the *Southern* and *Sewanee* reviews (I am thinking of such makers and interpreters as Malcolm Cowley, Cleanth Brooks, R. B. Heilman, R. P. Warren, and René Wellek), the job of literary restoration that Simpson eloquently describes will be immensely more difficult to sustain. The writers of the generations since World War II have yet to produce literature and criticism that begins to rival the great works of literature and criticism that characterize the high modernist period.

III.
T. S. Eliot,
the South,
and the
Definition of Modernism

T. S. ELIOT and the AMERICAN SOUTH

Cleanth Brooks

In the years before Eliot took out British citizenship, his friend Sir Herbert Read was aware, he tells us, of "the struggle going on in Eliot's mind" between the claims of England and those of his native America. In the essay which Read contributed to *T. S. Eliot: The Man and His Work*, he does not state what he believes was the decisive factor in Eliot's ultimate decision; instead, he simply prints the following excerpt from a letter that Eliot wrote to him on April 23, 1928.

> Some day I want to write an essay about the point of view of an American who wasn't an American, because he was born in the South and went to school in New England as a small boy with a nigger drawl, but wasn't a southerner in the South because his people were northerners in a border state and looked down on all southerners and Virginians, and who so was never anything anywhere and who therefore felt himself to be more a Frenchman than an American and more an Englishman than a Frenchman and yet felt that the U.S.A. up to a hundred years ago was a family extension.

Just how seriously are we to take all this? Is Eliot simply being playful with his friend? Even if the account contains its grain of truth—and I believe it does—it also clearly contains a good measure of exaggeration. Nevertheless, it is Eliot's first and indeed, so far as I know, his only reference to his having a Southern connection. I think it very likely that the boys at the Milton Academy in New England did tease the new boy from St. Louis about his Southern drawl. That statement has the ring of truth, for in the 1890s, St. Louis may well have been a good deal more Southern in accent than I judge it to be today.

Read also writes that "on one or two later occasions in a mood of solemn gaiety [Eliot] would sing a ballad like 'The Reconstructed Rebel.' " Unless I am mistaken, this is a song of defiance from the lips of a thoroughly unreconstructed Southerner. It begins:

> O, I'm a good old rebel
> Now that's just what I am;

For the "fair land of freedom"
I do not care a damn

and it states that "Three hundred thousand Yankees / Is stiff in Southern dust," and follows with such bloodthirsty sentiments as

They died of Southern fever,
Of Southern steel and shot,
I wish it was three million
Instead of what we got.

If Eliot in his mood of solemn gaiety was trying to adopt the most extreme caricature of the hard-bitten, never-say-die Southerner, he couldn't have chosen better. Auden, too, was drawn to the ballad, apparently for similar reasons.

Eliot's singing this song does not, of course, prove very much of anything about his relation to the American South. But the Page-Barbour Lectures, which he gave in 1933 at the University of Virginia, can tell us a great deal about what he thought of the South. The lectures were published in 1934 under the title *After Strange Gods*. The first lecture, addressed specifically to the Virginians, is a carefully considered statement of ideas and principles that are integral to Eliot's later work and thought.

In this first lecture, he says that he had never visited the South until he crossed the Potomac in 1933 on his journey to Charlottesville. Though in his 1928 letter to Read he claimed to have been born in the South, we remember that he immediately went on to qualify this statement by telling Read that his parents were Northerners living in a border state; for Missouri, though it can claim one of the stars in the Confederate Stars and Bars, is in fact more accurately described as a border state in which the Union sympathizers were very numerous and soon gained control.

At any rate, Eliot makes it quite clear that he regarded this visit to Virginia as his first to the South whose tradition he meant to discuss as having proved special and important on the North American continent.

The close relation of these Page-Barbour lectures to Eliot's developing ideas is confirmed by his statement that he was taking this first visit to the Old South as an apt occasion for a reformulation of his early essay "Tradition and the Individual Talent." In that essay he had been concerned primarily with the individual writer. Obviously he meant now to discuss tradition in its larger terms as affecting a whole society. Because Eliot saw in the American South an example of what he meant by a tradition still alive and relatively coherent, his lectures in Virginia would offer a proper occasion for such a reformulation and for an extension of such an examination. True, Eliot avoided mere flattery. He described in more guarded terms the cultural situation as it now existed: he told his audience that he expected to find in Virginia "at least some recollection of a 'tradition' such as the influx of foreign populations has almost effaced in some parts of the North, and such as never established itself in the West," though he immediately added that "it is hardly to be expected that a tradition here, any more than anywhere else, should be found in health and flourishing growth."

So much for the opening paragraphs of Eliot's first Page-Barbour lecture. But before I go on to cite and quote from some of the other things he had to say about Virginia and the South, it may be wise for me to answer a question that may already have arisen in your minds.

Just how seriously can we take the compliments that Eliot addressed to his Southern hosts? Eliot is known for his civility and his courtesy. Besides, a lecturer is not only tempted but licensed to give a certain amount of praise to his auditors, especially if they are people of another nationality or even of another pronounced regional difference. An American addressing a British audience or a Japanese audience is aware of this and will usually take some pains to appeal to traits that he and his audience share. Eliot does show his acute awareness of his cultural difference from his hosts. Thus, at one point he tells his Virginia audience that a complimentary remark that he had just made "should carry more weight for being spoken by a Yankee."

Nevertheless, I believe that what Eliot says in *After Strange Gods* on the subject of Southern culture he did mean very seriously, and especially what he says about tradition, about the relation of the region to the nation, and about the nature of culture and the character of the good life. But he speaks as a realist. In fact, in his first lecture he fully recognizes the intense pressure on the South to change its ways and the difficulties that it would find in preserving its own identity. It is not too much to say that *After Strange Gods* amounts to a grim warning rather than an invitation to self-congratulation.

How can I be so confident of this estimate? Because of two considerations. The first is that Eliot had evidently read with deep interest and sympathy *I'll Take My Stand,* which had been published three years earlier. So he was well aware of the analysis that a group of Southerners had recently made of the present plight of, and future prospects for, the region.

In short, the Yankee visitor, now a British subject, had not simply succumbed to the charm of Charlottesville and Mr. Jefferson's University of Virginia. Very early in his first lecture he refers to *I'll Take My Stand* by name, and throughout the course of that first lecture he refers to Agrarianism and to what he chose to call the neo-Agrarians.

Yet he could not have been unaware of the fact that many Southerners thoroughly disagreed with the Agrarians and that the University of Virginia itself could hardly be considered to be a stronghold of the Agrarian movement. For instance, Stringfellow Barr, a historian at Virginia and a close friend and associate of Eliot's host at Charlottesville, Scott Buchanan, had in 1930 debated John Crowe Ransom as the spokesman for the twelve contributors to *I'll Take My Stand* on the merits of the Agrarian position. The debate, by the way, had been held in Richmond and had attracted many literary people and public figures from Virginia and elsewhere. This circumstance does not, of course, impugn in any way the sincerity of Eliot's tribute to Scott Buchanan in the preface to *After Strange Gods*. Eliot there thanks Buchanan "for conversation and suggestions" out of which, he tells us, his Page-Barbour lectures grew. But it should make plain that in his first lecture, Eliot knew that he could not take for granted that he was preaching to the converted and had no reason to assume agreement from his listeners when he praised the virtues of the older Southern culture.

There is a second and far more cogent reason for taking seriously Eliot's praise of the South's regional culture. Fifteen years later he would publish his *Notes Toward a Definition of Culture,* a much more elaborate formulation and development of the position he sketches in the first of his Page-Barbour lectures. In spite of the modesty of its title, the *Notes* constitutes a detailed elaboration of Eliot's ideas on the nature of a culture and the mode of its transmission from one generation to another. Its third chapter, entitled "Unity and Diversity: The Region," has a particular relation to what Eliot told his Virginia audience about the relation of Southern culture to American culture generally considered. Naturally, in the *Notes,* a book that was calculated to the longitude of Great Britain, the regions with which Eliot is principally concerned are Ireland, Wales, and Scotland. But the principles involved apply fully to the relation of America's most self-conscious region, the South, to the United States as a totality.

So it was not the tradition-laden atmosphere of the Old Campus at Charlottesville, Jefferson's beautifully planned arrangement of buildings and grounds, that drew from Eliot as visitor indulgent comments on regionalism and culture of the South's older day. On the contrary, Eliot obviously did see in the American South at least some residue of habits of mind and of a traditional way of life which he regarded as having universal value.

To take a particular instance of links between what Eliot said in the Page-Barbour lectures and what, years later, he included in his *Notes* on culture, consider these two passages.

He told his Virginia audience in 1933: "The Civil War was certainly a disaster . . . from which the country [and here he means the whole of the United States] has never recovered, and perhaps never will: we are always ready to assume that the good effects of war, if any, abide permanently while the ill effects are obliterated by time." In the later book, published in 1948, he writes, "The real revolution [in the United States] was not what is called the Revolution in the history books, but is a consequence of the Civil War; after which arose a plutocratic élite; after which the expansion and material development of the country was accelerated." Eliot then proceeds to mention other consequences of what he regards as the "real revolution"—consequences that he regards as deleterious to the development of a flourishing culture. Thus, in the *Notes* he not only confirms his earlier statement but indicates what he had meant in saying that the American Civil War was a disaster, not merely to the South, but to the whole of the United States.

That Eliot regarded as fully relevant to the American South his discussion of the relation of the cultures of Ireland, Wales, and Scotland to the dominant culture of England becomes fully clear in the following passage from his first Page-Barbour Lecture: "No one, surely, can cross the Potomac for the first time without being struck by differences so great that their extinction could only mean the death of both cultures . . . to come into Virginia is as definite an experience as to cross from England to Wales." Eliot argues that a national culture would be poorer if it were strictly uniform in its makeup. Variety among its various parts constitutes a stimulating force. A strict uniformity lacks the richness and depth that come from a measure of diversity. Thus, in obeying the natural instinct of human beings to realize themselves, the people of a region are actually nourishing the national culture. If a regional culture is suppressed or obliterated through some facile notion of cultural uniformity, everyone loses.

Eliot provides a concrete illustration by pointing out the ways in which the poets and fiction writers of Scotland, Wales, and Ireland have enriched the literature written in the English language. It would be easy to make the same case for our Southern writers. Imagine the impoverishment that American literature would suffer if one subtracted from it Katherine Anne Porter, Eudora Welty, William Faulkner, and R. P. Warren. If these writers had kept silent or, almost as damaging, if they had ignored their Southern cultural material and tried to imitate scrupulously Washington Irving, Henry James, or Sinclair Lewis, American literature would not be what it now is.

Eliot's *Notes Toward a Definition of Culture* is a closely argued book. I shall make no attempt at a full examination of it here. It will serve my present purpose well enough simply to call attention to some of the issues in which it closely resembles the Agrarians' *I'll Take My Stand.*

First, both books call for resistance against economic determinism. Our reasonable goals and ends ought to determine our means, rather than the most efficient means forcing upon us the ends we are to pursue.

Second, both see a very close relation between a people's religion and its culture. Indeed, in a very meaningful sense the culture is an extension and expression of a people's ultimate values—something that neither Eliot nor the Agrarians hesitate to call by its true name: religion.

Third, both emphasize an actual community in being. No amount of planning or social engineering can create a community. The community is the reality with which one must deal. It cannot be ignored, and if it is destroyed, the possibility of developing a genuine culture may well be destroyed with it.

Fourth, the transmission of cultural values is best done through the family, and the family must be preserved.

In the interests of economy I have stated these matters in my own terms, but I believe that I have not too much simplified what is said in the "Introduction: A Statement of Principles" of *I'll Take My Stand,* and in the essays by Allen Tate and Lyle Lanier. I am equally confident that I have not distorted Eliot's views as expressed in his *Notes,* though I have obviously left out much that is in that rightly freighted book.

I must now turn back to *After Strange Gods.* One large question about that book still remains to be answered: Why did Eliot never allow it to be reprinted? It is, I believe, the only one of his books that has never been reissued. I think that I know the answer, and if I am correct, his decision not to reprint it had nothing to do with his approval of regional cultures and regionalism, but something to do with what he had to say in the second and third Page-Barbour lectures.

In writing a book entitled *After Strange Gods,* with its provocative subtitle, *A Primer of Modern Heresy,* Eliot was risking trouble and almost certainly inviting misunderstanding. The phrase "After Strange Gods" is itself provocative. It has a definitely biblical ring, though I have not been able to find this exact phrasing in either the Old Testament or the New. The phrase would seem to be an amalgam of a number of texts found in the Scriptures, texts which reproach various persons or peoples for going "a whoring after" gods other than the true God, and of several other texts which carry a similar reproach for seeking after "strange gods." I expect that the phrasings "after other gods" and seeking "strange gods" simply fused in Eliot's memory. The amalgamation probably sounded so right that he didn't take the trouble to look it up. I, for example, was so certain that "after strange gods" was an exact quotation that I was shocked when I couldn't find it listed in Cruden's *Concordance.*

Yet the title would probably not have aroused so much hostility had Eliot not added his subtitle. By declaring his book to be "A Primer of Modern Heresy," Eliot was here surely trailing his coat as if inviting a fight. Our age in particular is sensitive to anything that smacks of heresy hunting. We associate it with intolerance—some priestly group turning over a victim to the secular arm for dire punishment. In a permissive age, the person who even appears to be himself intolerant can expect to be treated with intolerance.

Worst of all, in his second and third lectures, Eliot illustrated his statements about the heresies of the age with examples from the works of living (or only recently deceased) writers, such as Katherine Mansfield, D. H. Lawrence, and Thomas Hardy. With these illustrations the fat was indeed in the fire.

It did not avail that Eliot pointed out that he was not in this instance judging their literary art—which he conceded to be great—but was writing as a moralist, concerned with the moral disorder of our world as reflected in their art. Nor did the fact that Eliot made it plain that he regarded Lawrence and Hardy, for example, as distinguished literary artists, even though their fiction revealed the disorder and growing cruelty of the world in which they and he lived. Nor did it apparently help very much that he made a related judgment of the mind and sensibility of his old mentor at Harvard, Irving Babbitt, and of Ezra Pound, his warm friend, whom he tells us in his second lecture is "probably the most important living poet in our language."

Eliot had actually given rather precise notice of what he was planning to do in this book by quoting as a long epigraph a passage from Theodore Hacker's "Was ist der Mensch." Here Hacker writes of the chaos revealed in present-day literature, though he attributes it to tendencies in our age and not to evil in our writers. He cites them because their art furnishes a faithful mirror for what is going on in the culture.

Surely this is also the use to which Eliot puts the works of the contemporary writers whom he invokes. Perhaps he believed he made his purpose plain when he wrote in his second lecture that he was not concerned here "with the author's *beliefs,* but with orthodoxy of sensibility and with the sense of tradition." He also mentioned in this second lecture the "alarming cruelty in some modern literature," but the general context indicates that he meant the alarming cruelty of our world as reflected in modern literature. If so, this is very close to Yeats's remark on the "growing murderousness of the world"—certainly not an unwarranted observation.

Most damaging of all, Eliot made a remark in his first lecture that seemed distinctly anti-Jewish: unity of religion, he wrote, made "any large number of free-thinking Jews undesirable." As far as his argument is concerned, *free-thinking* is the key word. Thus, even the ultraconservative Old South got along with its God-fearing Jews very well. There was perhaps less anti-Jewish feeling in the Old South than anywhere else in the United States. *Freethinkers*—whatever the final merits of Eliot's argument—would have been the accurate term. And if freethinking was the issue, whether the ancestors of the freethinkers were of the Jewish, Catholic, or Protestant faith would not matter. Yet Eliot, in the light of his later statements, must have bitterly regretted what he had earlier set down.

As a matter of fact, the anti-Jewish passage aside, the argument advanced in the last two lectures could not be expected to thrive in the intellectual climate of the 1930s or, for that matter, in that of the 1980s. In any case, whatever has merit in Eliot's position is better stated in the *Notes,* with the appropriate reservations and qualifications to be found there. Clearly Eliot later on preferred to write *Notes Toward a Definition of Culture* than to reissue *After Strange Gods.*

There is an additional epigraph on the title page of *After Strange Gods,* which so far seems to have attracted no notice at all. As we know, Eliot liked to employ epigraphs. He frequently used them to preface individual poems, including even some of his short lyrics. The epigraph I am concerned with here amounts to two and a half lines of verse from Sophocles' *Oedipus Rex*. As usual, Eliot prefers to quote the Greek original, but I shall set down here Bernard Knox's translation. My own Greek is too rusty these days to provide a translation entirely accurate, much less elegant. The Greek seer Tiresias speaks as follows: "Go think this out. And if you find that I am wrong, then say that I have no skill in prophecy."

We have encountered Tiresias before in Eliot's poetry. In *The Waste Land* Tiresias is made to witness the lovemaking that is not loving or fulfilling or life-giving, but sterile and meaningless.

> (And I Tiresias have foresuffered all
> Enacted on this same divan or bed;
> I who have sat by Thebes below the wall
> And walked among the lowest of the dead.)

In the notes to *The Waste Land* Eliot tells the reader: "What Tiresias *sees* . . . is the substance of the poem." I propose here that what Mr. Eliot sees in the modern world is indeed the substance of what he has to say about it, not only in *After Strange Gods,* but also in his *Notes Toward a Definition of Culture.*

Are we to conclude then that in *After Strange Gods* Eliot means to assume the mantle of the prophet Tiresias? Well, at least Eliot seems to see a parallel between Tiresias and himself. Both are conscious that their predictions are almost certain to be disregarded. The ears on which the words of each will fall are deaf indeed. If none are so blind as those who will not see, none are so deaf as those who will not hear.

Yet I mustn't make Eliot seem too serious here. He had an excellent sense of humor with which he is not often credited. His reference to Tiresias is so well hidden as to seem sly: only for the observant eye is the admission apparent. Though aware that what he is going to say will not be understood, he will make his statement anyway. In that matter at least Eliot has proved to be a true prophet: he has been regularly misunderstood.

Yet now in the 1980s the content of the prophecy is worth reexamining. Modern Western man, and especially his American version, is predisposed to hubris—an overweening pride in his own powers and achievements. Now he may be threatened by the very success of some of his most brilliant achievements. Eliot was probably aware that even his choice audience of traditional Virginians were also Americans and might stand in need of such a warning. To have solved, as Oedipus did, the riddle of the sphinx does not mean that one knows the whole nature of man or that one can accurately read one's own future.

It would be foolish to claim too much. Eliot was never the unregenerate Southern rebel, and long ago he had put away his Southern drawl in favor of an impeccable British accent spoken after the manner of Oxenford. His visit to Virginia in 1933 was apparently his last to the old Confederacy (with the exception of a brief visit to the University of Texas in 1958). Nevertheless, his concern for the older Southern culture was considered and genuine, and he established a lasting friendship with one of the most thoughtful of the Southern Agrarians, Allen Tate. When Eliot's letters are finally published and the remainder of Tate's, that correspondence, though probably not extensive, may tell us a great deal about a warm and enduring relationship and one founded on common sympathies and understandings of our twentieth-century world.

T. S. ELIOT: The SAVAGE COMEDIAN
and the SWEENEY MYTH

Ronald Schuchard

T. S. Eliot has never enjoyed a public reputation as a comic poet, or as an obscene poet, but his new friends in London in 1915 were well acquainted with the lusty characters who peopled his bawdy ballads and limericks. Eliot playfully interspersed the narrative of his letters to Conrad Aiken with stanzas on the escapades of King Bolo and his Big Black Kween, "that airy fairy hairy-un, who led the dance on Golder's Green with Cardinal Bessarion." He sent poems entitled "Bullshit" and "Ballad for Big Louise" to Wyndham Lewis, and wrote to Pound from Merton College, Oxford, that Lewis' "Puritanical Principles seem to bar my way to Publicity. . . . I understand that Priapism, Narcissism etc are not approved of, and even so innocent a rhyme as '. . . pulled her stockings off / With a frightful cry of "Hauptbahnhof!"' ' is considered decadent." Lewis, who saw the poems as "excellent bits of scholarly ribaldry," jokingly told Pound that he was trying to print them in his periodical, *Blast,* but stuck to his "naif determination to have no 'words ending in -Uck, -Unt, and -Ugger.' "

There is much in Eliot's juvenile graffiti that is vulgar and coarsely humorous. That said, it is of interest that the impulse to sexual caricature was accompanied by an equally strong impulse to poems of spiritual martyrdom. It is of even greater interest that the bawdy element not only survived his twenty-fifth year but, with the appearance of Sweeney in 1918, became one of the most "serious" and "personal" elements of his art. Between 1915 and 1925, as he read deeply in comedy, myth, and ritual, Eliot created around Sweeney a comically sordid poetic landscape of brothels, lowlifes, and exotic types: Doris, Mrs. Turner, Mrs. Porter, Fresca, Grishkin, Rachel, and others. Collectively, they inhabit the phantasmagoria through which Eliot expresses his moral convictions about the world of vanity, fear, and lust.

Eliot wrote most of his bawdy poems prior to his precipitous marriage in June, 1915, to Vivien Haigh-Wood. But the marriage quickly placed them in a rather humorless financial plight, somewhat relieved by the generosity of Bertrand Russell, who took the couple into his London flat for several months and assumed an avuncular role in the struggling marriage. Two years of marital difficulty and poetic dryness were to elapse before Sweeney appeared among Eliot's new quatrain poems of 1918. Where did he come from, this apeneck brothel browser? What prompted Eliot to make a sort of generic slide from martyr to whoremonger, to slip from the tragic and spiritual to the comic and carnal? What is the relationship of the Sweeney poems of 1918 and 1919 to *The Waste Land,* where Sweeney makes a cameo appearance in "The Fire Sermon," and to *Sweeney Agonistes,* where Eliot's mythic figure reenacts an ancient ritual of death and resurrection? These are some of the questions that I want to address this morning in discussing a group of modernist poems that have troubled critics for almost seventy years.

Pound and Lewis knew the witty practical joker in Eliot, but they did not know in 1915 that he was already a serious student of the comic spirit. He had studied Aristophanes at Harvard, and he kept Bekker's five-volume edition close at hand. During his year abroad in Paris in 1910–1911, where he says he underwent a "temporary conversion" to Bergsonism, Eliot read Bergson's book-length study, *Laughter: An Essay on the Meaning of the Comic,* published in 1903, where he develops his belief in the moral function of comedy. "Any incident is comic," Bergson argues, "that calls our attention to the physical in a person when it is the moral side that is concerned."

Bergson's analysis of the comic pervades the quatrain poems, but Eliot subsequently encountered a more arresting discussion of the comic poet in Baudelaire's essay "On the Essence of Laughter, and Generally of the Comic in the Plastic Arts," published in 1855. Baudelaire argues that laughter, which is satanic and based on pride and the individual's feeling of superiority over other beings, is the experience of contradictory feelings—of infinite greatness in relation to beasts and of infinite wretchedness in relation to absolute being. He distinguishes what he calls the "absolute comic," whose work "has a mysterious, a durable, an eternal element, even as the work is destined to show men their own moral and physical ugliness." The absolute comic is the superior artist, one who is receptive to absolute ideas and who brings those ideas to bear on the moral degradation of fallen humanity. In playing with the ideas of pride and superiority in his audience, the absolute comic works with laughter that is provoked by the grotesque, which carries the audience beyond its feelings of superiority over other men to its feelings of superiority over nature. In depicting the human slide toward the bestial, the absolute comic reveals not only the guttering moral consciousness that separates men from beast but the horror of man's separation from absolute being.

Eliot seized upon Baudelaire's definition of the absolute comic, and with it he was directed by Baudelaire to its most ferocious practitioners in England. "To find the ferocious and ultra-ferocious comic," wrote Baudelaire, in a passage quoted by Eliot, "we must cross the Channel and pay a visit to the misty kingdoms of the spleen," where the distinguishing mark of the comic is violence. As he began to write the Sweeney poems in 1918, Eliot immersed himself in the savage and violent tradition of English comedy, from Christopher Marlowe and Ben Jonson to Charles Dickens, thence to the most contemporary manifestation of the ferocious comic in England—his bawdy friend Wyndham Lewis.

In his essays on Marlowe and Jonson in 1918 and 1919, Eliot defines in his masters the techniques of caricature that inform his own work. He focuses on *The Jew of Malta* to characterize Marlowe's genius for achieving serious moral thought through caricature, identifying him, in effect, as an absolute comic. Arguing that in Elizabethan drama "the more farcical comedy was the more serious," Eliot holds that the play should be read as a farce. "I say farce," he writes, drawing directly upon Baudelaire, "but with the enfeebled humour of our times the word is a misnomer; it is the farce of the old English humour which spent its last breath in the decadent genius of Dickens." Marlowe's style, says Eliot, "secures its emphasis by always hesitating on the edge of caricature at the right moment"—a technique that Eliot employs repeatedly in the Sweeney poems, as when Rachel Rabinovitch "Tears at the grapes with murderous paws."

Eliot continued to explore the comic techniques of *The Jew of Malta* by comparing it with Jonson's *Volpone,* where the vice-ridden characters are all linked to the appropriate animal: Volpone the Fox and so on. Jonson's "type of personality," Eliot observes, "found its relief in something falling under the category of burlesque or farce." In examining Jonson's comic methods of achieving moral seriousness, Eliot praises his mastery of grotesque caricature. To Eliot, Jonson was also an absolute comic, and he wrote admiringly in a neglected essay on "the Comic

Spirit" (1921) that Jonson's drama is therefore "a criticism of humanity far more serious than its *conscious* moral judgments. 'Volpone' does not merely show that wickedness is punished; it criticizes humanity by intensifying wickedness."

This lost art of serious English caricature, Eliot had discovered, could now be found anew in the fiction of Wyndham Lewis, particularly in his novel, *Tarr,* published in 1918, which Eliot reviewed on several occasions. "Mr. Lewis's humour is near to Dickens," he wrote, "but on the right side, for it is not too remote from Ben Jonson." Eliot identified in Lewis those aspects of savage humor that were most important to his own work, singling out, for example, Lewis' mastery of humiliation, which Eliot described as "one of the most important elements in human life, and one little exploited." He subsequently praised *Tarr* for possessing "an element of that British humour, so serious and savage, to which Baudelaire once devoted a short study." Lewis was Eliot's single visible ally; and in connecting himself and Lewis to Baudelaire on the one hand, and to Dickens, Jonson, and Marlowe on the other, Eliot felt that they had revived the absolute comic in England. Each was, to use Lewis' title, "A Soldier of Humour."

Thus, in his criticism leading up to *The Waste Land,* Eliot clearly sought to prepare a favorable climate for the ferocious English humor of which he had become both proponent and practitioner. Indeed, we should begin to see that the early thrust of Eliot's literary modernism was in the revival of this comic mode. Ironically, as Eliot began his experiments against an enfeebled humor, his modern audience misread his comic signs. But now the questions press again: what happened in Eliot's personal life to turn the bawdy balladeer into a savage comedian in 1918? What emotional relief, as he described it in Jonson, did his type of personality seek in turning to the comic quatrains? The intellectual, almost evangelical interest in comic theory did not in itself lead him to the new mode; rather, the poems grew out of an urgent need to find an artistic form for the preoccupations of a deeply wounded sensibility. A distinctive feature of humor, he wrote in discussing *Tarr,* is "the instinctive attempt of a sensitive mind to protect beauty against ugliness, and to protect itself from stupidity." What ugliness and stupidity, we want to know, motivates these difficult, stripped-down poems of sexual grotesques involved in adulterous and other illicit encounters, with constant allusions to lechery, cuckoldry, and betrayal? Perhaps we shall never know the full story, but a recent study lays out the bitter truth of a long-rumored situation, Bertrand Russell's sexual affair with Vivien

Eliot. Russell, who had sworn himself to a platonic relationship, had restrained himself for two years, but he wrote to another mistress, Lady Constance Malleson, that he began having sexual relations with Vivien in the autumn of 1917. The evidence at hand makes it all but certain that Eliot knew or had strong intimations of the affair by the summer of 1918, when Russell provided the Eliots with his summer cottage. He later wrote to Ottoline Morel that "the spectacle of Bertie" had been a significant factor in his eventual conversion. There is no doubt that in 1918 Eliot's vision of sexual humanity was terribly darkened, little doubt that Russell's lustful betrayal and Vivien's adulterous desire were the cause. To cope with the humiliation, to protect himself from the moral ugliness and stupidity, Eliot turned savagely to the sexual caricature of Sweeney and his friends. In so doing, he gradually created a personal myth of sexual betrayal, psychological retribution, and moral regeneration. We begin with "Sweeney Erect."

In assigning *The Maid's Tragedy* to his night class of adult students in 1918, Eliot told them that the gifts of Beaumont and Fletcher as dramatists were "on the whole better exhibited in the scene than in the complete play." Little did those students know how much one scene meant to him—the scene that provides the epigraph for "Sweeney Erect", the betrayed Aspatia's bitter lament of her desertion by her lover for the king's mistress. "But man—O, that beast man!" she cries, asking her waiting women to be sad with her as she recounts stories of lost heroines. She asks to see one woman's needlework of Ariadne and Theseus, who abandoned Ariadne on the waste shores of Naxos. Complaining bitterly that the scene does not show the depths of Ariadne's misery, she commands the woman to rework the mythic portrayal. "Do it by me," she exclaims. "Do it by me the lost Aspatia." Eliot thus prefaces the poem with Aspatia at the height of her hysterical state, deeply upsetting her waiting women. "Dear madam!" one exclaims. We approach the poem at the conclusion of Aspatia's frantic identification with Ariadne:

> and behind me,
> Make all a desolation. Look, look, wenches,
> A miserable life of this poor picture.

"Sweeney Erect" begins with the poet's recasting of Aspatia's hysterical imperatives in the first two stanzas—Paint me Ariadne; Display me the "perjured sails" of Theseus—as though the poet would, like

Aspatia, harshly rework the betrayal. But the summoning of Ariadne's pathos is suddenly, in a jarring shift of myth and style, deflated and displaced by some sheet-covered lovers, with only their feet and hands protruding for dawn's searching light. It is as though the poet, in his abrupt redirection of the poem, cannot continue the pathetic mode, is forced to shift to burlesque, dissolving his original impulse in lowlife comedy. The declension of the mythic dimension is swift: if not Ariadne and Theseus, then perhaps Nausicaa and Polypheme? No, all the way down to Sweeney and Doris. Sweeney's prehensile arm, arched over Doris, erupts from the sheets in a "gesture of orang-outang" as he rises in steam from their torrid undercover rendezvous. Torpid, tousled, and detumescent, he becomes a great gaping yawn, an "oval O cropped out with teeth," and immediately begins his posterectile performance, his aubade, as it were. A violent scissor kick jackknifes him from the supine to the prone in so ungainly a manner, in such exaggerated clumsiness, that he desperately pushes the bedstead for support and, with Eliot's Marlovian touch, "claws" at the pillow slip to regain his balance. Newly and safely erect, our brothel comedian continues the morning entertainment with his madcap ablutions, in the pink. Sweeney, who "Knows the female temperament," prepares to shave, lathering not just his cheeks but his whole face, setting the comic mood for Doris' arousal. Her laughter, we may imagine, is spontaneous and delighted, recalling her later reminiscence in *Sweeney Agonistes:* "He's like a fellow once I knew. / *He* could make you laugh." Even the absolute narrator joins the fun; so grotesque is the silhouette of broad-bottomed Sweeney at his toilet that the pedantic intruder cannot resist a double-edged gibe at Emerson's noble depiction of man as the shaper of history. Eliot's own unequivocal attitude toward Emerson surfaced in a review that preceded the poem: "Neither Emerson nor any of the others was a real observer of the moral life."

For his *pièce de résistance* Sweeney begins toying with his razor, testing its sharpness on the hairs of his leg, an acrobatic gyration that elicits a shriek of animal laughter; indeed, Sweeney's Chaplinesque, music-hall pantomime throws Doris into a paroxysm of uncontrollable laughter, making her clutch breathlessly at her aching, bursting sides. (She recalls the canceled passage on Fresca's entertainment in *The Waste Land:* "The Russians thrilled her to hysteric fits.") In her seizurelike extremity, Doris is appropriately caricatured as "The epileptic on the bed." The riotous laughter brings the house down, however, and Doris' room is

quickly crowded upon by the alarmed "ladies of the corridor." When
they discover that they have mistaken hilarity for violence, their solic-
itude turns sharply to indignation and high-minded propriety. And if
Madam Turner is personally perturbed and professionally concerned,
Doris is nonchalant and wholly unrepentant in dismissing them. She
soon returns, happily spent, washed, and toweled, to her sometime
fancy man, Sweeney, "padding" like a lioness, bountifully toting those
old restoratives, those creature comforts, "sal volatile / And a glass of
brandy neat." The poet's caricatures of their movements—Sweeney's
orangutan gesture and his "clawing," Doris' hyenalike shrieks and her
"padding"—are individually comical, but collectively they viciously
imprint the bestial on Sweeney's and Doris' actions, implying at poem's
end that they will now curl up in their lair with no moral disturbance,
with no disquieting metaphysic to trouble their animal coupling, however illicit.

   This brothel burlesque is, however, so skillfully amusing on the
surface that we forget its tragic origins—forget to recall Aspatia at the
crucial moment of misunderstanding in the corridor. In the awkward
uncertainty about Doris' hysteria the tragic and the burlesque intersect,
and it is here that we sense the poet's comic debasement of Aspatia's
grief in a personal myth. Whereas Aspatia, decrying the bestiality of
man, rises to hysteria in her grief, Doris, laughing violently at the
grotesque antics of Sweeney, rises merely to hysterics. The figures of
Aspatia and Doris come together as their separate cries reach a similar
pitch, and the parallels force the reader to recognize the sexual bestiality and moral blindness common to both the tragic and the comic
action. Eliot's comic creations seem blissfully unaware of their moral
natures in this poem, but the absolute comic is aware of them, just as he
is painfully unforgetful of Aspatia, whose betrayal was brought about by
a lust that drove the king and his mistress to facilitate a convenient
sexual arrangement at Aspatia's expense. The poet himself is not
amused by Sweeney and Doris. His personal voice is unmistakable; this
is Aspatia's poem, written for her with great empathy.

   When Eliot was collecting his quatrain poems for a limited edition
entitled *Ara Vos Prec,* he wrote to his brother about them in February, 1919:
"Some of the new poems, the Sweeney ones, especially *Among the
Nightingales* and *Burbank,* are intensely serious, and I think these two are
among the best I have ever done. But even here I am considered by the
ordinary newspaper critic as a wit or satirist and in America I suppose I

shall be thought merely disgusting." This rare volume contained a unique printing of "Sweeney Among the Nightingales," which included a second epigraph from an anonymous Elizabethan play, *The Raigne of King Edward the Third*. In the play King Edward becomes infatuated with the virtuous Countess of Salisbury while her husband is away at war. In contemplating her beautiful features he compares her voice to the music of the nightingale. His second thought about the comparison provides the epigraph: "And why should I speake of the nightingale? / The nightingale sings of adulterate wrong." The amorous king thinks it too self-satirical to conceive of his desire as adulterous, and he rationalizes semantically that to be virtuous with such a lady would be sinful, and to be sinful with her would be virtuous.

The epigraph was printed in bold block capitals, typographically disproportional to the title and text. However appropriate for the poem, it seems to be deliberately, intemperately emblazoned on the page, as if to catch a guilty eye. Eliot inexplicably stripped the epigraph before the poem reappeared the next year in the first American edition of his work, but in the textual history of the poem, it remains a telling emblem of mind during composition. The succeeding action of the play, which traces the Countess' unyielding constancy before the lecherous king, illuminates Eliot's ironic personal attraction to the play. When the king begs her to lend her body to him "to sport with all," she eloquently refuses to relinquish the bower of her "intellectual soule": "If I should leave her house, my Lord, to thee, / I kill my poore soule and my poore soule me." When she learns of his further plots to seduce her, she takes up a knife, swearing to kill the husband sleeping in her bosom. Only then does the king awaken from his lust and bow to her fidelity and moral integrity. "Arise," he commands her,

> and be my fault thy honors fame,
> Which after ages shall enrich thee with.
> I am awakened from this idle dream.

For Eliot, however, the sexual nightmare continued.

The other, retained epigraph comes, as you know, from the *Agamemnon* of Aeschylus—the moment when, shortly after his return to Argos from Troy with his unwilling concubine, Cassandra, Agamemnon is brutally slain by his wife, Clytemnestra, who acts in adulterous league with her lover, Aegisthus. Entrapping him in the folds of his robe while he bathes, she slays the king with an axe as he cries out, "Alas, I am struck a mortal blow!" This epigraph and the allusions to Agamemnon's death in the final stanza provide a crucial tragic frame for Eliot's low comedy.

We find Sweeney in a brothel again, on a stormy, threatening night, presumably the object of ribald teasing by the nightingales. Laughing in compound caricature, his simian gestures and the changing coloration of his face make him a figure of protean animal shapes—ape, zebra, giraffe. The absolute narrator, in contemplation of the epigraph's tragedy, tries to envelop his own comic scene in portent. But the ominous atmosphere, in which Death and the Raven seem to await entry, is laughably deflated by the image of Sweeney guarding the hornèd gates of pleasure—a debunked image from the *Aeneid* by way of Dryden that Eliot reworked in a fragment of *The Waste Land:* "the human engine waits . . . To spring to pleasure through the horn or ivory gates." But the sexual engines in this brothel are run down, and though Sweeney is the object of sexual solicitation by the two conspiring ladies, he is curiously indifferent to their automatic advances. When the mechanical approach of the woman in the Spanish cape results in a clumsy, boisterous pratfall, the seduction becomes a farce. So apathetic are the bodily appetites of this "silent vertebrate" that he comically contracts into a concentrated ball of refusal when the waiter offers fruit. And when the ravenous Russian, Rachel *née* Rabinovitch, tears at the hothouse grapes in a bestial exaggeration of her adulterous appetite, Sweeney declines her histrionic advance with a gesture of fatigue and removes himself from the sexual game of chess. He feigns good humor, but what, we wonder, has happened to his libidinous ways? He may be spent, but he also seems preoccupied, even disturbed, his weariness as much mental as physical, his golden grin forced. Does Sweeney have that sense of foreboding, "of something about to happen," that Eliot says he wrote the poem to show? We leave him looking in as his host, presumably Mrs. Porter, admits another customer and the nightingales resume their seductive song of adulterate wrong.

The portentous voice that earlier acquiesced to the more insistent description of sexual intrigue now resumes authority over the banal scene. Adopting again a constellational perspective, the absolute narrator makes the ironic observation that the siren songs of the nightingales are near another human community, the Convent of the Sacred Heart, where the chaste brides of Christ sublimate desire in devotion. The observation itself charts the moral distance between brothel and convent, nightingale and nun; and the narrator continues to elevate the perspective with a more distant, more mythical association of Sweeney's nightingales with the nightingales of the "bloody wood." In an uncollected letter Eliot wrote, "The wood I had in mind was the grove of the Furies at Colonus; I called it 'bloody' because of the blood of Agamemnon in Argos." This striking revelation almost forty years after the fact explains why the allusions of the final stanza have been so unyielding. In perhaps the clearest example of the modernist technique of dislocating and conflating myths, Eliot purposefully fused scenes from Sophocles' *Oedipus at Colonus* and Aeschylus' *Agamemnon,* borrowing the nightingales from Sophocles for Agamemnon's death scene. "It was a simple matter," he continued, "to bring the dead Agamemnon into the open air, and to transfer the nightingales from one place to another." Singing above the dead Agamemnon, wrapped in his blood-stained robe-*cum*-shroud, the nightingales in this very personal, seemingly vindictive poem, defecate on the sinful king, their "liquid siftings" staining the shroud already dishonored by Clytemnestra's adultery. But their song also awakens the Furies, the All-Seeing Ones, and *that* is the borrowed association that bears upon the poem. Indeed, the sense of foreboding that weighs upon Sweeney's libido, unconsciously felt by Sweeney but strongly perceived by the absolute comic, is a sense that the Furies, the inflexible agents of retribution who pursue men into atonement, are now at hand. The nightingales follow Sweeney into *The Waste Land,* where the song that cries "'Jug Jug' to dirty ears" again signals the arousal of the Furies, whose pursuit, we shall see, has wreaked a terrible metamorphosis upon the protagonist of *Sweeney Agonistes.*

At the time he wrote "Sweeney Among the Nightingales," Eliot was absorbed by what he called "the phantom-psychology" of Aeschylus, Sophocles, and Shakespeare; and in the Sweeney poems he begins to trace the psychological transformation of promiscuous characters possessed by moral agents. Human beings may tend, comically and tragically, toward the mechanical and bestial, but to Eliot human beings cannot escape the horrible consequences of sensual abandonment. He knew that sexual tragedy brings the greatest spiritual horror, unleashes the Furies, the Dark Angel, the hoo-ha-ha's. So pursued, Sweeney becomes a study in the phantom-psychology of sexuality, in sensual-spiritual transformation.

Eliot develops this agon between the physical and the spiritual in his seventy-line portrait of Fresca, an excised passage that served as a prelude to Sweeney's brief appearance in "The Fire Sermon." Fresca, languidly dreaming of "pleasant rapes" in her boudoir, has not yet undergone her inevitable transformation into a Mary Magdalene, is herself unaware of the Dark Angel latent in the sexual urge, but the absolute narrator identifies the treacherous chemistry of her desire: "The same eternal and consuming itch / Can make a martyr, or plain simple bitch." In contemplating Fresca's sexual reveries, the narrator hears at his back, or at her back, not time's wingèd chariot, as does Marvell's artful seducer, but the haunting "chuckle" of death. This chuckle, he knows, brings more than a carpe diem awareness of mortality; it brings a horrific awareness of the void that underlies illicit sexuality. Implicitly, the All-Seeing Ones have found her out.

The wasteland quester, musing on the rat-infested, infertile land, then hears behind his back the blaring horns and motors that herald Sweeney's annual return to Mrs. Porter in the spring. Since the earlier poems, Sweeney and Mrs. Porter have become such personal mythic figures in Eliot's imagination that they can make their appearance in the poem without introduction, casually displacing Acteon and Diana in a mythic parade of passion. Heard in the fanfare are lines from a bawdy ballad.

> O the moon shone bright on Mrs. Porter
> And on her daughter
> They wash their feet in soda water.

Yet Sweeney and Mrs. Porter are but fleeting figures in the phantasmagoria of this section, this "cauldron of unholy loves," where the montage of images and allusions will not hold in the quester's mind, flooded as it is with associative fragments of high and low passion, constancy, and betrayal. As Sweeney and Mrs. Porter fade out of the disturbed procession, the wail of the "ravish'd nightingale" marks their departure and awakens the Furies, who will drive them toward their ritual deaths.

Even in this brief scene in "The Fire Sermon" we can see that Eliot had already discovered a ritual frame for the moral regeneration of Sweeney and his wayward friends. Since 1916 he had been reading the Cambridge anthropologists, all of whom were making the case that comedy and tragedy had their origins in ancient fertility rituals. As an absolute comic, Eliot had become particularly interested in F. M.

Cornford's *The Origins of Attic Comedy,* published in 1914, which argues that a phallic fertility ritual of death and resurrection underlies the development of comedy and that elements of this ritual provide the framework for the plays of Aristophanes. Meticulously following Cornford's reconstruction of the Aristophanic plot-formula, with its strong sexual element, Eliot turned immediately from *The Waste Land* to fully ritualize Sweeney's annual visit to Mrs. Porter, making them adversaries in an agon of life and death, making her murder, resurrection, and marriage to Sweeney the modern equivalent of an ancient drama.

Beginning in 1923, *Sweeney Agonistes* went through a succession of titles, subtitles, epigraphs, and scenarios. The earliest title, "Pereira; or, The Marriage of Life and Death, a Dream," not only defines the agon of the play; it points to the dreamlike state of being which Doris has entered in the prologue and which Sweeney tries to describe in the agon. Doris has come home with "a terrible chill." "I *think* it's only a chill," Dusty tells Pereira on the telephone, but we discover that she suffers from a vague apprehension and fear not unlike Sweeney's in "Sweeney Among the Nightingales." Superstitiously cutting a deck of cards, she turns up the two of spades, the coffin, a ritual symbol of death. "I know it's mine," she says frantically. "I dreamt of weddings all last night." She thereby forecasts the ritual death, resurrection, and marriage that she must soon undergo. As the epigraph from Aeschylus' *Choephoroi* (*The Libation Bearers*) now implies, the Furies are aswarm in her consciousness.

When the agon begins, we discover that Sweeney's purgation and metamorphosis have already taken place, and in the ritual drama he appears symbolically as a risen god or king to deliver Doris and Mrs. Porter from their death-in-life. He engages in flirtatious but threatening banter with Doris about the manner of her death—her ritual cooking—preparatory to the sacramental eating of her flesh on a "cannibal isle," where her rebirth will take place. "You wouldn't eat me!" exclaims Doris. "Yes I'd eat you!" Sweeney savagely replies, "In a nice little . . . missionary stew." Sweeney then begins to instruct, no, remind Doris of the transformation of consciousness that takes place on that isle of regeneration—the recognition that there is nothing at all in life but "Birth, and copulation, and death." Sweeney, who has evidently slain her before, gives her a hint of his own horrific transformation.

> I've been born, and once is enough.
> You don't remember, but I remember,
> Once is enough.

His subsequent story of a man who once did a girl in, and of the innate desire of any man to do a girl in, is told by way of analogy to reveal a dispossessed state of mind. "I've gotta use words when I talk to you," he says in frustration, knowing how horribly inexpressible is a mind that is neither dead nor alive, that no longer has any "joint" with the ordinary plane of reality. The chorus, chanting "The Terrors of the Night," chuckle the phantom laugh that signals sexual death: "You've had a cream of a nightmare dream and you've got the hoo-ha's coming to you."

The fragment stops abruptly with the insistent "Knock Knock Knock" of death, but we now know from Eliot's synopsis and extant scenarios that the play would follow the Aristophanic formula. In the scene to follow, Mrs. Porter makes her riotous entrance, singing a bawdy refrain from the ballad of Casey Jones: "And the neighbors knew by the shrieks and the groans / That the man at the throttle was Casey Jones." Sweeney, a reborn Casey Jones who, as a canceled epigraph relates, "In the red light district . . . found his fame," then murders Mrs. Porter. Her subsequent resurrection is followed by a marriage and feast, with Sweeney the Cook scrambling the eggs for the wedding breakfast of life and death. "It may not be too fanciful," one critic has recently observed, "to see in the fictional severance and reunion an image of the spiritual condition and the spiritual destiny of Eliot and his wife, as Eliot perceived them."

The Aristophanic ritual thus became Eliot's experimental model for comic purgation, for the dramatization of what we can now see as the Sweeney myth. From the outset there is a thin line between horror and laughter in this myth, but "in the end," says Eliot, "horror and laughter may be one—only when horror and laughter have become as horrible and laughable as they can be . . . then only do you see perceive that the aim of the comic and the tragic dramatist is the same: they are equally serious." Eliot tinkered with *Sweeney Agonistes* for productions in the 1930s, but he finally abandoned it—perhaps because the human drama that motivated it had ended and the comedian had lost his ferocity, perhaps because his marriage itself had died, not to be reborn. The fragments of *Ash-Wednesday* had turned his poetry back to the spiritual quest, and with the announcement of his Russell-inspired conversion in 1928, he was ironically cast into the role of public martyr. But the bawdy side of Eliot had not died—evidenced in 1939 by his contribution to a pamphlet of verse, twenty-five copies of which were printed strictly for private circulation. Entitled *Noctes Binanianae,* it contains, the subtitle says, "Certain Voluntary and Satyrical Verses and Compliments, as were lately Exchang'd between some of the Choicest Wits of the Age . . . now printed without castration after the most correct copies." The pretentious Latin title, according to my esteemed colleague, William Arrowsmith, translates, appropriately, "Buggery Nights." This late collection of doggerel reminds us that Eliot was not, by temperament, a savage comedian. In his bawdy, lighthearted moods, his more natural moods perhaps, he would beg us, on the occasion, as 'Possum, as Tom, not always to take him so seriously.

MODERNISM and ITS CANON

Denis Donoghue

I should say a little about Modernism before coming to the question of its canon. We have a choice. We can regard Modernism as a recurrent sentiment, a distinctive type of feeling, and find it in many historical periods; or, we can deem it to refer to a particular cultural formation which emerged toward the end of the nineteenth century—1880 or thereabouts—and persisted till some agreed date in our own time— say 1945. If we choose history rather than typology, we might agree that Modernism was a recognizable feature of modern literature and thought from Pater's *Studies in the History of the Renaissance,* published in 1873, to T. S. Eliot's *Four Quartets,* published in 1943. Post-Modernism would then refer to a nuance, a mutation, or indeed a refutation of the sentiment we call Modernism.

As an example of Modernism in the first sense, denoting a type of feeling, a mood likely to recur, I have in view Matthew Arnold's preface to the 1853 edition of his poems. Explaining why he had decided to omit "Empedocles on Etna," he said that the situation the poem treated was one "in which the suffering finds no vent in action; in which a continuous state of mental distress is prolonged, unrelieved by incident, hope, or resistance; in which there is everything to be endured, nothing to be done." His intention in writing the poem was clear.

> I intended to delineate the feelings of one of the last of the Greek religious philosophers, one of the family of Orpheus and Musaeus, having survived his fellows, living on into a time when the habits of Greek thought and feeling had begun fast to change, character to dwindle, the influence of the Sophists to prevail. Into the feelings of a man so situated there entered much that we are accustomed to consider as exclusively modern; how much, the fragments of Empedocles himself which remain to us are sufficient at least to indicate. What those who are familiar only with the great monuments of early Greek genius suppose to be its exclusive characteristics, have disappeared; the calm, the cheerfulness, the disinterested objectivity have disappeared: the dialogue of the mind with itself has commenced; modern problems

have presented themselves; we hear already the doubts, we witness the discouragement, of Hamlet and of Faust.

I concede, if it amounts to a concession, that in other essays Arnold used the word *modern* in a different sense. In his inaugural lecture "On the Modern Element in Literature," he described as modern not predicaments but the capacity to deal with them. "The life of Athens in the fifth century of our era" was, he said, "one of the modern periods in the life of the whole human race." No matter: it is enough for my purpose that the "modern" is not solely an attribute of Arnold's time, an invention like the telegraph. It is a type of sentiment or a recurrent bearing in the world, characterized by a feeling of belatedness, of having been born pathetically out of one's time; or, in Arnold's alternative meaning, the sentiment of having somehow survived the incongruity.

But I have to concede that most students of Modernism have represented it as an event. They disagree on its precise historical moment: each claims a certain latitude in specifying its beginning and its ending. But they agree that there was indeed such a moment.

As an example of this second usage, I shall refer to Georg Lukacs' essay "The Ideology of Modernism" and to the context of debate which he shared with Adorno, Bloch, and Benjamin. My references can be fairly casual. I am concerned not with the validity of Lukacs' argument but with its historical predicate. His position is easy to describe. Lukacs praises realism in the novel and represents it as superior alike to naturalism and Modernism. According to naturalism, the external world is already complete and opaque, and the individual intelligence can only be a witness to that opacity; it cannot alter it. According to realism in the novel, reality is not separate from the characters and their experience of its force. It is typical of naturalism that the hero sees the world as alien because impenetrable. As a result, and to the degree to which the world is seen as alien, the self and its activities are presented as specious. In this respect there is no difference between naturalism and Modernism. According to Modernism—Lukacs' examples are Joyce, Musil, Benn, and Kafka—man is an ahistorical being, he is merely thrown into life, he does not develop through contact with the world, he is what he has always been. Realism, from Homer to Balzac, Gorki, Tolstoy and Thomas Mann, takes seriously the world and the people who live in it: it assumes that the transactions between people and their environments are real. Modernism prescribes conditions so defeatist that they can only issue in the attenuation of reality and the dissolution of personality; in this respect, "Kafka's *angst* is the experience *par excellence* of modernism." Lukacs associates Modernism not only with late-bourgeois ideological decay but with High Art's contempt for the masses—motives which culminated in 1914 and became virtually obsessive thereafter.

Lukacs' fundamental objection to Modernism was that it made no attempt to represent the totality of social relations: it proceeded as if history were merely the history of consciousness. Bloch, on the other hand, defended Modernism—in particular, Expressionism—on the grounds that it represented the future of mankind by expressing its desires; Modernism's allusions maintained the validity of the past as uncompleted experience, and testified to the "not-yet" of human life. Modernism's decision not to reflect man's social determination in the world was validly utopian. Benjamin defended Surrealism for similar reasons: it provided access to a dreamworld hitherto suppressed by worldly ratiocination; besides, it could still be used "to win the energies of intoxication for the revolution."

Benjamin's argument for the profane illuminations of Surrealism did not convince Adorno, who found surrealist images dead and fixated upon death; they were the *nature morte* of Modernism, testifying not to the subject's freedom but to his collapse into passivity.

These few sentences are not meant to clarify a dispute but to show that Modernism, in this second sense, was thought to have arisen from particular historical conditions and to constitute a response to them.

What those conditions were is a matter of some dispute, but again I need not be precise. The most persuasive account of them, so far as my reading goes, is Georg Simmel's *The Philosophy of Money,* published in 1900, especially in its argument that the central feature of any economy is exchange, not production. Society, according to Simmel, is not an abstract concept or a hypostasized sentiment; it is the universal which is alive, embodied in the interaction of exchange relationships. In modern society, money represents pure interaction; it embodies and sublimates the practical relations of man to the objects of his will. The modern division of labor "permits the number of dependencies to increase just as it causes personalities to disappear behind their functions, because only one side of them operates, at the expense of all the other sides, the composition of which would make up a personality." These are the most favorable conditions for bringing about a feeling that one's autonomy must be sought within an embattled self and not in one's relation to the world.

If we add to these conditions a strategy first described by Max Weber—the separation of morality, science, and art, and the consignment of each to a separate compartment and a separate system of values and authorities—we infer that individuals are virtually required to see their lives as divided into a true part and a false. My life is divisible into two parts, the private and the public. In my public life I make a living, deal with other people, and negotiate conventional expectations. In my private life I truly live, choose the constituents of my experience, fill my life with images for which I take responsibility. The strategy which Weber describes makes it easy for people to identify themselves with their subjectivity and to regard their public lives as merely circumstantial. It follows that I regard the interests arising from my subjectivity as spiritually far superior to those imposed upon me by my daily circumstances.

Jürgen Habermas has remarked, in Weber's context, that recourse to subjectivity in a strategically divided life would also favor experiences different in every respect from those of one's public life, which are chiefly characterized by predictability and repetitive force. My subjectivity would place correspondingly higher value upon experiences transitory, elusive, and ephemeral. It is easy to see that Habermas came to this emphasis by way of Baudelaire and Benjamin.

It follows, too, that Modernism, seen in historical terms, would include various forms of art directed mainly by their revulsion from the daily enforcements of repetition, technology, bureaucracy, and positivism. Specifically, it would include Aestheticism, Art for Art's Sake, Decadence, Symbolism, Expressionism, Surrealism, and various forms of utopian fantasy. It would repudiate Lukacs' realism on the consideration that the forces he wants to see in a dynamic exchange—individual subjectivity and the real world—are inauthentic. The one is divided from itself for its own protection, and the other is already opaque. Hence, in literature, those "strategies of inwardness" which Fredric Jameson has ascribed to Eliot and Joyce as techniques for converting an alien world into oneself, turning its degraded images into private rhythms and self-absorbing cadences. Jameson could have included Pater with Eliot and Joyce, since Pater's elaborately tremulous sentences are just as desperately in the service of an embattled subjectivity as any gesture in "Prufrock" or the first few chapters of *Ulysses*. In these writers, the relation between self and world is not dynamic: the given world is deemed to be already degraded, and the self merely uses it as the raw matter of provocations which become experience only by being converted to privacy.

The process by which the predicament described by Simmel, Weber, and Habermas issued in the literature of Modernism and was recognized in that character can now, I hope, be described. The description should also lead us toward the question of the canon and the current disputes on that issue.

It is my understanding that of the various movements and tendencies I have listed as included in Modernism, the crucial one is Symbolism. The character that Symbolism found for itself in modern French poetry exemplified, more completely if more desperately than in any other form, the impulsions of a self sustained mainly upon vulnerabilities and repudiations. Symbolism, in poetry, dance, and theater, spoke of a desperately sought purity of being—of essence purified from the existence its adepts despised. Arthur Symons' *The Symbolist Movement in Literature,* published in 1899, was the book which articulated these fragile desires for Yeats and Eliot: it gave the sentiment of distaste its literary provenance and encouraged young poets to believe that they might persist in its ambience. But it was *Axel's Castle,* published in 1931, that first defined a literary period in terms of its relation to French Symbolism. Edmund Wilson's book carried the subtitle *A Study in the Imaginative Literature of 1870 to 1930,* and made Symbolism not only the theme of its first chapter but the cardinal term of reference for its subsequent chapters on Yeats, Valéry, Eliot, Proust, Joyce, Gertrude Stein, and Rimbaud. Wilson's sense of Symbolism was that it was the second wave of Romanticism, complicated by the fact that it broke upon French rather than upon English shores. He was convinced that modern English, Irish, and American literature could only be understood in its relation to Rimbaud, Mallarmé, and Valéry.

Wilson's book established Modernism in literature as a particular set of affiliations and procedures. But it was F. R. Leavis who convinced a generation of readers that T. S. Eliot's early poems—the poems culminating in *The Waste Land*—provided the most complete embodiment of the new possibilities. In 1932 Leavis published *New Bearings in English Poetry* and founded a journal, *Scrutiny,* to develop the case made in that book. His main argument was that despite the significant achievements of Yeats, Hardy, and a few other poets, the workable traditions of English poetry had exhausted themselves. The situation in 1914 was such that "English poetry in the future must develop (if at all) along

some other line than that running from the Romantics through Ten-
nyson, Swinburne, *A Shropshire Lad,* and Rupert Brooke." The only line
of development that seemed at all productive was in Eliot's poetry: "He
has made a new start, and established new bearings."

Leavis' book was, in its main emphasis, an attempt to gain for Eliot's
poetry a particular form of recognition. Eliot was already, indeed, a
famous poet. His early poems had been acknowledged as distinctive
achievements by Ezra Pound, Marianne Moore, Wilson, I. A. Richards,
and many other poets and critics. It cannot be claimed for Leavis that he
was among the first to bear witness to Eliot's significance. But *New
Bearings* was directed toward a far larger case; not only that Eliot was a
poet of an extraordinarily telling kind but that English poetry would
have to work out the possibilities he had disclosed. It was because of
Eliot that Leavis presented the true direction of modern English poetry
as involving Hopkins and Pound, recognized as of Eliot's company. "It is
owing to Mr. Eliot," Leavis wrote in *New Bearings,* "that Pound and
Hopkins can be discussed as having the significance here attributed to
them, and can be associated with him in terms of a revised tradition."

Leavis' book not only insisted on the understanding of modern
poetry as issuing from Eliot's procedures but prescribed the terms in
which *The Waste Land* should be read. The unity the poem aims at, he
said, "is that of an inclusive consciousness"; its procedures involve "the
co-presence in the mind of a number of different orientations, fundamental attitudes, orders of experience." Eliot's capacity to focus such a
consciousness made it possible for Leavis to say that in *The Waste Land* "a
mind fully alive in the age compels a poetic triumph out of the peculiar
difficulties facing a poet in the age." In the same spirit, Leavis pointed to
"The Love Song of J. Alfred Prufrock" and the other early poems as
having expressed "freely a modern sensibility, the ways of feeling, the
modes of experience, of one fully alive in his own age."

It may be said that Leavis' account of *The Waste Land* merely worked
out the consequences of Eliot's note about Tiresias: "Tiresias, although
a mere spectator and not indeed a 'character,' is yet the most important
personage in the poem, uniting all the rest. Just as the one-eyed
merchant, seller of currants, melts into the Phoenician Sailor, and the
latter is not wholly distinct from Ferdinand Prince of Naples, so all the
women are one woman, and the two sexes meet in Tiresias. What
Tiresias *sees,* in fact, is the substance of the poem." But I doubt if any
qualified reader in 1932 could have made much of these meltings,

dissolvings, and unitings if Leavis hadn't translated these processes into the more available idea of an inclusive consciousness. Without the translation, it would have been virtually impossible for a reader to divine where, if anywhere, the peremptory fragments, the elusively memorable phrases and transitions in the poem, could be resolved. Eliot's note on Tiresias points the reader in the right direction but doesn't go far enough because Tiresias can only see the world as one alienated from it. As I have remarked in *The Sovereign Ghost,* Tiresias does not give or sympathize; he does not participate in the suffering and transformation of "What the Thunder Said." There is a state of consciousness beyond Tiresias. As Eliot wrote in *Knowledge and Experience in the Philosophy of F. H. Bradley,* "We are led to the conception of an all-inclusive experience outside of which nothing shall fall." I assume that such an experience would be the subjective form of totality—a "violence within," to use Wallace Stevens' terms—corresponding to, and answering with its own power, the gross totality of an alien world.

It is true that the idea of a perspective beyond that in which we deal with our daily lives was already available to readers. A mild form of it was available in James's preface to *The Lesson of the Master,* where he speaks of operative irony as the capacity to imply and project "the possible other case"—the case "rich and edifying where the actuality is pretentious and vain." It was available, too, in Eliot's essay on Marvell, where he describes wit as involving "a recognition, implicit in the expression of every experience, of other kinds of experience which are possible." Available, too, in Ransom's account of the metaphysical impulse in poetry as "committing the feelings in the case . . . to their determination within the elected figure." Ransom appears to say that the figure, the trope, is wiser than the poet who resorts to it, and not only wiser but more generous in its recognitions and allowances.

These several citations are in the spirit of *The Waste Land,* and would be the better if they were developed further. But what Leavis did—and I refer to the formula of "inclusive consciousness" only to suggest the far more complex process of reading which it merely epitomizes—was to turn the predicaments which led to Symbolism into opportunities featuring a distinctively modern accomplishment. The sentiment of belatedness, the fragility of the sense of self, the felt excess of consciousness over experience—these conditions, which issued in the world-weariness and debility of Yeats's early poems, could be turned to a different and far stronger account by a poetic imagination of a different order. Eliot's early poems do not capitulate to the fears and lassitudes they seem, in a superficial reading, merely to express. The idea of an inclusive consciousness marked a triumph, whereas the idea of an embattled subjectivity pointed only to a predicament or a malaise.

It was Leavis, then, who defined the kind and the degree of the significance to be ascribed to *The Waste Land*. But his constituency, in 1932 and indeed later, was almost entirely English: his influence was immense, but it was to be found in a generation of English schoolmasters who brought his particular values and preoccupations into virtually every school in England. His influence in America was slight, partly because he was indifferent to the recognition of a distinctively American literature and an American language, partly because he regarded the native possession of the English language as a privilege by definition unavailable to Americans and Irishmen. So the work he did in England and for English readers had to be done in America by other critics.

The work was begun—but hardly with Leavis' particular emphasis and insistence—by F. O. Matthiessen. It is true that Eliot's poetry was already discussed by the most alert college teachers and their brightest students. The disputes between John Crowe Ransom and Allen Tate about the form of *The Waste Land* were the most spirited but not the sole episodes of their kind. But Matthiessen's publication of *The Achievement of T. S. Eliot* in 1935 gave Eliot's poetry official status in American colleges and universities. *Understanding Poetry,* by Cleanth Brooks and Robert Penn Warren, published in 1938, and Brooks's more avowed reading of Eliot in *Modern Poetry and the Tradition,* published in 1939, carried the work further and applied to the history of English poetry the critical principles and procedures Eliot had outlined in *The Sacred Wood* in 1920. When Matthiessen published his revision of *The Oxford Book of American Verse* in 1950, he gave authoritative recognition not only to Eliot but to the Modernism in poetry which Eliot most fully articulated.

The reception of Eliot's poetry in the years from 1917 to 1950 has normally been regarded, I think, as an edifying matter. Those who played a part in it had cause to feel at least quietly gratified. They ensured that an extremely difficult poetry gradually gained access to colleges and universities, and eventually to men and women at large—a remarkable critical and pedagogical achievement. But a year or two ago we began to hear that Eliot's reception must be given a different construction. We are now told that the intellectual community, faced with a new and exacting body of work, merely appropriated it and used it to exhibit, once again, its own authority. Why were Eliot's academic critics so concerned to show that *The Waste Land* cohered and was not the heap of fragments it seemed to be? We are now to believe that the academy has a resolutely vested interest in maintaining the sentiment which associates meaning and value with unity. Why did Eliot's poems, obscure as they appeared to be, comport themselves agreeably enough in seminars? Because Eliot, under an ostensibly revolutionary surface, had a powerful interest in signs of order—indeed, in the order he first called Tradition and later Orthodoxy.

The clearest statement of the position to which I refer is John Guillory's essay, "T. S. Eliot and Cleanth Brooks," included in *Canons,* a collection of essays on the politics of canon formation, edited by Robert von Hallberg. Guillory's essay is extremely intelligent and urbane, but it argues that the New Criticism put itself at the service of the liberal pluralism which is "the regnant ideology of the academy." The argument, up to this point, is one I would be pleased to accept: I can't think of any ideology more suitable to universities. But Guillory refuses to let me enjoy that conclusion. "The technique of formalist interpretation," he maintains, "subtends the larger ideology, satisfying within a narrower domain of practice the longing for consensus, for a metaphysics of the same—a longing expressed by the posited 'unity' of the literary work."

I shall say a few words about "unity" in a moment, but first I have to interrupt Guillory's argument when he refers to "the academy." He means to say that there is an institution, single-minded and authoritative, and that it has interests as you and I have interests. In many contexts, it can be recognized as the enemy. But there is no such institution. The academy exists in that sense only when questions of funding and endowment are raised. Day by day, there are teachers who teach undergraduate and graduate students. They are not told what to teach or how to teach it. If I am designated to teach a course called "The Modern Novel," I am left entirely free to choose the novels, and equally free to teach them as I please. In none of the three countries in which I have taught has it ever been suggested to me that I should assign a particular book and teach it according to certain assumptions. To refer to such a miscellany of purposes and decisions as "the academy" is to invent a monster and proclaim a program lurid enough to accompany the invention.

As for the "longing expressed by the posited 'unity' of the literary work," Guillory's implication, I assume, is that when a teacher demonstrates that a poem which seems chaotic or arbitrary—*The Waste Land,* again—is in fact profoundly unified, he insinuates to his students that unity, in social life as in poetry, is the natural state of things. Students thus persuaded are likely to be docile both inside and outside the classroom. But Guillory knows well that a desire for unity is not a modern university's invention. At least since Kant's *Critique of Pure Reason,* philosophers have sought to define the Beautiful as the reconciliation of multiplicity into unity. "The Beautiful," according to Coleridge, "contemplated in its essentials, that is, in kind and not in degree, is that in which the many, still seen as many, becomes one." In the search for the Beautiful, symbols have often been given a certain privilege. To many philosophers, a symbol has seemed to be an episode of reconciliation, a momentary if vulnerable glimpse of unity—organic unity, it is sometimes claimed, as in Yeats's great-rooted chestnut tree in "Among School Children." But it would be a desperate argument to claim that a sinister politics issues, even in Yeats's case, from the fact that a tree is one thing and that it has many branches. Indeed, I note a charming remark by Northrop Frye in a recent *Times Literary Supplement,* dated January 17, 1986: "We may postulate a verbal world intermediate between subject and object, but that creates a fresh set of difficulties: one may easily treat a verbal structure as though it were a natural object, as the 'formalists' do when they make a cult of organic wholeness. Poems are organic wholes for the same reason that pills are round: not because roundness is their essence, but because that shape favours assimilation." As a teacher, I can live with that.

Besides, Guillory also knows that the unity traditionally ascribed to symbols, by regular contrast with the severances of allegory, is now so commonly rejected that the rejection constitutes an orthodoxy. It is no longer startling to quote Walter Benjamin's attack on the allegedly theological character of symbols and his advocacy of the doomed integrity of allegory, in *The Origin of German Tragic Drama;* or Paul de Man's attack, in "The Rhetoric of Temporality," on the alleged mystification in Romantic theories of the symbol; or Fredric Jameson's denunciation, in "*Ulysses* in History," of "the practice of symbolism itself, which involves the illicit transformation of existing things into so many visible or tangible meanings." Hazard Adams' *Philosophy of the Literary Symbolic,* published in 1983, is an attempt to move the argument about symbolism and allegory beyond the stage at which rival teachers scowl at each other, apparently, as they pass along the corridor.

The same scowling is going on, it appears, on the question of the canon. I have as much difficulty in recognizing "the canon" as in knowing where to find "the academy." The only aspect of the matter which seems clear to me is that reference to the canon is misleading; it is based upon a false analogy with canonicity as an attribute of the Catholic Church and its founding texts. The canon is the collection of books of the Bible which the Church has accepted as genuinely inspired rather than apocryphal. The word *canon* is also used to mean the list of persons canonized—formally admitted to the calendar of saints. Jews and Protestants accept as canonical only the books of the Hebrew Bible and exclude those books of the Greek Bible which they call apocryphal and which Catholic and Orthodox Christians call deuterocanonical. Jews don't accept the New Testament as canonical, and so on. Now it is evident that nothing in the syllabi of universities corresponds to the canon in the founding texts of the Church. There are no poems which must be read. Nothing taught in an English department is supposed to have the authority the New Testament and certain patristic commentaries are supposed to exert upon Christians. To confine the question to modern poetry: there is no canon.

There are critics who exhibit a canonist's ambition. I have referred to Leavis, who wrote *New Bearings, The Great Tradition,* and several other books with the clear intention of establishing a canon in English fiction and poetry. In fiction, certain works by Jane Austen, Dickens, George Eliot, Henry James, Conrad, D. H. Lawrence. In modern poetry, Eliot, Hopkins, Pound, Empson rather than Auden, with Yeats and Hardy as marginal figures, though superb writers in their own idiosyncratic ways.

Hugh Kenner's ambition is also a canonist's. He has written many books to enforce his view that there is what he calls "International Modernism"; that its achievement compels acknowledgment of Pound, Eliot, Wyndham Lewis, Joyce, and Beckett; that, in relation to modern poetry, the crucial figure is Pound, the proper indication of his force is Imagism, and the trajectory of that force may be traced in William Carlos Williams, Marianne Moore, the Objectivists—Louis Zukofsky and George Oppen, especially—and Charles Olson and the Black Mountain poets. Stevens doesn't come into the reckoning because he had no part "in the only story that I find has adequate explanatory power: a story of capitals." Kenner means London, Paris, and Dublin. Like Virginia Woolf and William Faulkner, Stevens "seems a voice from a province, quirkily enabled by the International Modernism of which he was never a part, no more than they." As for modern England, the only poets Kenner has endorsed are Charles Tomlinson, who has read Williams and Moore, and Basil Bunting, who has read Pound.

To Kenner, Stevens is nothing, or at best a nonsense poet; to Harold Bloom, he is nearly everything. Bloom, too, has canonical ambition. He wants to convince us that there is one story and one story only: it begins, so far as English poetry is in question, with the agon of Milton and Blake and Shelley, enters its crucial American phase in Emerson, Whitman, and Dickinson, gathers unto itself whatever its agonistic will requires of Nietzsche, Pater, Freud, and Yeats, and proceeds as a constantly renewed Freudian drama through Hart Crane, Stevens, Elizabeth Bishop, John Ashbery, A. R. Ammons, and John Hollander. What the story discloses is at every point "the self-revelation of a profoundly subjective consciousness." There is no sign, in that story, of Eliot, Pound, or Robert Lowell.

We are not done with canonical zeal. In his rueful way, Philip Larkin proposed to tell a different story. His *Oxford Book of Twentieth Century Verse* is predicated not upon Eliot, Pound, or Stevens but upon Hardy, whose *Collected Poems* Larkin declared (in 1966) "many times over the best body of poetic work this century so far has to show." The implication of the *Oxford Book* is that Hardy maintained modern poetry in such an irrefutably creative relation to the English language that the interventions of Eliot and Pound were merely local disturbances.

I have mentioned four canonists, and indeed the list is incomplete. None of them command the field. None of their books have been accepted as the Summa. These men are rhetoricians, trying to persuade their readers by telling, each of them, a different story. None of the stories amount to heresy, for the sufficient reason that there is no orthodoxy to be rejected. If you find one story more persuasive than the others, you accept it: well and good.

In practice, what happens? Modern poetry is taught in our colleges and universities mostly by recourse to anthologies. Graduate students are expected to go much further, into the collected poems of many poets, but undergraduates are initiated through anthologies. The standard anthologies—the *Norton,* for instance, edited by Richard Ellmann and Robert O'Clair—are mainly characterized by their omnivorous hospitality: they try to represent every kind of poetry that has come to editorial attention. It is left to individual teachers to choose which of the hundreds of poems they will assign to their students. Special interests tend to be expressed in smaller anthologies and to make their way gradually into the standard ones. Alan C. Golding has estimated that the poets represented in the two most famous rival anthologies a generation ago, *New American Poetry*, published in 1960 and edited by Donald Allen, who liked his poems rough and casual, and *New Poets of England and America*, published in 1957 and edited by Donald Hall, Robert Pack, and Louis Simpson, who liked well-tailored poems, are now equally on show in the big anthologies. Feminist complaints about the exclusion of women poets from the standard anthologies are now being appeased. And there is, to make amends, the *Norton Anthology of Literature by Women*.

But I am not sure that I have met John Guillory's argument. If he believes that universities have invested so heavily in decorum that they want to see their teachers disclosing unity in a poem where every visible sign speaks of chaos, I can only say that such has not been my experience. If I were to choose to emphasize chaos rather than order in modern poetry, and speak in favor of open form rather than closure, I can't flatter myself that my masters would take any interest in my preference. The current argument about canon formation and the alleged exercise of institutional power in such formation is, I assume, an expression of the misgiving many teachers feel about institutions. Everything I have said may be interpreted as offering to justify the "repressive tolerance" which, twenty years ago, enraged Marcuse and other critics. I have no wish to revive old factions. But I don't believe that the conditions in which we read and teach modern poetry are sinister or repressive. Nor do I believe that universities are up to any monkey business.

NOTES on CONTRIBUTORS

JAMES W. APPLEWHITE, associate professor of English, Duke University, has published three volumes of poetry: *Following Gravity, Statues of the Grass,* and *Foreseeing the Journey.*

HOUSTON A. BAKER, JR., Albert M. Greenfield Professor of Human Relations, University of Pennsylvania, is the author of *Blues, Ideology, and Afro-American Literature: A Vernacular Theory,* and *Modernism and the Harlem Renaissance.*

CLEANTH BROOKS, a founding editor of the *Southern Review,* 1935–1942, Gray Professor of Rhetoric, Emeritus, Yale University, is one of America's major literary critics.

GEORGE CORE, editor of the *Sewanee Review* and well-known scholar and critic, was for several years the chief editor of the University of Georgia Press.

THOMAS W. CUTRER, associate director of the Texas State Historical Association, is the author of *Parnassus on the Mississippi: The "Southern Review" and the Baton Rouge Literary Community, 1935–1942.*

DENIS DONOGHUE, holds the Henry James Chair in English, New York University. His numerous books include *Ferocious Alphabets* and *The Sovereign Ghost.*

CHARLES EAST, former director of the Louisiana State University Press and former editor of the University of Georgia Press, has recently published *New Writers of the South: A Fiction Anthology,* edited with an introduction (1987). He is the editor of the Flannery O'Connor Award for Fiction series, University of Georgia Press.

HENRY LOUIS GATES, JR., professor of English, comparative literature, and Africana studies, Cornell University, is the author of *The Signifying Monkey* and *Figures in Black.*

WILLIAM C. HAVARD, chairman of the political science department, Vanderbilt University, is the author of *The Changing Politics of the South* and *The Recovery of Political Theory.*

ROBERT B. HEILMAN, author of *Tragedy and Melodrama* and numerous other works, was a member of the Department of English at LSU from 1935 to 1946.

DANIEL C. LITTLEFIELD, associate professor of history at LSU, is the author of *Rice and Slaves: Ethnicity and the Slave Trade in Colonial South Carolina*.

HUEY P. LONG (1893–1935), governor of Louisiana from 1928 to 1930 and United States senator from 1930 to 1935, was the author of an autobiography, *Every Man a King*, and *My First Days in the White House*, published in 1933 and 1935, respectively.

GLORIA NAYLOR is the author of three novels—the award-winning *Women of Brewster Place, Linden Hills*, and *Mama Day*, scheduled for publication in February, 1988.

LESLIE E. PHILLABAUM, director of the Louisiana State University Press, was president of the Association of American University Presses in 1984 and 1985.

LOUIS D. RUBIN, JR., scholar, author, and University Distinguished Professor of English, University of North Carolina, Chapel Hill, is the founder of Algonquin Press.

RONALD SCHUCHARD, Emory University, is currently editing two volumes of *The Collected Letters of W. B. Yeats* for Oxford University Press. He delivered the 1985 T. S. Eliot Memorial Lecture at St. Louis.

ELIZABETH SPENCER, distinguished American novelist, after a long residence in Montreal, Quebec, Canada, has moved to Chapel Hill, North Carolina. Her latest novel is entitled *The Salt Line*.

WALTER SULLIVAN, novelist and critic, is professor of English, Vanderbilt University. His books include two novels—*Sojourn of a Stranger* and *The Long, Long Love*—and a critical study, *Death by Melancholy*.

ROBERT PENN WARREN, a founding editor of the *Southern Review*, 1935 to 1942, was named America's first poet laureate in 1986. He has received many awards, including two Pulitzer prizes, and is the author of the widely known novel *All the King's Men*.

The SOUTHERN REVIEW:
A SELECTED BIBLIOGRAPHY

Brooks, Cleanth. "The Life and Death of an Academic Journal." In *The Art of Literary Publishing,* edited by Bill Henderson. Yonkers, N.Y., 1980.

Brooks, Cleanth, and Robert Penn Warren. Introduction to *An Anthology of Stories from the Southern Review.* Baton Rouge, 1953.

_____. "The Origin of the *Southern Review.*" *Southern Review,* n.s., XXII (Winter, 1986), 214–17. Reprinted in this volume.

Cutrer, Thomas W., ed. "Conference on Literature and Reading in the South and Southwest, 1935." *Southern Review,* n.s., XXI (Spring, 1985), 260–300. Reprinted, with abbreviated introduction, in this volume.

_____. *Parnassus on the Mississippi: The "Southern Review" and the Baton Rouge Literary Community, 1934–1942.* Baton Rouge, 1984.

East, Charles. "The Death of Huey Long: A Photographic Essay." *Southern Review,* n.s., XXI (Spring, 1985), 247–56. Text reprinted in this volume.

Heilman, Robert B. "Baton Rouge and LSU Forty Years After." *Sewanee Review,* LXXXVIII (Winter, 1980), 126–43.

Long, Huey P. "Politics and Education." *Southern Review,* n.s., XXI (Spring, 1985), 257–59. Reprinted in this volume.

Montessi, Albert J. "The *Southern Review* (1935–1942)." *Chicago Review,* XVI, No. 4 (1964), 201–12.

_____. "The *Southern Review* (1935–1942): A History and Evaluation." Ph. D. dissertation, Pennsylvania State University, 1955. Published by the author under the title *Radical Conservatism: The Southern Review (1935–1942), ca.* 1984.

Simpson, Lewis P., ed. *The Possibilities of Order: The Work of Cleanth Brooks.* Baton Rouge, 1976. See especially Robert Penn Warren's "Conversation with Cleanth Brooks," 1–124, a meditation on the meaning of literature that bears retrospectively on the motives for all the literary endeavors of Brooks and Warren. Also, see Robert B. Heilman, "Cleanth Brooks: Some Snapshots from an Old Album," 128–49.

———. "The *Southern Review* and a Post-Southern American Letters." In *The Little Magazine in America: A Modern Documentary History*, edited by Eliott Anderson and Mary Kinzie. New York, 1978. (This book reprints a special issue of *Triquarterly*, XLIII [Fall, 1978].) The introduction to the present volume is adopted from "The *Southern Review* and a Post-Southern American Letters."

Southern Review: Index to the Original Series, Volumes I–VII, 1935–1942. Compiled by Cherri M. Pancake and Sarah S. East. Baton Rouge, 1973.

Southern Review: Index to the New Series, Volumes I–VII. Compiled by Sarah East and Cherri M. Pancake. Baton Rouge, n.d.

Southern Review: Index to the New Series, Volumes VIII–XIV. Compiled by Maureen O. Carleton, Sarah S. East, and Susan Polack. Baton Rouge, n.d.

Southern Review: A Commemoration, 1980. Baton Rouge, 1980.

"Southern Letters and Modern Literature: A National Literary Conference." Program. Baton Rouge, 1985.

Tentarelli, Ronda Cabot. "The Life and Times of the *Southern Review.*" *Southern Studies: An Interdisciplinary Journal of the South*, XVI (Summer, 1977), 129–51.

———. "The *Southern Review*, 1935–1942: The Intellectual History of a Cultural Quarterly." Ph.D. dissertation, Louisiana State University, 1980.

Webb, Max. "Ford Madox Ford and the Baton Rouge Writers' Conference." *Southern Review*, n.s., X (Autumn, 1974), 892–903.